SPY/
COUNTERSPY

SPY/ COUNTERSPY

The autobiography of
DUSKO POPOV

Foreword by Ewen Montagu

GROSSET & DUNLAP
PUBLISHERS
New York

FOREWORD

Even those of us who are addicted to the fantastic excitements of the fictional spy story—whether it be about James Bond or a William le Queux hero of prewar days—turned with relief and interest to the more realistic story of the strains and risks of actual spying, such as Somerset Maugham's *Ashenden*.

In this book Dusko Popov gives us the best of both types. In addition, his story is *true,* and the more fascinating because of that. Reading him one can get all the thrill of real danger—not of James Bond's alligators and man-eating fish—but of something even more ruthless, evil, and dangerous: the German Secret Service.

I knew Dusko Popov well during the war, when he risked and achieved so much for the Allied cause. He could, in some respects, have been an Ian Fleming hero—one of the bravest and gayest of men, possessing immense charm and personal magnetism. He enjoyed a carefree and luxurious life. As he was wont to say: "Why not, if the Germans are paying for it? And that life is me. If I didn't live it I would be 'blown'; the Germans would realize at once that there was something strange."

At the same time, he exhibited a basic common sense that James Bond never displayed. For instance, he knew what was going wrong during that ghastly period in America when Hoover and his FBI could not realize that to deceive the

Germans would win victories and save thousands of lives but preferred to make arrests—if possible, publicized arrests, so as to gain funds and influence—in the peacetime "policeman" tradition.

When I went overseas, at the start of that trouble, to try to help by getting British Service information for Dusko to send to his spymasters (if we could not get the American information that they really wanted at the time), I remember him saying to me in his Park Avenue apartment, "They need not trust me right away simply because the British say that I am O.K.; but they are so ridiculous. Microphones everywhere and planted so obviously. Why, if I bend over to smell a bowl of flowers, I scratch my nose on a microphone."

Yet he also had the steel within, the ruthlessness and the cold-blooded courage that enabled him to go back to the German Secret Service Headquarters in Lisbon and Madrid time and again, when it was likely that he might be "blown"; it was like putting his head into the lion's mouth. Bravely, in cold blood, he risked torture and death to reestablish German confidence in him so that he could continue to make his great contribution to the Allied victory.

Having worked with Dusko Popov (then known to me as Tricycle) from the time he arrived in war-battered London, I have read with absorbing interest his angle on the exploits of which I knew, and with fascination of those which were concealed from me at the time by the basic security principle of "no need to know." From the start, I fell under the spell of his personality, his sincerity, his gaiety, and his courage. I am sure that he will have the same effect on all those who read this book.

The Hon. Ewen Montagu, C.B.E.,Q.C.
London, February, 1974

PROLOGUE

To survive the multiple hazards of espionage it is better not to be too serious. The trick, I believe, is to be light-hearted without being superficial. I never took life, myself, or other people too seriously. I was criticized for this and for having "too many devices" on my banner by none other than Major General Stewart Menzies, the head of British Intelligence, who added that it was nevertheless ideal for my job. For a while, I considered the phrase for the title of this book.

In the same vein, I was advised by many that the story I have to tell is a serious one, that I have a contribution to make to history, and that the style of writing should reflect this. I was warned that to use the conversational form would make the book read like a novel and, cardinal sin, would be taking liberties with real-life characters. Moreover, it would diminish the book's credibility.

I've taken that liberty anyway. Agreed, it is impossible to quote people textually, to remember their exact words. But I do remember the spirit of conversations, and I believe the spirit is what counts. I want to give the reader as accurate as possible a feeling of what certain people were like, of what it was to live through the times I describe while doing the job I did. I don't think a dry tome would accomplish this as effectively.

Another thing, I was in my late twenties and early thirties when this story took place and impelled to live to the hilt. It would be false to imbue with the gravity of a grey-beard the recountal of a young man—insouciant, romantic, adventuresome, albeit sufficiently mature to be entrusted with a critical mission. Anyway, maybe I'm still not enough of a greybeard to pontificate. I've read much non-sense about the metier, both dry stuff and derring-do, and have no patience with either. Granted, spying is both a ser-ious and dangerous business, but it is also boring with its eternal waiting and infrequent action. It would be impos-sible to endure, at times, if one could not exhibit a light-hearted exterior.

Although I decided to try to tell the story as it was, to paint the picture as I remember it, I also checked as pains-takingly as possible all the facts involved, so I would not neglect what my friends deem its historical importance. Memory does play tricks, and I spent several months travel-ing and researching, speaking to old friends in the field, delving into files, both British and German.

Most governments nowadays have laws that make it a crime to reveal their secrets. Perhaps their secrets conceal their crimes. But in many instances, too, bureaucratic leth-argy and the philosophy that it is safer to take no action have perpetuated secrets that no longer have legitimate *raisons d'être*.

Until recently my mouth was sealed, my pen kept dry. I couldn't reveal my wartime activities. Not so much that they had been classified secret. More insidious, they hadn't been declassified. Fortunately, circumstances at last brought about the revelation of my wartime existence. My friend Sir John Cecil Masterman charged the barriers and cut through the red tape sealing his tale and incidentally mine.

PROLOGUE

Perhaps the timing is providential. I had been keeping a brake on my patience ever since the end of World War II, wanting in particular to reveal the circumstances as I knew them concerning Pearl Harbor and my encounter with J. Edgar Hoover. Although it is too late to alter the event, to bring back to life the hundreds of thousands, perhaps millions, who died needlessly as a result of the mishandling of the information I brought to America concerning the impending Japanese attack, I was persuaded that the world was entitled to know about it. Today in particular, perhaps a lifting of the curtain may alter our perspective salubriously.

There are also a few secrets that this book doesn't reveal. To protect some publicity-shy individuals, I have given them pseudonyms. But the reason is simply one of privacy, in some cases even modesty.

And there is one commonly assumed secret which I shall try to lay low right now. Secret agents do retire. At the end of the war, I was issued two suits of mufti and a change of linen, and I said goodbye to it all. I had a life to make and a living to earn.

It is true that field-grade officers in intelligence are never officially terminated and are only placed on leave. But that is so that they may be kept under thumb. Occasionally though, one of us does manage to bend back the finger.

SPY/
COUNTERSPY

1

Nothing is really thrust upon you. You have to accept it as well. You have a choice, even of life or death. When my best friend, Johann Jebsen, the man to whom I owe my life, was maneuvering me into becoming a Nazi spy, I became aware of the situation rather rapidly and accepted because it suited my plans.

At first I did feel some resentment, mainly because Johnny wasn't playing aboveboard. But I wasn't shocked. I sensed that Johnny was motivated by a complicated set of reasons, some even altruistic. And if some were for personal gain, I made no moral judgment. One shouldn't demand the ultimate of anyone, not when his own skin is involved.

Johnny's opening move was to send me a cable, which found me in Dubrovnik. I had come down from Belgrade for the week of festivities in honor of our patron saint, Saint Blaise. It was the gayest time of the year in my home town, with parties and costume balls every night. And the freest time of the year, too. Under the anonymity of masks and costumes, conventions could be flouted with more impunity than usual. I had gone to bed late. I was awakened by my charwoman pulling back the curtains, grumbling in her old-woman way under her breath.

"Look at this place. Girls. Drinking." She was deliberately mumbling loud enough for me to hear. "And on Saint Blaise day. I told your father he should never have given you your own place."

"Enough," I said. "I've told you a thousand times, that's exactly why he gave it to me. For privacy. So why are you waking me?"

Katerina approached the bed holding her hand out, an envelope in it. "A telegram, Gospar Dusko." She knew me almost all my life and called me by my first name, adding the local Dubrovnik equivalent of "Master" to it out of convention, not respect.

I ripped open the envelope and noticed first the top and bottom of the flimsy yellow form it contained. The telegram came from Berlin. It was signed "Johann Jebsen" and was dated 4 February, 1940. It read: "Need to meet you urgently. Propose 8 February, Hotel Serbian King, Belgrade."

Except for its brevity, the message was not characteristic of Johnny Jebsen. Usually, there was little in life he would consider urgent, yet I knew it was no mistake. His precision in language would preclude his employing a word that did not express his exact meaning.

I started to pick up the telephone to send a return message, then put it down and hopped out of bed. It would be better to go to the telegraph office myself. A message dictated in German over the phone might be garbled. Katerina hastily left the bedroom as I started to look for my clothes.

Under any circumstances, urgent or flippant, I was bound by friendship, and more, to go to meet Johnny. Even during Saint Blaise festivities. But this summons was obviously not to a romp. I was worried about its urgent character. I could think only of the scrape, to understate, that Johnny had gotten me out of three years before and surmise that he was in some sort of similar predicament himself.

Even before the telegram came, I had been wondering how Johnny was reacting to the war, now five months old. Although he was anti-Nazi, he was presumably safe because his background was above suspicion. Johnny was heir to a great fortune and so seemed likely to identify with the status quo. His was an old Hamburg family steeped in the naval tradition of the ancient Hanseatic state. But knowing Johnny as I did, knowing his independence, his unpredictable character and quixotic way, I wouldn't have been surprised if he had run afoul of the Nazis.

Anyway, safety in Nazi Germany was theoretical at best. I had learned that three years before. Even as a foreigner—almost an innocent—I had had a run-in with the Gestapo and, had it not been for Johnny, would have ended my days in a concentration camp.

The road from Dubrovnik to the capital was long in 1940. Yugoslavia was not famous for its highways. But I was somewhat proud of my driving ability and of my machine, and I felt I was keeping a rendezvous with destiny, so I pushed my BMW, avoiding potholes as I could, reliving all the while my acquaintanceship with Johnny.

It was in 1936 that I met Jebsen. I had finished my law studies in Belgrade and enrolled in Freiburg University in Breisgau in south Germany to prepare my doctorate. This choice was dictated by a couple of reasons. Germany always had dominated southeastern Europe culturally and economically. In the early days of Hitler it was using any and all means to extend this domination . . . and succeeding. Any ambitious person in the small Balkan nations had to speak German, and that language was the weak point in my linguistic accomplishments. I had already been to schools in England and France. Another reason for my choice was Freiburg. It was a beautiful, small city at the foot of the Black Forest, close to marvelous ski slopes, and close to home. It had one of the liveliest campuses in Europe. Freiburg also had an excellent scholastic reputation. My intention was to combine study, sports, and pleasure, to all three of which I devoted myself with equal passion.

Obviously, I was politically amorphous, or almost so. The Nazis had been in power for nearly four years and although I was repulsed by them, that didn't stop me from going to study in Germany. It seemed to me that the pros outweighed the cons.

My naiveté didn't last long. One could feel the disturbing influence of the Nazis in the streets, at the university, and even in private homes. It is true that many people—mainly white-collar workers and the *petit bourgeois*—did speak enthusiastically about the Nazi regime. But those who didn't feel that way fast learned to control their tongues.

At centers of learning such as Freiburg, the Nazi influence was felt more strongly than elsewhere in those early days of Hitlerism. Most professors not in sympathy with the regime were eliminated. The few who remained did so only by being circumspect and teaching in strict conformity with official thinking. All Jewish professors had been ousted without exception, but at that date a small number of classes for Jewish students still existed—for international face-keeping, undoubtedly. The Jewish students were allowed no privileges whatsoever apart from attending classes, and most of them were flunked out deliberately.

German students, too, were under no illusions of liberty. Their first practical, nonacademic lesson was to control their behavior and conform. They also knew without being told that they could not expect a prosperous career after graduation unless, at the very least, they joined one of the paramilitary cells in the university. The more ambitious ones signed up with the S.S., the Sicherheitstaffelin, or Security Section, whose uniforms bore the dreaded lightning flash insignia. Others went into the Brown Shirts, the so-called S.A., or Sturmabteilung, the storm troops.

As for the foreign students, of whom there were well over a thousand in Freiburg, the regime courted them sedulously. They came from all over the world, but in the majority they were English, some Americans, and some French. Then there also were the Ausland Deutscher, those from the German minorities in Yugoslavia, Czechoslovakia, and Hungary. They were foreign citizens but Germans still.

The foreign students were afforded many facilities: inexpensive restaurants, lodgings, organized sports, particularly winter sports, and, for many, free tuition. Another free facility was Nazi propaganda, always present though at times subtle. This was where I came a cropper.

Since no foreigner could join a German student club or association, we were given one of our own, the Auslander —or Foreign Student—Club. The club's quarters in the Badenstrasse were plush, even luxurious, and had nothing to envy their German counterparts. The prettiest girls in Freiburg frequented the club and membership dues were extremely low or even free to some. Germans, too, could be members of the Auslander, but, as I learned later, they usually were hand-picked by the party for this distinction.

In addition to the quarters and the girls, our club afforded another attraction not to be found at the German clubs: free speech.

Johann Jebsen and I met at the Auslander Club. Perhaps because our proclivities and possibilities were similar. Johnny early accepted me as a friend. More than that, I was one of the few at school he seemed to respect as an equal or, it could be, as a mentor. I was a few years older than Johnny. We both had some intellectual pretensions, but on the side, we were addicted to sports cars and sporting girls and had enough money to keep them both running.

Our backgrounds were somewhat similar too, although

Johnny's people were big fish in a big pond and mine were only big in a little pond. Johnny was the orphan son of a rich Hamburg shipowner. My father, an industrialist rich only by Yugoslav standards, was nevertheless fairly indulgent. In later days, Johnny figuratively adopted my family and formed a friendship almost as strong as mine with my older brother, Ivo.

Johnny was an idol at the university. Most students, unable to compete with him intellectually or otherwise, revered him and were completely under his charm. He was a complex, many-faceted character, simultaneously an aristocrat, even an autocrat, and a democrat. He was a man of whims and surprises, devious.

Another of his and my close friends at the university was Freddy von Kaghaneck. Freddy fell in the same pattern. It was Freddy who displayed the most aplomb the day we three decided to lend our support to our favorite konditorei owner in his disobedience to a Nazi decree. The local party boys had ordered all café and restaurant owners to post a sign declaring "Jews and Dogs Not Allowed." Herr Billinger, who ran the Billinger Café on Bertholdstrasse, refused to comply. Two S.S. types in uniform took up stations at the door of the konditorei to intimidate customers by requesting their names.

"Johann Jebsen," Johnny said highhandedly, staring down from his six-foot height at the short, pugnacious agent.

"Dusko Popov." I sneered.

"Graf von Kaghaneck," Freddy cited his illustrious name. He was a descendant of one of the most influential Catholic families in Germany. "But you wouldn't know how to spell it: Graf . . . G-R-A-F . . . von . . . V . . ."

The S.S man turned apoplectic. We brushed by him to take a table in full view of the street.

At the time it was a lark. We three couldn't bring our-

selves to take the Nazis seriously. It was about on a level
with Johnny's habitual treatment of the police. Johnny drove
a supercharged Mercedes 540K convertible. He handled the
machine with skill but also with utter nonchalance and disregard for traffic regulations. He was never stopped because
he had had the foresight to make an arrangement with the
police. On his arrival in Freiburg, Johnny had paid a visit to
the police chief, handing him two envelopes. "One," he
explained, "is for police charity. The other is payment in
advance for my fines. When that runs out, let me know.
Saves time to pay in advance." I don't know whether the
chief pocketed both or neither, but the trick worked.
Johnny drove as he liked and parked where he pleased, and
no policeman ever flagged down the driver of that distinctive 540K with its burbling chrome pipes flaring out of
the hood.

If I speak about Jebsen often it is both because he affected my life more than any other person and because I'm
trying to make him understandable. That's not easy, not
even for the closest of his friends. His coldness, aloofness,
could be forbidding, yet everyone was under his spell. Actually, he had much warmth too, but it was expressed only by
action and attitude, rarely verbally. He spoke abruptly, in
short phrases, hardly ever used an adjective, and was, above
all, ironic. His intelligence was reflected in his face, in the
alertness of his steel-blue eyes. His knowledge was ency-
clopedic and his memory infallible. In dress, he was like a
young Anthony Eden, conservatively elegant. He would no
more go out without his umbrella than without his trousers.
His only Germanic touch was a monocle screwed into his
right eye. Otherwise he reflected his semi-Danish origins,
having high cheekbones, very blond hair, and regular fea-
tures. In all he was handsome, strong, wiry, not muscular.

With all this, Johnny was a complete person, fun-loving,

woman-loving, open to all conversations, and intensely curious about human reactions. One of his tricks was to deliberately stir up situations to see what would happen. He delighted in sticking pins in people, particularly in the pompous, who had need of a bit of deflation. I afforded him one of his great opportunities in this respect.

It happened one afternoon that I was sunning myself at a swimming pool with a girlfriend. Undoubtedly to arouse me, she complained that another student, Karl Laub, whom I liked rather well as a matter of fact, had been chasing after her. She told him she wouldn't go out with him because she was my girlfriend.

" 'How long will that last?' " she quoted him as saying.

"That's a dreadful thing for him to have said, isn't it, Dusko? You love me, don't you?"

I answered "Ugh" to both her questions, too lulled by the sun to pay her any serious attention.

"Well, then, I think you should do something about it."

"Yes, darling." I sought to appease her. "Next time I see Karl I'll knock his block off." I turned over on my stomach to sun my back.

Next thing I knew she was nudging me in the ribs. I twisted around to see Karl standing above me. I hardly wanted to argue with him about what to me was a casual affair, but I had committed myself. I tried to get out of it as easily as possible.

"Go away, Karl," I told him, "you're in my sun and I hear you've been saying nasty things to Anne-Lore. Now just apologize and stop making shadows."

"I meant whatever I said." Karl was an infatuated idiot. "And if you don't like shadows, you can get on your feet."

I sprang up, and the next thing I knew my hand had slapped, more resoundingly than hurtfully, his face. I was shocked by my reaction and tried to lessen its import by telling him, "Let's not be foolish, Karl. Anne-Lore should be appeased now, so we can forget it."

"My seconds will call on you." Karl pronounced the set formula, turned, and walked away stiffly.

Dueling was having a revival on the campuses of Germany. Hitler encouraged saber fighting as a demonstration of virility. The bouts were fought between two parallel lines beyond which one could not retreat, and small masks over the eyes and nose were the only protection allowed. This accounted for the scarred faces of so many German students.

I chose Jebsen as my second, and not thinking my looks would be improved by a bright red cicatrix, I instructed him what to say. As the one being challenged, I had the choice of weapons. It violated the conventions, but I selected pistols. It was well known on the campus that for two years running I had won a snap-shooting contest in which the target was a moving figure. I had been taught to shoot by the commandant of my regiment in Yugoslavia. His method, which proved infallible after practice, was to use the middle finger on the trigger and the index finger laid along the barrel as a pointer.

As foreseen, Karl's seconds objected to my choice of weapons. Following my instructions, Johnny told them I was honor-bound as a cavalry reserve officer of my particular regiment to fight only with pistols. Who could check on an outfit based in Bosnia?

A student court of honor decided the case. I couldn't be required, it declared, to break my regimental code, but neither could Karl be required to duel with pistols. Karl and I were declared enemies for life. But that wasn't the end of the story.

Jebsen saw in the incident an opportunity for a bit of fun at the expense of some of our more obnoxious comrades.

He would intimate to one of these that I was set on provoking a duel with him. No one was daring enough to want to trade pistol shots with me or to accept the disgrace of refusing to do so. I was given a wide berth, many times without even knowing why.

Our flouting of the Nazis took on a more serious aspect when I learned what was going on at the Auslander Club. In addition to the alluring girls, the elite of the pro-Nazi German student intelligentsia were chosen by the party machine as members of the club. Their function was to propagandize us by indirect methods, one of which was the "Herren Essen." This was a formal candlelight dinner, black tie obligatory, every second Friday night. The dinner was exclusively for men, the girls joining us only after eleven for dancing so as not to inject their frivolity in the dinner-table conversation. With the promise of girls afterward, however, and with free and excellent food and unlimited vintage wine, these functions never lacked for attendance.

Seemingly by chance, the dinner-table conversation invariably would turn into a public debate. At first, the custom seemed innocuous enough, since we were permitted, even encouraged, to say whatever we pleased, insults to the Führer excepted. After a while I was surprised to find that the Nazi thesis was regularly winning the most votes.

"Why is that?" I asked Johnny. "The majority of the students at the dinners are foreigners. Surely most of them can't be in sympathy with the Nazis."

"You're as innocent as they are," he laughed. "They're bending over backward to be fair. Haven't you noticed it is always one of the German students who suggests the topic? They bone up on it in advance. Now do you understand why they are more convincing?"

I cursed myself for not figuring out the trick before. "Johnny, old boy"—my tone caused him to look at me sharply—"do you think you could find out the topics in advance?"

"Nothing easier." His eyes took on a rare warmth reserved for mischief.

Not to expose Johnny to unnecessary jeopardy, I prepared the antithesis for our fortnightly contest in conjunction with a couple of British and American friends. For the next year and a half the Nazi viewpoint never again won a majority.

It was fun, and like most fun there came a day when the piper claimed his due. It happened shortly after I took my doctorate. To celebrate this event, I planned a trip to Paris. At six the morning before my announced departure I was awakened by heavy pounding on the door of my apartment. I opened it to find four Gestapo men, who ordered me to dress and prepare to accompany them.

While one kept me under surveillance, the three others ransacked my apartment. They seemed to take particular delight in the job, probably because I was one of the few students to have his own quarters, and even in the university there was some jealousy about that.

I did the usual protesting and inquiring what it was all about but got nothing for my pain except a bit more pain. Rather roughly, the Gestapo men hustled me down to their car and conducted me to their headquarters.

For eight full days and nights, a relay of agents questioned me almost constantly. For some reason they didn't beat or torture me. It wasn't simply because I was a foreigner. As I was to learn later, such a subtle distinction didn't phase them. Probably they thought their method more adapted to my case. The questioning would continue until they brought me to the point of incoherence and fainting, then they would allow me a snatch of sleep, resuming as soon as they could bring me around again.

They started by accusing me of being a Communist. "You went out with a girl factory worker," one of them charged in substantiation. I explained that in Dubrovnik we had an ancient tradition of democracy. Bootblacks and lords associated with each other, attending the same school and remaining on familiar terms ever after. This probably made me even more suspect.

"You hung around the factory," they accused, "didn't you? Why?"

"I came to pick up the girl, if you want to call that hanging around the factory."

"Admit it, you're a Communist," insisted a Gestapo man who looked like a schoolteacher type of disciplinarian.

"I'm not a Nazi, if that's what you mean," I said, determined to keep up my resistance. "Your propaganda is no good for the export market."

"Ah, propaganda." He glared at me through steel-rimmed heavy glasses that magnified his eyes, making him look fanatic. "That's your game, isn't it? You go around lying about us. You said . . ." He fumbled in his breast pocket and drew out a small notebook. "You said, three weeks ago at the Auslander Club, that food is rationed here. That was a lie. There is no rationing in Germany."

"I said one can't buy as much as one wants and that that amounts to rationing. Didn't you hear Goering's speech on guns or butter, mein Lieber Herr? My answer should be in your notebook. What else do you have in it?"

If he had had a ruler, he would have hit me on the knuckles with it. "I have that you made nasty remarks about a patriotic parade. And that comes not from a German but from a good Swiss boy."

I knew the boy and why he was considered good. He was Swiss only by birth. By conviction he was a Nazi.

"I only said the girls smelled afterward. It was a joke and

you know it. Now come to the point. What do you really want from me here?"

"Here we want you to answer with the truth, not sexy wisecracks," he fumed, turning me over to a colleague who took up a different line.

This one held up a book that I recognized as mine, a first play by Ernst Toller, *Man and the Masses*. Soon after Hitler's takeover, Toller came to Dubrovnik as German delegate to the International Pen Club meeting, which was being held there that year. Toller was a Socialist and a Jew. The German government sought to override the Pen Club selection and sent a man named Müller to Dobrovnik to replace him. The convention refused to seat Müller, and Toller remained as representative. After the convention Toller stayed on in Dubrovnik for a while, obviously being unable to return to Germany. Toller was a brilliant and amusing man; naturally enough he drew to him the young intellectuals of the town. We became rather good friends and he gave me a few of his books.

"You can't deny this is yours." The Gestapo man pointed to the flyleaf. "It is dedicated to you, dedicated by that Jew Communist Toller. You have brought forbidden propaganda into the country. Admit you're a Communist agitator."

"I've read *Mein Kampf* too. Does that make me a Nazi agitator?" I replied with what I realized was unwanted logic. There was no point in answering at all, but I was doing so hoping that I would get the ordeal over with that way.

In general they asked me nothing of any seeming importance, questions to which they could obtain the answers easily without my cooperation. The session went on for days because they wanted to know how I had spent nearly every hour of my nearly two years in Germany.

"With whom did you speak on that day?" they would

ask. "What about? What girl did you go out with? What did you do? What book did you read that night?" Even feigning cooperation, straining my memory for details, precise or not, was reducing me to exhaustion, to a subhuman state. I was trying to avoid giving names of those I thought they might not know and who might be hurt.

While I was undergoing this interrogation, the gentlemen from the Gestapo were questioning simultaneously everyone who had ever come into contact with me in any capacity whatsoever. They hauled in waiters in restaurants I frequented, my tailor, my garage mechanic, and others of that nature, in addition to those who knew me more intimately. It was a lesson in terror . . . and in the product of terror. Bosom friends pretended to barely know me. Professors who two weeks before had praised my work declared I was an anarchist, useless and snobbish. To whitewash themselves, some acquaintances invented compromising declarations they accredited to me and covered me with slander and worse.

In all, I later calculated the Gestapo questioned over two hundred persons on my case. Only two stood up for me: Freddy von Kaghaneck and Johann Jebsen.

When a few weeks had passed and I was still being held prisoner, incommunicado, Johnny at last realized the gravity of the situation. He hadn't taken this sort of miniature tempest growing out of a student prank too seriously. It had seemed unimaginable that it could have a serious outcome.

Powerless to intervene himself, not trusting the German lines of communication, Jebsen drove to Switzerland and telephoned to my father in Dubrovnik. My father hadn't been worried at not hearing from me, believing that I was unwinding in Paris after my examinations. He was accustomed to single-mindedness in such circumstances, it being a trait I acquired from him.

In addition to his business activities, my father was president of a provincial political group and, as such, had considerable back-room influence. When he learned what was happening, he went directly to the Prime Minister, Dr. Stojadinovic. And the Prime Minister went directly to Goering. On the latter's intervention, I was freed immediately but given twenty-four hours to leave Germany. I was not at all loath to comply.

After my eight days of unremittent questioning in Gestapo headquarters I had been transferred to the Freiburg prison. A red-brick round building in the northeast section of town, it had no resemblance whatsoever to the attractions that characterized the resort in publicity brochures. I did have a private room, however—solitary. My clothes were taken away and I was given a rough gray convict suit, no permission to receive visitors or letters or to write to anyone. I was allowed into the prison yard for exercise a few minutes each day. It was there—out of the corner of the mouth of a fellow prisoner—that I learned my probable fate.

Since I had done nothing punishable by law, there could be no real charges brought against me. Therefore, I would be shipped in secret to a concentration camp. No bothersome formalities such as a trumped-up trial. I would never be heard from again. The usual exit was made feet first.

I thought it was incredible that this could happen to a foreigner. There would be inquiries, families and friends protesting. "You'll be listed as missing," my prisoner friend explained.

With my twenty-four hour eviction notice, the chief of the Gestapo warned me, "Don't communicate with anyone." I went directly home to snip off the odd strings of unfinished affairs dangling after two years at the university. I arranged for the sale of my BMW, which had German plates, sold or labeled for friends my books, settled my bills with the local tradesmen, and packed up my belongings.

I couldn't spot anyone following me, but I was sure that I was under surveillance, so I avoided contacting anyone. I did meet a few acquaintances on the street to whom I mentioned, without embellishment, that I was taking the train for home the following afternoon. They surmised the rest and didn't tarry to talk.

Taking courage in my release and apparent whitewashing, some friends who had heard the news did attempt to see me off at the train station. Only two girls succeeded. They cunningly told the Gestapo men stationed at the platform entrance that they were there to see someone else off. When the others presented the platform visitor's ticket required for nonpassengers, they naïvely told the truth and were advised that I was not frequentable. It was a sad parting. No Johnny. No Freddy.

To go to Belgrade from Freiburg one had to change trains in Basel. There, unexpectedly, I found Johnny at the station—or rather he found me. When refused access to the platform in Freiburg, he had jumped into his 540K and raced the train to Switzerland.

Appreciating what he had done for me, I said to Johnny emotionally, "If you ever need anything, Johnny, you know you only have to say the word. I mean it sincerely, and you know I usually keep my promises," I added pompously. I was to fulfill that one in more ways than one.

2

The Johnny I found in the bar of the Serbian King Hotel in Belgrade had changed visibly in the three years of our separation. That was not unexpected. Naturally, he would feel some onus for his country's actions. World War II had started some five months before. Poland was already ravaged, and Hitler was preparing to cross the Maginot Line in France and destroy still more civilizations. Johnny's maturity, if you can call it that, had the unhealthy aspect to be expected from such nourishment.

As we talked, his sharp intelligence evinced itself more than ever, but so did his cynicism and dark humor. His eyes, always expressive of his feelings, now often showed apprehensiveness. The exterior signs of unease were there, too. He ordered his whiskies double, neat, and frequently. He smoked a lot. In style and neatness, his clothes still rivaled Eden's, but his blond hair was no longer so closely trimmed and he had a neglected mustache, reddened by tobacco.

His concern showed itself by the words he blurted out almost in response to my "How are you?"

"Hitler is making fools out of the Germans," he followed up his greeting, "and with their help he may take over the world."

Johnny didn't habitually say the obvious, and my answering glance was one of perplexed curiosity.

"Okay, we'll leave that talk till later when we're sufficiently drunk," he said. "Right now, here's my problem. It needs fast action. Germany has five ships blocked in Trieste. One of them is mine. I've managed to obtain authorization to sell them all to a neutral country."

I knew more or less the background to the story. The five ships in Trieste weren't the only ones rotting in a Mediterranean port. English and French warships controlled these waters entirely. As an Axis partner and the only other naval power in the "Mare Nostrum," Italy would have gladly traded with the German ships, but she was not yet in the war and so couldn't attempt to force the blockade.

"What neutral country will chance buying those ships?" I objected. "If the French and English refuse to recognize the sale, they'll seize them at the first opportunity."

"Righto, any idiot can see that, even those idiots in Berlin . . . eventually. But for the moment all they're asking for is a firm engagement from a neutral country that the ships will not be used in trade with England or France. That's why we have to act fast before someone at the Admiralty sees the catch."

"That's where I come in, eh? The specialist in firm engagements—or bilge water, to keep it in the proper metaphor."

"Right again, my lad. You have to use your excellent contacts and set up a deal that I can shove through before anyone starts getting curious."

"You know where the ships will end up?" I asked.

"They can row them in the Henley regatta, for all I care."

"Not worried about getting into trouble?"

His blue eyes turned steely. "I'm beyond that. Either

I do what I think is correct or . . ." The eloquence of
his raised hands finished the sentence. "Dusko, you are one
of the few persons I can tell it to. I had some difficult mo-
ments before deciding. Deciding not on a line of reasoning
but on a line of action. I'm caught, anchored by my roots
like most of us but with the difference that I'm not wearing
blinders. I don't owe obedience to a bloody tyrant. On the
contrary. But to be completely truthful, old friend"—
Johnny smiled ironically—"maybe some of my love for my
country has to do with so much of it actually belonging to
me. I'm not about to give that up, and what's more I intend
to have it on my terms. So, as I told you, one of those ships
is mine. . . . "

I felt sorry for Johnny. He was being pulled so many
ways. Under that mask of a snob and a cynic and under his
playboy manners, he was a man with very basic honesty.

"Tomorrow morning, first thing, we'll see about the
ships. Tonight," I said, feeling Johnny needed diversion,
"I'll show you Belgrade."

Where we were sitting in the glassed-in bar of the Serbian King, we overlooked the Danube and the Old Turkish
fortresses. Viewing these remnants of previous conquerors
recalled to Johnny the misery of any thinking man who had
to live in Hitler's Germany so we rapidly fled the place for
a round of Belgrade's nightspots. Somewhere en route we
enlisted the company of two girls from the chorus of one of
the clubs, and we wound up having a lovely brawl with the
director of our hotel, who threatened to throw us and our
company out—not for moral reasons but because we insisted on champagne and steak for breakfast in the public
dining room.

After winning our battle, I followed this restorative with
several cups of strong Turkish coffee, which is one of the

pleasant heritages left us by the Turks. A cold shower on top of that and I was in form to accomplish Johnny's mission.

On my return from Freiburg I had started practicing law—business law mainly, with a few banks as clients. Occasionally I did some governmental missions, but above all I was closely connected with the most powerful financial figure in Yugoslavia, Bozo Banac. Banac was in league with influential British business interests. Through him I had met the British Commercial Attaché for the Balkans, a Mr. Sturrack. Sturrack was competent and well liked, and we had become friendly. I chose him as the ideal intermediary for Johnny's mission.

"How would you like to add five bottoms to the British Merchant Marine," I proposed to Sturrack, "at the expense of the Germans?"

"What are you up to, Dusko?" he asked, very wise and very fatherly. He was used to treating the younger set of Belgrade that way. He had two beautiful daughters who were driving half the town's eligible men to learning English. The other half, of course, spoke it already.

I explained how we might hoodwink the Germans by purchasing their ships through a Yugoslav company and later transferring them to the British. Sturrack grasped both the situation and the opportunity in a flash. On his own responsibility he gave me the go-ahead to start negotiations immediately, saying he was confident he would secure London's blessings.

The next person I visited was a great friend of my family and I knew her to be 100 percent pro-Allied. I had no doubts about securing her aid. Mrs. Djurdjina Racic was the widow of a shipowning magnate and the daughter of the man revered as the founder and father of Yugoslavia, Nicola Pasitch, who in 1918 became our first prime minister.

Mrs. Racic was indeed willing to have her shipping company serve as cover for the transaction. Her only reserve was that the project be presented to the Yugoslav government as genuine.

"They are so eager to be neutral," she complained, referring to the government, "that they would either prevent its realization or disclose our true intentions to the Germans."

The ridiculous part was that if either the German or Yugoslav government had been wide awake they would have realized there was some skulduggery afoot. A guarantee not to trade with the Allies wasn't worth the paper it was written on.

Within a few days, London sent its agreement, money for the purchase, and the Admiralty's thanks for some thirty thousand tons of shipping. Johnny and I rushed to complete the transaction before anyone got wind of it. He flew to Berlin to secure the necessary documents while I completed all the formalities in Belgrade.

Two weeks later, Johnny came back to Belgrade and we held a quiet celebration. The deal was signed and sealed. At the same time, Johnny gave me a first glimpse of his real occupation and of the vast panorama of activities that were to develop in the following years.

We were in my quarters at the family winter home in Belgrade. The heavy curtains and thick Persian carpets contributed to an atmosphere of privacy and conspiracy. Johnny opened up.

"As you have undoubtedly imagined, I had no desire to be dragged into the armed services of the Third Reich. To avoid that—and for other reasons—I joined the Brandenburg Division." Seeing my puzzled expression, he explained, "That's a kind of sabotage outfit under the control of the Abwehr." I nodded to show that I was following. At least I knew what the Abwehr was: the major German intelligence establishment, a part of the OKW, the high command.

"For an antimilitarist"—I converted my puzzlement to irony—"you sure chose the right branch."

He ignored my snideness. "I myself have good friends in the Abwehr, and Dr. Hjalmar Schacht is on very close terms with Admiral Canaris."

Schacht, of course, I knew, as did anyone who read a newspaper. As president of the Reichsbank he had revaluated the mark and earned an international reputation as a financial genius. In fact, his nickname was "Financial Wizard." I also knew that Johnny admired him greatly and had served a sort of apprenticeship under him, during which he learned most of his financial know-how.

Admiral Canaris, on the other hand, meant nothing to me. Johnny obligingly explained.

"Admiral Canaris—Wilhelm Canaris—is the chief of the Abwehr. I met him through his personal assistant, Colonel Oster, whose political ideas and philosophy are identical to mine."

"And how about Canaris? What is he like?"

Johnny considered for a moment, stubbing out an old cigarette and putting the flame of his gold lighter to a new one. Heavy smoker as he was, he was never inelegant. He didn't light one cigarette from another.

Johnny described the Admiral as a sensitive man, unobtrusive, short in stature but tireless. He credited him with much curiosity, vast intelligence, and a first-class sense of humor. "He gives the impression of preferring to listen rather than to speak, yet when he eventually does speak, it is like a blitz," I recall Johnny saying.

I asked, "Is he a Nazi?"

"He has the reputation of not being one even though he is regularly closeted with Hitler. That's an unavoidable adjunct to his post of Chief of Intelligence," Johnny said.

"He's also in close contact with Reinhard Heyndrich, who is head of the S.D. and one of the heads of the Gestapo as well." The S.D., I learned, was the Sicherheit Dienst, the internal political intelligence and security branch. Counter-intelligence, in other words.

Johnny poured himself another half-tumbler of scotch from the fresh bottle I'd left on the table between our arm-chairs. It was about two-thirds down but Johnny was cold sober. Still, he wasn't making much sense to me. I'd been dabbling in politics in Belgrade and understood some of its subtleties and contradictions, but I couldn't see the point of Johnny's running with his diametrical opposites.

"I told you already that I want to keep out of uniform. I also want to be free to travel, to keep in touch firsthand with what is happening in the world outside of Germany. I couldn't do that if I were in a military unit destined for cannon fodder. I won't be able to do it either unless I'm well established in the Abwehr. If you want to stay in, you can't pretend or exist on the fringes. You have to entrench yourself, and to do that you've got to produce results."

"Like what, Johnny?" My tone was somewhat sharp. He ignored the implied criticism.

"Oh, nothing spectacular to begin with. Well, for in-stance, just before I left for Belgrade, Hans von Dohnanyi —he's another of Canaris's friends and advisers—von Dohnanyi was preparing a report about the most suitable French politicians to be in touch with when France is van-quished."

"Don't you mean 'if and when'?"

"Dusko, I'm afraid it's 'when.' Germany's enemies all make the same mistake. They underestimate her strength and Hitler's aggressiveness and determination. They think all France has to do is sit comfortably behind the Maginot Line. It's not going to happen that way."

"Okay," I countered, "but if Germany is that prepared,

you should know the French politicians who'd be willing to collaborate with you. Your ex-Ambassador in Paris should be able to answer that question offhand."

"I'm sure he can. And has. But the Abwehr was asked to give an independent opinion and I'd like to contribute to it. In intelligence they say, 'An information is no information unless it is confirmed from several independent sources.' " Forthright, as usual, Johnny explained that it would serve his purpose to contribute to the report and to do so he needed my help. He warned me that he would have to furnish my name and sources to his superior.

All things considered, it was a loaded request. Johnny was putting as a personal favor what was in reality a job of work—of intelligence work—for the Nazis. Still, the question sounded innocent enough. The answer could be obtained easily by anyone mingling in diplomatic or political circles. I didn't see the harm in it, and besides, I was developing a little idea of my own.

"Okay, Johnny," I said after a large swallow of scotch. "I'll do it for you with one proviso. Don't ask for more than that. I'll be delighted to help you ride out the war, but it's like sticking a knife in my own guts to think that I'm helping your Nazi friends even a little."

Johnny's head nodded a few times to express what he couldn't put into words. I turned businesslike and arranged the *modus operandi*.

"How much time do I have?"

"You can take a few weeks. I'd like a comprehensive report."

"And how do I get it to you?"

"Send me a telegram in Berlin. I'll come down."

Obtaining the information was no trick at all. I had all the contacts necessary—personal friends, friends of my father's and relatives—many of them high-ranking members of the Yugoslav Foreign Office, some of them experts on French affairs, some ex-ambassadors or even active ministers. I also was well acquainted with a number of French officials in Yugoslavia. The task was time-consuming only because I couldn't come out and ask the question directly. It had to be done in the course of dinners, luncheons, social conversations.

Despite my reservations, I warmed to the job because the subject was fascinating and the opinions amazing in that they all coincided. Leaving aside the leaders of the overt Fascist factions in France, who were ultimately discarded as having no real influence or prestige, the same few names occurred to all. Sometimes it was the former Prime Minister and Minister of Foreign Affairs, Pierre Flandin, occasionally Marshal Pétain, but the first candidate on everyone's lips was another ex–Prime Minister, Pierre Laval.

Laval's past spoke for him, it was felt. Whenever he was in power he espoused the line that France must avoid war at all cost by making arrangements with Hitler and Mussolini. He sacrificed the Franco-Soviet Pact to that end by blocking its ratification in Parliament even after having signed it himself. His flirtations with Mussolini broke the spirit of the Petite Entente, a defensive alliance among Czechslovakia, Romania, Yugoslavia, and Greece, leaning chiefly on French support. The main reason for his selection as collaborator number one was his bitter hate for England. He was convinced there was no possibility of defeating Germany; my informants believed that he would welcome the opportunity of changing sides and, together with Hitler, vanquishing the common foe across the Channel.

That was the gist of the long report I wrote for the Abwehr in duplicate. I had another recipient in mind for the second copy, but I was hesitant to make a direct approach, wanting the contact to be unobtrusive. I was fearful that I might be considered a meddler.

One evening at an embassy dinner I got the opportunity I was waiting for. I was a fairly regular figure at the various foreign social functions. I think I was invited to add local color. I was one of those natives with whom one could mix safely. I didn't drink out of the finger bowl, I could carry on a conversation in several languages, and I did as a bachelor fill a certain lacuna.

My quarry was the First Secretary of the British Embassy, Mr. Dew. I cornered him at one of these soirees when he went out on the terrace for a breath of air. It was a chilly evening so we were not likely to be disturbed. I took advantage of that to tell him about Johnny's assignment. Mr. Dew asked a lot of questions, among them, would I mind if he reported the matter to his superiors? That, of course, was precisely what I had in mind. He also requested a copy of my report, which I turned over to him before handing the original to Johnny. I pointed out to Mr. Dew that Johnny's assertion that the Germans were sure of taking France was more important than my report. As a Francophile, that worried me, but the First Secretary didn't seem ruffled at all. "Interesting," was his comment. "Be a good thing for you to keep in touch with that chap."

"That chap" came to pick up my report, but except for transmitting to me, a bit later, official thanks and compliments for its accuracy, I was out of touch with him. I did notice though, a distinct change in the attitude of the German Embassy toward me.

In the course of business, I at times had had to call around at the embassy, and the staff's attitude had been cold and stiff. Undoubtedly they knew I was *persona non grata* in the Fatherland. After doing the report on France, I smelled of roses. Someone must have given them the word. Suddenly, they became full of little attentions, and previous obstructions vanished. I think this was due not only to an official change in attitude: with their guilt complex, the Germans were particularly sensitive to, or appreciative of, any sign of sympathy or friendship.

The prognostication implicit in the minor job I had done came true: France capitulated. In Yugoslavia, the reflection of that victory was painfully visible. The Germans, along with their friends and sympathizers, strutted their arrogance. Fearing Hitler, the Yugoslav government tried even more desperately to prove its neutrality. It felt that it was isolated from any help and would either have to bend or be crushed. Not so the Yugoslav people. During the course of some five hundred years their country had been invaded and occupied periodically, and they had long training in, and a tradition of, resistance. Taking to the mountains was an old Yugoslav tactic. Despite the government's attempts to control it, the population, almost unanimously pro-Allied, was ready to burst at the smallest provocation, singing "La Madelon" in cinemas and booing the Nazi hierarchy in newsreels.

To confirm our plight for me, Johnny told me gloomily on one of his trips to Belgrade, "With the fall of France, every hope we had of getting rid of Hitler by internal action vanished."

Johnny became a permanent visitor and guest in our townhouse toward the end of the summer of 1940. Ostensibly he was in Yugoslavia because he had undertaken several commercial and financial propositions in Belgrade. It was true that Johnny was an indefatigable businessman. He couldn't go anywhere without seeing the possibility of a good deal. In our small circle we coined the word "Jebseniade" to indicate a sure business proposition or clever trick.

The family had gone to Dubrovnik for the summer and I wanted to go sailing there, but Johnny had involved me in his business deals and I couldn't get away unless he dropped things and came too. No amount of urging would get him out of Belgrade. That wasn't the Johnny I knew.

"What's eating you?" I finally asked. "You're not the little businessman who can't leave the shop. What is it?"

He pleaded preoccupation, telling me how practically every German was now 100 percent for Hitler since he took France, how you had to be careful not to show antagonism, how you had to make double sure of even close friends. He went on with what seemed to me a lot of defeatist twaddle: Hitler's reputation for infallibility was perhaps correct, he'd never been wrong so far. "He's the undisputed master of Europe," Johnny said, echoing Goebbels. "In a few months' time, he'll probably finish off England, and then America and Russia will be glad to come to terms with him. Hitler's promise to change history for the next thousand years may come true."

"You propagandizing me, Johnny?" I asked jokingly. He kept on being serious.

"Like it or not, we have to accept the facts and adapt ourselves to them," he defended himself. "We may have to become part of Hitler's new world or be crushed."

I was exasperated and puzzled. "Christ, Johnny," I said impatiently, "what are you leading up to? Do you want me to go down on my knees and lick boots?"

"Sorry," he apologized. "I guess I was being heavy-handed." He gave me one of his rare smiles and tempered my harsh thoughts. "I was leading up to something, something I know you won't exactly like."

I waited for the disclosure without comment.

"Would you dine with a friend of mine, a member of the German Embassy? Or better, may I bring him home for dinner? Perhaps it would be more discreet not to be seen with him."

"Is he that bad?"

"You judge after speaking to him."

I didn't pursue the questioning any more. It was the first and only time I had ever seen Johnny at a loss.

The friend Johnny brought home for dinner was about what I would expect of an Embassy official. His name was Major Müntzinger—a Bavarian, by his accent. He was very sure of himself and of an ultimate German victory. It made my blood boil to have him sitting at my table, eating my food and drinking my wine, but I didn't show it.

I liked it still less when he said, "The service you have rendered us," and I concluded he meant the Laval report, "was clear and reasoned and it proved to be exact. You have a talent for seeing what is important. Your wish to help us is proof of your political wisdom and your ability for adaptation."

Shades of what Johnny had been lecturing me about! I washed my mouth out with a swallow of wine, but the taste was still there.

The major continued. "In the future you will find that you are going to need us. Right now, may I tell you frankly, we need you." The major was starting to head somewhere.

He wiped his mouth briskly and put his napkin on the table, although we weren't finished eating. I didn't think he'd come just to sample our cook's food.

"There is no better alliance than one of mutual interest," Müntzinger continued, very satisfied at having produced this philosophical gem. "Now, you have the reputation in Belgrade of being a liberal, and your misadventure in Freiburg as a student was well advertised. Nobody knows your real feelings, and we'd be obliged if you would keep things that way. In spite of the temptations nowadays, please don't let anyone know you are a friend of ours. You can help much more if everyone thinks you are anti-German. And by the way"—he tried to be charming—"I'm sure the unpleasantness you had may be blamed largely on the zeal of the provincial Gestapo."

I avoided looking at Johnny. Müntzinger's speech had been planned and rehearsed, and I had the feeling that Johnny was the coauthor, if not the director.

I passed that off and asked, "What help do you want?"

"I shall come to that," he replied. "In a couple of months, certainly not much later, England will be invaded—unless, that is, she sees reason and sues for an armistice. No country can resist the German army. To facilitate the German task and to make an eventual invasion less bloody—to save many German and English lives—you could help."

He may have expected applause. "Ah," was all I said, but that seemed to satisfy him. I was following my grandfather's dictum. "Let people talk," he used to say. "You will learn more than by questioning them. And don't let your face say what your tongue doesn't want to."

The major got down to specifics. "You are a good friend of Mr. Banac's. You met the Duke of York at Banac's home and entertained him during his stay in Dubrovnik."

That wasn't accurate but I wasn't going to tell it to Müntzinger. I had met the Duke at Banac's but I hadn't really entertained him. I had arranged honorary membership for him at the Dubrovnik yacht club, the Argosy, of which I was one of the founders, and had shown him around a bit.

I thought I could see what Müntzinger was leading up to. With the Laval report in mind, I was prepared for some similar proposition, but he proceeded to outline something far different.

"We have many agents in England, quite a number of them excellent," he said. "But"—the truth came—"we would like someone who has entry everywhere. Your connections would open many doors. Some types of information are not obtainable in the street. You could render us a great service. And we could do the same for you, Herr Popov. The Reich knows how to show its appreciation with generosity. You will become an important person in the future of Yugoslavia."

This was something else again, not simply the writing of a corroborative report. In no uncertain way he was asking me to join the German espionage service. "Shocked" would be the wrong word for my reaction; so would "surprised." Subconsciously, given Johnny's occupation, I must have been prepared for the offer. But I did feel a burst of adrenalin coursing through me.

Johnny hadn't uttered a word since Müntzinger took over the stage. He was avoiding my eyes, contemplating the smoke of his cigarette and the color of his cognac.

"What kind of information would you expect from me?" I knew the answer but I wanted him to spell it out.

"General. Political." A slight pause. "Military. But really that is not in my province. I'm here to seek your agreement. Johnny will introduce you to the proper people when and if you accept."

"You don't require an immediate answer?"

"Certainly not," he said heartily, as though displaying generosity. "Think it over. There are some risks involved, but as a good gambler, I can tell you that they are minimal in the light of the advantages. But weigh all the elements yourself. I am staying in Belgrade a few days. Let me know through Johnny what you have decided and we shall have a long talk afterward." He was quite sure of himself—or was it of me?

He rose from the table. We hadn't bothered moving from the dining room. I showed him out and returned immediately to the salon, where I knew Johnny would have installed himself. When I walked in he was pouring himself a drink, his back toward me. I closed the door and he turned around, his explanation ready without my having to ask.

"I would have chosen another way of doing this, Dusko," he said, "but they were in a hurry."

"Let's put our cards on the table, Johnny. You've been laying the groundwork for quite a while." My tone wasn't accusatory, merely a statement of fact.

"That's right," he said. "I figured you'd realize it. Makes things easier."

Johnny took the scotch bottle and his glass and put them on the coffee table in front of the couch. Then he arranged the pillows to his liking and stretched out. We were in for a long talk. I crouched on the tiger-skin rug in front of the fireplace. That's my favorite position.

"Müntzinger is my immediate superior," Johnny began. "He is well considered by Canaris, enjoys his full confidence. He is the chief recruiter for the Abwehr in Central Europe.

"As he told you, the Abwehr has men in England but no one capable of operating on a high level. And that's what the gentlemen from the Tirpitzufer want."

"The Tirpitzufer?"

"Sorry, I forgot you don't know Berlin very well. Tirpitzufer No. 74-76 is Abwehr headquarters. It has its reputation."

I could imagine for what.

"They've been looking desperately for a man who can move in the upper stratum of British society. The man has to have other qualities as well, as you can imagine. Many other qualities. In essence, he has to have the makings of a superspy. I took a great liberty, I suggested you. It was in the heat of the moment. I regretted it later but . . . too late to back out."

I came off my haunches and paced the room, partly to escape proximity to Johnny.

"When did you put my hat in the ring? Before or after the Laval business? Or was it at the time of the shipping deal?"

"No, it was after all that."

"You were testing me with those." It was a statement, not a question. I almost said "suckering me in" but I wasn't mad enough to do so. I thought I should have been, but as a matter of fact I really wasn't mad at all. For a few reasons. One, I had confidence in Johnny. Two, the situation wasn't without interest, nor was it that unexpected. It was only the scope that took me by surprise. I was expecting some more little assignments, not to be asked to play the role of a master spy.

"Yes, if you wish. I was testing your reaction," Johnny admitted. "And theirs. Your French report made an excellent impression in Berlin. They termed it as clear as a Generalstab paper. Then they dug out your file and got additional information, too. . . ."

"From you?"

"Mainly from me."

"And were they really convinced I've had a change of heart since Freiburg?"

Johnny laughed. "People—even tough politicians like the Nazis—believe what they want to. Judging by your conduct, you are an ambitious man. You're the son of a wealthy family; you don't really have to work, yet you do. And hard. So if you're ambitious, you have no place to turn except to the Germans. Economically, we have always controlled the Balkans. Now we're winning the war, too."

"Great character analysis," I said.

"Freud was a Jew." Johnny laughed for the first time that evening. "You don't expect them to apply his theories and to deduce that you—me too, perhaps—are trying to compete with your father."

I grinned in return. "I haven't figured it out myself."

"So"—Johnny breathed easier—"to get on, the Tirpitz-zufer ordered me to convince you, to recruit you. I couldn't bring myself to do so right away. Not fast enough. Müntzinger got impatient and decided to handle it himself."

I wanted to think, to be my myself. I poured a nightcap and slugged it back. "I'll sleep on it, Johnny. Goodnight."

"I hope you'll forgive me, Dusko," he said softly. "I'm using you. I'm sorry. I can't survive otherwise." There was no doubting his sincerity, but I couldn't concede that easily. I half nodded and waved my hand at him.

"One more thing," he added, as I opened the door. "If you want to destroy a team, the best way is to become part of it."

I shot him one glance and went on to my room. Why the hell hadn't he said that earlier? Complex character, my friend Johnny.

That was no night for sleep. Not that I had to make up my mind. I do that quickly. No use going over the same ground fifty times. Facts don't change. But there was one piece missing to complete the game. Would the British play? If they wouldn't, I'd have to turn down the Germans, and one didn't refuse their sort of offer with impunity.

I rushed off first thing next morning to Milosa Velikog Street, where the British Embassy was located. "Do you realize fully what you are letting yourself in for?" Mr. Dew asked, after listening keenly to my recital of the previous evening's events. "Not that I want to discourage you. Fighting the Nazis is the only proper thing to do, we all feel that way. But this bit of business you are volunteering for is sort of on the nasty side. One mistake is more than you're allowed."

"One does what one can, Mr. Dew," I answered, shrugging off the warning. Both it and my reply rang in my ears like stage dialogue.

"Good for you," Mr. Dew approved. I had been accepted into the club. "Now, this sort of thing is out of my competence," Mr. Dew admitted graciously. "I shall ask a friend of mine to see you. He'll be interested, I'm sure. He'll ring you up first thing to arrange a meeting."

The man who phoned that afternoon "at the suggestion of Mr. Dew" introduced himself as Spiradis. He asked me to come right around to see him at the British Passport Control Office.

For the second time that day I found myself on Milosa Velikog. Passport Control was located in a building about 300 yards down the street from the embassy. On being ushered into the office of the man named Spiradis, I found that I knew him vaguely. Our paths had crossed at social functions, so briefly that neither recalled the other's name, but I was sure that his wasn't Spiradis. I realized that he was certainly more than a passport control officer. When I was initiated to the game, I found out that he was the chief of M.I.6 for the Balkans, and Spiradis was his cover name.

Spiradis had me repeat the story I'd told Mr. Dew. I went through it dutifully, although I was sure Mr. Dew had acquainted him with it. That, I was to learn, was standard Intelligence technique. Spiradis questioned me down to the finest details, particularly in reference to names.

"Well," he pronounced at last, smoothing the long hairs

combed sideways over his bald scalp, "we are very interested indeed." Spiradis's speech was very British, yet there was something foreign about him. "I shall have to ask for instructions from London, but you may take it for granted we shall pursue the matter."

Communications between Belgrade and London were notoriously slow at any time and worse now that the war was on. Spiradis had his own channels. Only a couple of days later, he summoned me to his office again. Relieved at the rapid action, I jumped into my brand-new BMW and roared off for Milosa Velikog.

"London wants you to continue your conversation with the Germans," Spiradis informed me.

"Do I accept the job or do I have tea with them?" I asked. Bureaucratic doubletalk always annoyed me.

Spiradis's eyes twinkled. He rubbed his large nose between thumb and forefinger, probably to hide a smile.

"You are to accept their proposition. Be friendly but don't overdo it. Ask for time to liquidate your affairs and to prepare the trip."

"That will be legitimate enough," I agreed.

"Yes. We also want you to suggest that you have a friend in London—say, a Yugoslav diplomat—who is in need of money. You think you can get him to help you and to send information through the diplomatic bag."

I objected to that one. "What's his name? Müntzinger will want to know. He's got as much appetite for names as you have."

Spiradis dismissed my objection with a shrug. "Oh, invent something. Say you are not at liberty to reveal his name. Now"—he pointed a pencil at me—"to get down to cases: your voyage to London. I don't know what the Germans have in mind, but you must have a plausible pretext for it. Presumably, you're taking us in. A genuine pretext is the best cover. In your case there is not much of a problem. As a lawyer, you've been active in negotiating business deals with the British. You can carry on with that on an enlarged scale, a scale requiring you to go to London. You should be able to find some clients who'll agree to your representing them. We'll give you all assistance possible, particularly in the way of Navy Certs."

"In that case," I assured him, "I'm sure I can get all the clients I want."

Navy Certs were certificates of approval for goods traveling on seas controlled by the British. Without them ships were liable to seizure. The British were particularly careful and stingy about issuing Navy Certs for Yugoslavia. Foreseeing a possible Axis invasion of my country, they feared the building up of large stocks that might fall into enemy hands, to say nothing of the possibility that goods might be resold to the Germans.

Leaving the most delicate matter to the last, Spiradis said, almost casually, after we concluded our arrangements, "Oh, of course, you won't say anything to Mr. Jebsen about your connection with us."

"He practically sent me here," I objected.

"Practically," Spiradis gave the word a whole other meaning. "In this business, the less said the better."

I was reluctant to admit it, but Johnny was becoming a bit of an enigma to me. Sometimes he blew one way, sometimes another. Perhaps he was a pragmatist, playing both sides.

"At any rate," I conceded, "he'll probably guess."

"Let him."

I did. I told Johnny only that I had arranged to go to England and that I had a diplomat friend who would help. Johnny didn't ask any questions, and I was sure it was because he preferred it that way.

My next meeting with Müntzinger, arranged by Johnny, riled me more than the first. As I had noted before, he was cocksure.

"I'm a fine psychologist," he crowed. "I knew you would come to the right conclusion. Jebsen here says you have even started things rolling on your own initiative. Very good. That is what we require in a job such as yours. Who is your diplomat friend?"

"An old friend. I can vouch for him."

"I'm sure you can, but what is his name?"

"The one condition he insisted on is that I don't reveal his name."

"In intelligence," Müntzinger explained, "information is useless if there is no name attached to it. We can't judge its reliability."

"I can promise you you'll know the source of the information," I hedged. "My friend will only be the intermediary."

"Well, all right for the moment, but later I will probably have to insist on his name."

"I'll try to get him to change his mind."

Fortunately, we never locked horns on this issue. I was able to drop my phony diplomat friend before it came to that.

While talking, Müntzinger had been caressing a fine crocodile attaché case. It was new and looked like those I had seen in the Hermès shop window on the Faubourg St. Honoré in Paris. The fruits of the occupation were falling already. He undid the clasp, reached his hand in, and pulled out a metal vial.

"Here," he held it as though he were giving me a treasure. "You will give this to your friend. Secret ink. When does he go back to London?"

"In a couple of weeks."

"Good. I shall be leaving here myself shortly, but I will be placing you under Jebsen's tutelage. He will give you a set of questions that you are to transmit to your friend. He will reply in that." He pointed to the ink, pleased as a child with the trapping of his profession.

"Jebsen will also be indoctrinating you, training you in codes, informing you of the contacts you will have, many things. You will be busy between now and the time you leave."

Müntzinger bade me goodbye with a great deal of warmth, as if I were a member of the clan, shaking my hand while he assured me how much faith they had in me and told me not to worry about funds. They would keep me amply supplied. My thanks were comparatively stiff, but I don't think that fine psychologist noticed.

Within only a few days, via Johnny, Müntzinger forwarded to me an exhaustive questionnaire for my friend in London. I passed it along to Spiradis together with the secret ink. He was more impressed with the questionnaire, the English having better secret ink, he said. The questions the Germans wanted to ask were useful because they showed what they perhaps didn't know. The questionnaire also indicated what areas the Germans were interested in. They particularly asked about defense measures on the south coast from around the Wash to Southampton. On the military side they wanted everything my friend could discover, a sort of shotgun technique: the locations of divisions, brigades, and commands, the names of officers. They were specifically interested in antitank guns but also wanted to know about other weapons, the armament industry in particular, and industry in general. And then there were many political questions similar to those they had asked me about France.

Who were Churchill's enemies? Who in Britain thought the war should be ended quickly? Who was in favor of starting to negotiate peace with Germany?

Having a memory that is photographic—although not always retentive for a long period—I didn't have to waste much time learning my lessons with Johnny. My business cover took more time and much running around. I actually had to create an import organization. I canvassed my Yugoslav banking connections to get a list of goods most urgently needed by their clients. Then I visited the clients and prepared dossiers on all of them for the English.

While in the midst of this frenzied activity, my BMW broke down. My mechanic diagnosed it as piston trouble. It would take some time to repair, since parts were difficult to obtain, and also the engine would have to be taken down completely.

My father's chauffeur, Bozidar, volunteered to drive me around in my father's Buick. The family was still in Dubrovnik, so he had little to do. That should have made me suspicious; Bozidar was lazy and usually wouldn't do more than the minimum. Yet we all were fond of him. He had taught me to drive when I wasn't yet fifteen, and he was a skilled chauffeur. He was cross-eyed, and we used to kid him about being able to see both in front and on the side.

A few weeks after I'd become a back-seat passenger, Johnny burst into my room one morning without bothering to knock. He was as upset as his cool nature would permit and was waving a sheaf of papers in his hand.

"You're being sold out by Bozidar," he cried. "Look at this." He thrust the papers at me.

I was just waking up and the curtains were drawn, so I couldn't see to read.

"What is it?" I asked.

"There are nine pages here listing almost every appointment, everyone you've seen in the last two weeks. I just found out about it a few hours ago. Müntzinger phoned to ask me to pick up the list. Before he returned to Vienna he hired Bozidar to spy on you. Your faithful retainer sold you out for two thousand dinars down."

I was still slightly drugged by sleep and could hardly believe what I was hearing.

"Bozidar?"

"Yes, Bozidar. I gave him another two thousand dinars this morning. I'm supposed to send the report on to Müntzinger."

"Bozidar," I moaned. "That S.O.B. sabotaged my car, then."

I switched on a lamp and glanced through the report. It was fairly comprehensive, but for the moment its real import didn't strike me. I shrugged.

"Except for a rather incomplete list of the names and addresses of my girlfriends, I don't see much harm in it."

Johnny took the list back.

"No? What about this?" He pointed. "And this and four more like it. All the same address on Milosa Velikog."

"Oh, that's the Passport Control Office where I applied for my visa for England." I had my excuse ready-made.

"Six times? Come off it, Dusko," Johnny snapped. "It is also the headquarters of British Intelligence in Yugoslavia."

"Damn." I swore more at Spiradis than at myself. I was a novice in the game, but he should have known better than to give me a rendezvous in his office.

"I hope this doesn't tear it, Johnny. I had plans."

"Tear it," Johnny snorted. "It's liable to tear you and everyone connected with you. Friends, family. You should know the Nazis by now. If they suspect the slightest thing about you, you're marked for the chopping block. And they'll take their revenge on your family later."

I ranted about my room, cursing the Nazis, myself, Bozidar. The idea of my family, and Johnny too, I realized, being involved in such a mess drove me up the wall. And not only was I not striking back at the Nazis, I was giving them another crack at me.

"Johnny," I said desperately, "how long have we got? When do you have to turn the report in?"

"It should go in today. Perhaps I can stall for a day or two but no longer."

"Supposing we write a false report?"

"I was thinking along the same lines," Johnny answered. "But there's Bozidar. We'd have to be damn sure he wouldn't talk."

"I'll take care of Bozidar," I promised. "Leave the report to me, too. I'll forge a new one and have it for you by tomorrow."

Various ways of silencing Bozidar occurred to me. I could threaten him, pay him off handsomely, have him imprisoned on a phony charge. Maybe the best, I finally decided, might be to send him far away and make sure he stayed there. I started figuring out ways to do that. The family would have to be brought in on it. They should know, at the very least, the potential risk they ran. Not all the family perhaps. My brother Ivo might suffice.

Ivo was married and had been practicing medicine in Belgrade for several years. I found him in his office on Dobracina Street, not far from our family house.

"The doctor still has another patient to see," Ivo's nurse told me.

"I'll wait, but tell him it is urgent," I instructed her. Like Johnny, I rarely used the word "urgent." I knew the message would get through to Ivo.

Ivo and I are very close, so close that when I revealed my

activities he didn't feel hurt that I hadn't told him about them before. He knew that I would have confided in him eventually. I hadn't done so to spare him the worry.

"So you think you can send Bozidar away and keep him silent?" Ivo chided me. "As easily as that?" he said, snapping his fingers. "Let's look at this practically. Bozidar is corrupt. I know we can both remember when he rode us around on his shoulders. That makes what he did all the more horrible. Bozidar is a cancer now. There is nothing we can do that will alter him. As long as he lives, he always remains a threat to you. No matter where, as long as he lives."

I knew Ivo was right. Subconsciously, I had had the same feeling.

"Let me take care of him," Ivo proposed. "It'll be safer if you are not involved directly, in case the Germans make an investigation."

"Don't be an ass, Ivo." I was very touched. "It's my job. No use your becoming mixed up in it."

"I want to be," Ivo answered. "We can't hide our heads in the sand. It's simple self-preservation. Either we fight or we get stepped on."

"This is still my job," I insisted.

"Okay, it's your job," Ivo answered half resentfully, "but count me in on anything else. Remember."

I had to wait until night to carry out my plan. Death seems to do better in the dark. Or at least, its practitioners.

In Yugoslavia, as in other countries, the courts usually assigned apprentice lawyers to defend the indigent. And frequently, if not usually, the indigent were young in their trade, too. Young hoodlums who had not yet earned enough to have their own lawyers. I had defended my quota of criminals, and one or two of my clients had appreciatively offered payment in kind, any time I needed them. It was the kind of proposition no one ever takes seriously, although it was given as such. My clients lived the sort of lives in which it might be necessary. I didn't. Or hadn't.

Before leaving the house that night, I tiptoed to the servants' quarters to check on Bozidar. The radio was on in his room. Through the keyhole I could see him sitting in an old armchair long ago discarded from the library. He was listening to a program of Yugoslav folk songs.

That accounted for the whereabouts of my tail. I was reasonably sure there wasn't another, but I took the precaution of sneaking out the back entrance. I was wearing some rough old clothes I used for hunting so I wouldn't stand out in the place I was going—a rough section of the Belgrade port on the Sava River.

My two clients were creatures of habit, faithful to the post in the bar where they had told me I could always find them after dinner. The one facing the door saw me as I entered. His face lit up in a smile. He was genuinely glad to see me. I had managed to secure suspended sentences for both of them on an assault charge, claiming self-defense.

"Have a drink and tell us your troubles," he said while his partner clapped me on the back. They were a wise lot. I sat down at their table and ordered a round.

"I'm being blackmailed," I explained. "My father's chauffeur."

"Do you want us to work him over?" one asked.

"Nah, won't do any good," the other told him. "He'll just run away and try to get at you later on."

"That's just what he'd do." I went along with him.

"Well then"—one of my friends raised his glass—"he's for the ditch."

We arranged that I would find a pretext, an errand, to send Bozidar out of the house that night. I told them I would supply an alibi if it came to that, but they treated the matter quite casually, sure they would get away with it. They protested, sincerely, when I pulled out a roll of bank notes. I knew that their kind of crime didn't pay well, so I insisted. For once in their lives, even if unknown to them, they were committing a socially useful act, and I figured they should be recompensed for it.

Strains of music were filtering through the door of Bozidar's room. It was 1 A.M. I knocked. Bozidar answered, scratching his chest through his open shirt.

"Sorry to ask you to go out at this hour," I said, handing him a sealed envelope and a hundred-dinar note. "I want you to deliver this immediately to Mr. Bogdan Savic. He's only a few blocks away . . . Car Dusana 195. You won't have to take the car out."

Bozidar was used to my erratic ways. He tugged his forelock, muttering his compliance. I turned to go, then felt squeamish.

"Ah, Bozidar," I said, quickly inventing a last chance for him to confess and appeal for mercy. "Have I been running you around too much these past few weeks? You look tired. Or worried. Is there anything?"

"Well, Gospar Dusko, you do run me around more than your father does," he said.

"You don't have to drive me any more if you're tired. I'll use taxis."

"Oh, no, no, no," he answered hastily. "I'm glad to be of service."

Of service to Müntzinger, I thought. Okay, you old bastard, you just lost your appeal. The court thanks you for signing your own sentence.

I hadn't asked my two clients for the details of their execution plan, only stipulating that I wanted his body found. Disappearances cause more investigation than deaths.

When the police called the next morning, I was able to act

genuinely surprised. My two ruffians had staged a masterful play. Bozidar, the police told me, had been shot to death at the scene of an apparent pillaging at the railroad yards. They thought he was implicated in the attempted theft, which had been foiled by some railroad guards.

As was expected of me, I paid for Bozidar's funeral. He had no immediate family and I was the only one who sent flowers. But only for the form. As far as I was concerned, he was Yugoslavia's first collaborator.

Jebsen sent the forged Bozidar report to Müntzinger, and we never heard any more about it, nor did he inquire about Bozidar. Johnny, who knew what had happened, did make a remark I found curious.

"You're a determined man, Dusko," he said. "Tell me, would you kill me, too, if you discovered I was playing dirty?"

"You'd never play dirty, Johnny," I answered, wondering what had prompted the question.

After the Bozidar alarm, things were too quiet for a few weeks. I was waiting for action from Berlin and London, and both were stalling. London wasn't sending the answers to the questionnaire, and Berlin was delaying permission to leave for London.

"You've got to deliver something," Johnny warned me. "Müntzinger is pressing for answers. Get him a few, even if not everything. It's a matter of proving yourself. But even when you do, never make the mistake of thinking you are in the clear. There will be more Bozidars."

"If they let me go to London, I could work on the questionnaire myself," I pointed out. "Why do you think they are holding back?"

"I can make an educated guess," Johnny said. "You, my lad, are slated to be a big wheel in our intelligence machine. It takes time to get one turning, to make sure there are no bugs in it. I suspect Berlin wants you here under its thumb until they've checked you from every angle."

When I tried to stir things up on the British end, Spiradis— whom I was contacting now with great precaution—insisted, "You'll have to be patient."

"We're almost at the end of August," I reminded him. "The Germans gave me that questionnaire in mid-July. It's a question of their patience, not mine. And I can tell you theirs is almost at an end."

"I'll send an urgent signal to London," he promised.

London came through with instructions several days later. They were anxious to have me there and had cooked up a scheme to get the Germans to move. I was to show them a letter from my diplomatic friend, explaining his situation.

The letter, written on the stationery of the Yugoslav Embassy in London, read:

Dear Dusko,

I understand your impatience. I have collected quite a number of the Ming porcelain you want as a present for your mother, but unfortunately, I cannot send it through the diplomatic pouch. For one thing, it is too fragile and too bulky. More important, the British Foreign Office is becoming sticky and we have been asked to limit our mail to the strictly essential.

I suggest you collect the porcelain yourself when you come to London or arrange for it to be collected. Otherwise, you'll have to wait until my next trip to Belgrade.

Incidentally, the money you advanced for the purchases has been spent. If you want to complete the collection, I suggest you bring more funds.

Yours,
Bata.

"Who is Bata?" Johnny asked when I gave him the letter to forward to Müntzinger. "I thought your correspondent was remaining anonymous."

He was. Johnny hadn't learned much of our difficult language. "Bata" means "Little Brother," an affectionate nickname in Yugoslav.

As London calculated, the letter provoked the green light from Berlin. Instructions came for me to make my travel arrangements—a time-consuming, tricky chore.

The first hurdle was that as a Yugoslav reserve officer I could not leave the country without a permit from the Ministry of War. Procuring that took much personal intervention. The rest required juggling. I had to pass through Italy but I wouldn't be allowed to leave there if I had a visa for England. On the other hand, Portugal would not allow me to enter unless I did have a visa for another country. The only way to do it was to carry a concealed letter from the British Foreign Office guaranteeing me a visa to be issued by the consul in Lisbon. These formalities accomplished, I had a last session with each of my spymasters.

To be absolutely sure of privacy, Spiradis and I met at Oplenac, a large park about twenty kilometers from Belgrade. It drew few crowds even on weekends and during the week was practically deserted. On top of the monument to the fallen heroes of the First World War—two hundred steps up, where we could survey the surrounding countryside—Spiradis saw fit to lecture me on my duties and obligations as a British officer. It surprised me that I was to be considered as such.

More pertinent, he warned me, "Act as if you are a real German spy. Forget you belong to us. While traveling, look as though you were worried that the English may suspect you. You can be sure the Germans will be observing you at every moment.

"Keep your eyes and your ears open and your mouth shut. Remember names and addresses and faces and every word you hear from or about the Germans, but put nothing in writing. Specifically, we are interested in anything you may hear about an eventual invasion of England. The German code name for that is Operation Sea Lion. Don't be skeptical," Spiradis said, noting my facial reaction. "You don't seem to appreciate fully what you've already accomplished. You've succeeded in infiltrating the Abwehr. Normally, that would require years of deliberate planning. You're on good or excellent terms with a few of their high-ranking officers. Pick their brains." He gestured as though he were trepanning them. "When you get to London, they'll put together what is already known with what you can supply, and any little thing may prove the missing piece in the puzzle.

"By the way, I don't know exactly what slot you're going to be placed in. British Intelligence is divided into two main units: M.I.6 and M.I.5. Overseas we're M.I.6—straight intelligence. M.I.5 are the counterintelligence crowd."

Actually, I later found myself working for both.

It was a beginner's lecture, but it was indicated. I hadn't realized the full advantages and scope of my position.

Spiradis also gave me my contact in Lisbon in case of need. Again, it was the chief of the Passport Control Office, a Mr. Davis. I decided to approach him charily. Johnny had already put me wise to the fact that Passport Control was frequently the cover for M.I.6 and that the Germans knew it.

After our conference, I conducted Spiradis to a meeting with the first agents I recruited for Intelligence. Spiradis was seeking to extend his net in Yugoslavia and had asked me for likely candidates. One was my brother Ivo, the other a university friend, Nichola Lùkas, a New Zealander by birth but of Yugoslav origin. Spiradis accepted them readily even though, like every other Yugoslav I was to recruit, they made one proviso: that none of their actions would ever be directed against Yugoslavia.

I lost direct contact with Nichola and only found him after the war in Trieste, a captain in the British Army. About Ivo, more later.

"Hello, Ivan," Müntzinger greeted me as he and Johnny arrived at the house to give me final instructions. I looked startled, and he explained laughingly that Ivan was my new code name.

Müntzinger was absolutely elated to have me leave for England. It reflected to his credit as a spymaster. He was expansive and voluble, so I had my first plunge at pumping an Abwehr officer for information, pretexting the necessity for learning about the country to which I was assigned.

"Ach, England, it had better come to terms with us soon," he boasted. "We have them on their knees, and the blitz will knock them out completely unless they come to their senses."

I said humbly, "I'm not a military expert, of course, but as I understand it, bombs will only soften up a place. You have to occupy it after that. What about the British Navy? We have to cross the Channel."

"The Luftwaffe will take care of the British Navy. And I know positively we have the wherewithal to cross the Channel. We have assembled over twenty-five hundred barges, nearly as many motorized boats, and over a hundred and fifty ships."

I whistled softly, appreciatively. Johnny shot me a fast, sharp look and a little smirk. He realized what I was up to and was amused.

"We also have troops trained and ready to go," Müntzinger added for my edification. "They await only the Führer's order to embark."

I tried to worm more specific details out of Müntzinger but got the impression that he didn't know much more, or any more. He carried on boasting about the invincibility of the German Army.

When we got rid of Müntzinger and Johnny and I were having our last chat, he said slyly, "When I'm in Berlin—which should be soon—I'll try to get some information to satisfy your 'natural' curiosity about Sea Lion." He said no more than that, and I didn't pick him up on it. He obviously didn't want me to. But every "sous entendu" confirmed that he knew I was a British agent.

With business cleared away, I faced up to the task of parting with my family and flew to Dubrovnik. Except for Ivo, they thought I was going to Lisbon and eventually to London on a business trip, which they found insane. London was under a continuous blitz, twenty-four hours a day, seven days a week. My family had no illusions that our country would escape the war, but it was difficult to countenance actually projecting oneself into such horrors while basking under the Adriatic sun.

My grandfather was the only one I didn't fool. He winked at me when I insisted that I couldn't drop my business affairs and told me later in private, "It's the war. You can't wait for it to come to you. You plan to stay in London, I know." He said nothing to the others.

3

An hour early, at ten in the morning, I walked out of the Hotel Ambassadori and up the Via Veneto to the Café de Paris. My "tref"—as the Abwehr called its rendezvous—was fixed at eleven but I had no better way to spend an hour than to sit on the terrace and watch the sights. As instructed, I displayed the Yugoslav newspaper *Politika* and placed a package of Morava cigarettes and Yugoslav matches on the table.

Well before eleven o'clock an elderly gentleman who looked like a retired professor strolled by on the sidewalk several times, his glance going to the foreign newspaper and cigarettes I was displaying. He selected a table next to mine, wriggled about so that his caned chair creaked, and cleared his throat. "Your first visit to Rome?"

I looked over at him. "No. I've been here several times before."

"Oh, but perhaps you're interested in visiting some place again. I could guide you," he suggested.

"No, thank you," I replied, then reconsidered. "Well, I would like to have a look at the Vatican."

"I'm an expert on the Vatican," my professorial type answered. "It's a lovely morning. We have plenty of time. Shall I hail a fiacre?"

He had answered exactly as prearranged.

"Do indeed." I gave the expected affirmative; the fiacre would take us to meet my Abwehr contact.

I glanced at my watch. It was ten thirty.

We went on a bona fide Cook's tour, missing nothing, from Saint Peter's toe to the Michelangelo frescoes. The professor was an expert on it all and was as tireless a walker as a talker. As I admired the frescoes, I also studied the face of every tourist, expecting one of them to conceal the man from the Abwehr.

At one in the afternoon, with the professor showing no signs of weakening or of leading me anywhere, I asked impatiently, "How about some serious business?"

His eyes lit up.

"Certainly, sir. It is a bit early, but I can arrange it for you after lunch. Make your choice."

He produced from his waistcoat pocket a dozen photographs of naked women, which he started showing to me one by one, accompanying each with a description of her specialty.

The Sistine Chapel reverberated with my laughter. Horrified, a group of nuns pantomimed for silence. I ran out of the chapel trying to suppress my laughter, leaving the old panderer to soothe the sisters.

In mid-afternoon the concierge of the Ambassadori rang to say that the guide I had ordered was waiting in the lobby. I broke out laughing again and told him I'd be right down. This time it was the real thing and he took a dim view of my not having punched in at the Café de Paris on the stroke of eleven. We abandoned the fiacre and Vatican gambit in favor of his Fiat and the Villa Borghese. He parked alongside the gardens, handed me two thousand dollars, and told me to expect a friend who was flying into Rome that evening.

Not unexpectedly, the friend turned out to be Johnny, coming directly from Berlin. I was delighted to see him but I felt that each meeting of ours took place on a tightrope. I was

99 percent sure of him, yet we had never had that final meeting of the minds that would have cleared everything up.

"What are we drinking, Dusko, scotch or schnapps?" Johnny teased as we settled into the leather armchairs in a deserted corner of the Ambassadori bar.

"Scotch," I told the waiter. And to Johnny, "I must get in the habit."

"Scotch for me, too," he ordered. The waiter left us. "Scotch to toast England. It will still be there tomorrow, according to the information I got for you in Berlin. To satisfy your curiosity, of course," he said, tongue in cheek.

"The invasion plan—Sea Lion—is off?"

"For the time being. I have it from the Admiralty." Johnny cited his sources for proper evaluation. "There is profound disagreement in Supreme Headquarters. The Army, the Navy, and the Luftwaffe can't get together. General Halder, the Army chief of staff, is confident he can smash England rapidly if the Navy and the Air Force give him the necessary backing. He envisions employing a hundred thousand men in the first invasion wave, to be followed immediately by a hundred and sixty thousand reinforcements. Halder's battle plan is to move in on a wide front."

Johnny was speaking rapidly, in a low voice.

I nodded to show that I was following.

"The Navy insists on a reduced front. It claims that is the only way it can guarantee the crossing in the face of British naval superiority. The Navy strategy would be to use mine fields and submarines to protect the invasion fleet."

"Are the figures that Müntzinger mentioned correct?" I asked. "Twenty-five hundred barges, nearly as many motorized boats, and over a hundred and fifty ships?"

"Substantially," Johnny answered. "Müntzinger wasn't exaggerating, but what he didn't say—or didn't know—was that twice that number are needed to transport an army the size

Halder has in mind. More decisive than that is the Luftwaffe. The Navy won't move unless the Luftwaffe will promise absolute control of the invasion area. And in spite of Goering's boasts, the Luftwaffe won't go that far out on a limb.

"The upshot is that Hitler is arbitrating the disagreement, trying to make compromises where they are impossible. So Sea Lion is being postponed from one month to the next, and meanwhile they all hope that certain elements in England— what they call reasonable and peace-loving elements—will sue for peace. Since Goering took over as Air Marshal and says he will annihilate the Royal Air Force and blitz the Britons to their knees, they are content to let him try it his way.

"I was told that Rudolf Hess is saying that some high personalities in the U.K. are seeking contact with Germany. As Deputy Führer, Hess has his own intelligence organization, you know, the Verbindungstab, which must have picked up that gossip. But it could come from other sources, too. The Abwehr is in touch with some supposedly powerful Welsh nationalist groups, and in those circles there's talk of Lloyd George coming back as Prime Minister and negotiating for peace."

"What's your personal opinion about all that, Johnny?"

"Wishful thinking probably stimulated by some truth. As a last resort they may attempt an invasion in the spring if the Luftwaffe smashes the R.A.F. Not during the winter in any event. Not with the fog and rough seas."

The form of Johnny's reply interested me: his use of "they," not "we." He wasn't identifying with the Nazis.

Johnny looked at his watch. "Enough business for tonight. I have a surprise for you. Freddy von Kaghaneck is in town. We're having dinner with him."

"Freddy!" It really was a surprise. "Is he in this, too?"

"No, nothing to do with the Abwehr. And he doesn't know

a thing of your activities. Hitler is trying to use the von Kaghaneck family's influence. He named Freddy a sort of special delegate to the Vatican."

Over dinner at Alfredo's, Freddy told me more about his appointment. "It is the most comfortable job anyone could dream of having during the war." Freddy laughed as though he were putting something over. "I'm cultivating cardinals and reporting their confidences. If they don't make any, I invent some. This is too good a job to lose."

Freddy's attitude struck me as extremely peculiar. As a Catholic aristocrat he was committing what amounted to *lèse majesté*. And he wasn't doing it under duress. Freddy didn't have to work for Hitler. He would never have been drafted into the military, since he had a game leg from birth. Nor would he have been bothered otherwise, thanks to the importance of his family. At least, I didn't think he would.

I didn't want to be questioned closely about my doings, so I didn't ask Freddy about his. There was a curious ambiguity about friendship for people in our positions. You tried to convince yourself that a friend would be on the right side, yet you couldn't dare trust that friendship far enough to reveal yourself.

Before leaving Rome, Johnny briefed me on Lisbon. "Your spymaster will be Major Ludovico von Karsthoff. He is the head of the Abwehr in Lisbon, which is one of the most important outposts in Europe. Lisbon and Madrid are the main centers for German and British intelligence now that Belgium and Holland are occupied.

"A word of warning about von Karsthoff. You may find yourself liking him. He's nearly a neighbor of yours, an Austrian born in Trieste. His real name—which I shouldn't use—is von Auenrode. You'll contact him by telephoning from a pay booth. Ask for Karl Schmidt and say his cousin from Stuttgart told you to call. Schmidt will ask you to call back in ten minutes and then will indicate he will be pleased to meet you at some specified time and place. Be there an hour early. A woman will pass and wink at you. Follow her. That I'm sure you can do without detailed instructions. The woman will lead you to a motorcar. You will enter without conversation and be driven to the tref."

"Sounds like a game," I said. "I hope the girl is good-looking."

"She probably will be. Part of the cover. Otherwise, why should you follow her? But I doubt if you'll see her again. Not that you'll lack for feminine company in Lisbon. Not nowadays. You'll have your choice of almost any nationality you want—except Portuguese, of course."

Wary since mucking up the Rome rendezvous, I followed Johnny's instructions to the letter. When I arrived an hour early this time, it was on orders. After only a few minutes of window shopping at a jeweler's on the Rua Augustus, a trim blond girl, obviously not Portuguese, gave me a broad, friendly wink. I followed her several blocks, turning a few corners, to an Opel sedan. Its motor was running, and a man was behind the wheel. My escort opened the door and ducked into the back seat, motioning me after her. The car started immediately. We didn't exchange a word. She said only "Stay" when the car stopped to let her out several blocks later.

We drove toward the Estoril. Near the Casino, the driver half-turned his head to say, "We are almost there. Crouch down on the floor, the house may be watched." I did as ordered. When the car came to rest and the ignition was switched off, I found we were inside a garage, the door of which was being closed by another man.

We walked through the garage into a house. The architecture showed the influence of the Moorish occupation of Portugal. A tall, slim, good-looking man awaited me in the salon. He held out his hand and advanced toward me.

"I am von Karsthoff," he said in German softened by a Viennese accent. "We are happy to have you here."

I shook his hand and assured him that I was equally happy to be there. Von Karsthoff offered me a drink, and we chatted about banalities, about my trip, about Lisbon. He managed to convey a feeling of genuine interest and concern, making me feel at ease.

"I have very specific orders concerning you," von Karsthoff said, a warm smile illuminating his face. "I have been instructed to handle you with love and care, to help you to the utmost. Now that I know you. I am sure it will be a pleasure to carry them out. You have inspired a lot of faith at the Tirpitzufer, and they are making ambitious plans for you."

I thanked him, adding, "I'm sure it is going to be a pleasure to work with you, Herr Major." This was a man to cultivate to the utmost. If I could win his confidence, he would be a source of much valuable information.

Von Karsthoff was explaining the methods we would use to contact each other in the future when the door opened and two dachshunds eeled their way to his knees. A young woman ran after them calling, "Ivan 1, Ivan 2." Karsthoff caressed the dogs and laughed heartily. "Nothing to do with your code name, pure coincidence."

I wondered if von Karsthoff was emulating Canaris. Johnny had told me that the Admiral owned two dachshunds.

The young woman handed von Karsthoff a slip of paper.

"My secretary, Elizabeth." He introduced us. "I'll be with you shortly," he promised her. There was something about his tone, a fondness, that made me think Elizabeth was more than a secretary. She was another one to be cultivated. Cautiously. And courteously. No competition with my spymaster.

"Pardon the interruption." Von Karsthoff waved the note Elizabeth had given him."Admiral Canaris is in Madrid and may come here. He will want to meet you," he predicted.

I left the villa the same way I had come, lying in the back of the sedan until we were well away from the immediate neighborhood and sure we had no tail. The driver dropped me off in Lisbon within walking distance of my hotel, the Aviz, Lisbon's most luxurious.

Berlin had instructed me to stay at the Aviz, and I learned from British Intelligence that the Germans controlled it. Small and set in a garden, the Aviz was impossible to leave without being seen or followed. Disobeying instructions, I changed hotels shortly, but twice during my stay I found telltale signs indicating that my belongings had been searched. I was "clean," so it didn't worry me. A third incident was more overt and more amusing.

On a few occasions when I ate in the hotel dining room I noticed a very beautiful girl, flamboyantly dressed. She was accompanied by an older woman whom I guessed to be her mother or an aunt, certainly not a duenna, since the girl left her immediately after eating to join one or another young man.

She probably noticed that I was intrigued by her, but although she cast many smiles and glances my way I wasn't sure they were for me. Not out of undue modesty. At a table next to me sat overwhelming competition: the Bolivian multimillionaire tin king, Patino.

One evening, alone in the elevator with her, the glances could have only been for me, but the brevity of our journey precluded anything much in the way of conversation.

"Room 25," I told the liftboy instead of giving him the floor number. I left the door to my apartment unlocked, as was my habit anyway, and retired to the bathroom to shower. I emerged to find the girl lying on my bed. She had done her toilette faster than I and was now wearing a sheer silk negligee of remarkable duality. It both covered and revealed her completely. She had mixed herself a scotch highball from the makings which I had ordered earlier and regarded me from over the rim of her glass.

I said, "Good evening," rather urbanely in my huskiest voice.

"Join me," she answered, flourishing the hand in which she was holding her glass.

I took the invitation to mean one thing, but it seemed she had a drink in mind. She eluded my embrace and prepared one for me.

"Let us talk a while," she objected to my directness. "You don't even know my name."

"Ilena Fodor," I answered. "Desk clerks are very helpful."

"Yes, they are, Dusko Popov." She showed tiny teeth made for nibbling. "But your name doesn't tell me much about you and I like to know a man first."

She kissed me on the cheek like it was a favor, pretending not to notice her breasts rubbing against my arm, and said, "Now fix me another drink and tell me about yourself."

Her phony coy game turned me off, but I wanted to know what she was up to, so I complied. We had many more drinks while I allowed her to pump me about my origins, my opinions, and my reason for being in Lisbon. Since I lied about the first two, there was no reason why I should even give her my cover story concerning the third. I concocted a tale about my being there to recover three stolen pictures for a Belgian client: a Gauguin and two other post-impressionists.

My story must have satisfied her, for as soon as I had finished it, her interest in me plunged to zero. Her sexy provocations stopped abruptly, but like the cheapest of whores she indicated she was ready to put out for payment received. She lay back in the bed with an empty, yawning, bored, you may-take-me now expression on her face. I handed her the almost empty bottle of scotch, saying, "Take this with you if you can't fall asleep. You've had your bedtime story."

The reprimand didn't phase her. She took the bottle.

The next time I saw von Karsthoff, after we had concluded our business and were having a drink he told me seriously that I should "stop trying to find those postimpressionist paintings." My job allowed no time for sidelines.

"No"—I laughed—"don't tell me you were taken in by that. It was a fairy tale for a not-too-nice young lady. But now I know, you're the one who cost me that bottle of scotch. I thought the checking was completed on me before I left Belgrade."

"No, I'm not the one," von Karsthoff reassured me. "I'm satisfied, but none of us is autonomous. I may be chief of intelligence here but Abwehr III—our counterintelligence section—likes to show its zeal. I happened to hear the story only because one of my subalterns in Abwehr III thought it was amusing how you threw the girl out."

The incident let me in on what was happening behind the scenes in German intelligence. Von Karsthoff went on to complain about other organizations operating parallel to the Abwehr. They were mainly political and therefore dangerous, he explained, the most insidious being the Gestapo group, the Sicherheit Dienst, run by Kaltenbrunner.

At another meeting, von Karsthoff introduced me to the chief of Abwehr III in Lisbon, Captain Kramer. Kramer was a professional police officer, the tenacious kind, a gray, silent, and thorough man. He never let up on anyone, including me. With Kramer in charge of spy busting, I could never relax. Von Karsthoff could give him orders to the contrary, Johnny could vouch for me—to Kramer it wasn't sufficient. He continued running checks on me constantly.

Associating with von Karsthoff was like being in the company of a domesticated panther. Physically there was a resemblance: he was tall and dark, and his movements were those of a big cat. Amiable as he was, you were constantly aware that you must not make a false move in his presence.

As Johnny had warned, I found myself liking von Karsthoff. In a way it helped. I didn't have to be too hypocritical in seeking his company. At the beginning I had done such things as arriving in the late morning so as to be invited for lunch or being especially courteous to Elizabeth, who I discovered was his fiancée. After a while such devices were unnecessary. An affinity developed between us, and von Karsthoff sought my company too. We were on a first-name basis.

Rather than turn me over to an underling, von Karsthoff undertook my education himself. He taught me codes and mail drops and gave me a Leica and instructions in its use. I learned to use the Leica but failed miserably in darkroom techniques. Taking pictures von Karsthoff's way was easy. His instructions were to always pose a girl in pictures of installations or similar objects. The idea was to make everything look like a tourist photo. As for the darkroom side, von Karsthoff spared me the chore, instructing me to bring my undeveloped film back to him.

For several days, von Karsthoff and his staff were tremendously agitated and busy about matters concerning Admiral Canaris. I never did learn if he actually came to Lisbon. At any rate, he certainly didn't ask to see me, and it would have been out of place for me to inquire directly about him. I picked up my information from bits of chatter and dinner-table conversation. It was sufficient to enable me to build a fairly complete picture of the admiral's mission in Spain and of its failure.

The admiral had come to Spain, I learned, to take over negotiations with Franco that Hitler had started personally three weeks earlier. Hitler was trying to persuade Franco to enter the war with an attack on Gibraltar. He had met the Generalissimo near Hendaye on the Franco-Spanish border on October 23 but had failed to get him to agree on terms. The gossip was that Hitler told Canaris he would rather have four teeth extracted than go through the experience again. Canaris was a personal friend of Franco's, but he apparently did no better.

According to von Karsthoff, the Germans wanted Franco to allow their troops to pass through Spain to attack Gibraltar on January 30. The Caudillo said "no" to German troops on his territory and offered to do the job with his own army if the Germans gave him guns and material. But not right away. He wanted a guarantee that the war would be short. Since Canaris couldn't give him a date for the invasion of Britain, Franco said he'd take Gibraltar after the Germans captured Suez.

Von Karsthoff gave me a tip-off on Hitler's intentions by commenting, "Unless the invasion of England is imminent, we shall have to start concentrating on getting information about North Africa."

When I forsook the Hotel Aviz I moved to the Palacio in Estoril, giving as my reason that I stood to meet more people there and perhaps pick up incidental scraps of information. Also, I told von Karsthoff, I preferred it for personal reasons. The Aviz was too staid.

Actually, the Palacio was much safer for me. Not only was it large enough to afford some sort of privacy, it also was managed by an Englishman, George Black, a person one could depend on. No one ever gave me his pedigree officially, and I don't know what he was told about me, but unobstrusively he acted as my guardian angel. If someone appeared interested in me or if there was someone in whom perhaps I should be interested, Black would tip me off.

The Hotel Palacio and the Estoril Casino nearby were the hub within the wheel of Lisbon. In 1940, Lisbon was a very special universe, a tiny enclave of neutrality where all sides in the war brushed shoulders. It was filled with refugees of all descriptions and all nations. Some were wealthy beyond measure, and they squandered their money like there was no tomorrow—as there might not have been. Some were impoverished to the point where they would sell anything, which usually meant themselves. In addition to the refugees, Lisbon was crowded with businessmen, various international officials, and agents and spies of all natures, including a number of would-be and free-lance ones. And if you weren't a spy, you were frequently suspected of being one anyway.

Most of the refugees were awaiting transport elsewhere— anywhere away from Europe. Space on ships was scarce, on airplanes almost unobtainable. So they were waiting, and the best places to wait were the Casino and the Palacio, if they could afford it. The rich came to relieve their boredom, wagering higher stakes than Monte Carlo or Las Vegas have ever seen. The poor came in a futile attempt to make a new life. And the others came to pass unobserved among them.

After several weeks in Lisbon, in late December, the Royal Dutch Airline informed me that that most coveted thing—a seat on an outgoing plane—was available for me. The reservation came through normal channels, but of course the hand of the Secret Service had pulled the string that procured it. Most travelers from Lisbon were relegated to passage by ship—if they were lucky—so the planes were the exclusive transport of VIPs or those with some claim to urgency. They frequently provided interesting material for observation.

The KLM plane took off from Lisbon airport in late afternoon. To avoid German fighters, the pilot headed west until far out over the Atlantic, then north to approach England from its lee side. To thwart possible spying or loose tongues, wooden panels were placed over the portholes as the plane neared the coast.

The plane touched down near Bristol at Felton Airport. Immigration and customs passed us through without difficulty, and a pink-complexioned man approached me as soon as I was through the gates.

"Mr. Popov, sir?" he asked in a soft voice.

"Yes," I answered, feeling safe on British soil to admit my identity to anyone.

"Jock Horsfall, sir," he said. "I'm to drive you to town."

He took my bags and I followed him to a new Citröen. Horsfall drove the Citröen at what seemed like a greater speed than the plane's, yet our passage didn't even ruffle the bucolic countryside. Horsfall was one of M.I.5's virtuosos of the wheel. He was a racing driver by profession, and whenever I had to make a particularly fast trip, Horsfall got the assignment.

We were some ten miles from London when Horsfall let the car's speed drop and turned to me, saying, "There it is." I looked ahead to see what he was speaking about. On the horizon, the sky was red. Every few seconds almost, a fire mushroom ballooned up. Goering's bombers were on their regular nightly mission.

"It's a rather hot night," he commented, but that didn't stop him from sending the Citröen speeding toward the blitz again.

Nothing seemed to stop the English from carrying on. Horsfall dropped me at the Savoy Hotel. It was fairly late, and I didn't expect anything more than my room to be awaiting me. The lobby and the public rooms beyond it were crowded, no one paying attention to the air raid going on around us. As I was signing in, I was approached by a man who looked like Hollywood's concept of a dashing British military type.

"Popov, hello." He held out his hand. "I'm Robertson." I hadn't expected to meet him until the following morning. Colonel T. A. Robertson was the head of the section of M.I.5 known as B.A.1, which dealt with the double-crossing of enemy intelligence.

Tar, as Robertson was known, took me into the Savoy bar, where we had a sandwich, a beer, and a "small chat." "Just wanted to get acquainted," Tar explained. "We'll get down to business tomorrow." He had come down from the country to meet me and was staying at the Savoy as well.

It was my first night under a blitz. The English calm must have infected me. I couldn't resist the temptation to have a look at it. After extinguishing all the lights in my bedroom, I opened the window and, despite the cold, sat there for a few hours. The antiaircraft guns were busy, and their flak sounded in counterpoint to the whistling of bombs and their explosions. Burning buildings crashed in gigantic explosions as well.

The sight stirred me as nothing before ever had. And I had thoughts that when related in a colder, calmer time seem overly emotional. I couldn't help wondering how people could live in the middle of such a hell. How they could carry on normally with gay dinners, flirtations, and polite conversations such as I had just witnessed in the bar. I was overwhelmed with admiration for the British and was sure that a nation with such self-control could not possibly lose the war. I was more resolute than ever to contribute my utmost to the winning of it.

Sitting there like a playgoer with the stage of London erupting below me, I admitted to myself that I had entered this game partially for reasons that were not the most admirable. I knew that I had been driven by adventure and ambition. I wasn't ashamed, but those drives now seemed unimportant. Only stopping this madness and slaughter was important. The values I had once had were secondary. My main weapons were to be lies and deceptions, and I would have to ask friends to commit treason—that is, what was considered treason and punished as such. I myself had already indulged in acts outside the normal social conventions, including murder. After this night of actually witnessing the legalized murder of war, I felt no qualms. It was my baptism by fire.

4

I had come to England and to Intelligence on the recommendations of Spiradis and Dew. I had been welcomed warmly by Tar in one of the posh hotels of London. Naïvely, I thought I was a full-fledged member of the "firm." It turned out that the Savoy was a gilded jail. I was free, I could go where I pleased, there were no locks on the doors, but I was not trusted. Not yet. I could be a genuine German agent who had slipped through the first line of defense. No one could afford to trust anyone in this business.

In the comfort of a suite specially rented by Intelligence, about a dozen officers subjected me to an interrogation just short of a third degree for four consecutive days. Far from resenting it, though, I actually enjoyed the experience. In parts, it verged on psychoanalysis. It also prepared me for similar grilling by the Germans. There in the Savoy, with a clean conscience and nothing to be caught up on, I could relax and merely try to answer to the best of my ability, but I realized that if I were in German hands, things would be far different. I would be far from relaxed. My story would be an invented one and its contradictions perhaps apparent.

The officers took turns posing me questions about everything and everybody who had to do with my mission—and many who didn't. They managed to extract from the depths of my memory events I no longer consciously recalled. They also made me see certain parts of my life and certain actions from angles I had never considered. Most of these men who were so adept at questioning were specialists in interrogation, and I rarely or never saw them again on operational missions. An exception was Ronnie Howe, then head of the Criminal Investigation Department at Scotland Yard, with whom I enjoyed a close relationship.

My inquisitors belonged to all the different branches of intelligence: M.I.5, M.I.6, Naval Intelligence, and Air Force Intelligence. Each one questioned me about things having to do with his particular section. Of necessity, there was some overlapping, and I couldn't help noticing certain rivalries among them, but nothing comparable to the jealousy and even hate that raged among the parallel German organizations I had studied in Lisbon.

When it came to relating what I knew about Sea Lion, I offered my "inside" information from Jebsen hesitantly, for fear of appearing ludicrous. The questionnaires the Germans had given me seemed to contradict Johnny's information. They asked specifically about matters which the Germans would have to know if they intended to invade. But hesitant or not, my interrogators—in this case, mainly M.I.6 and Naval Intelligence—drew from me every shred of conversation I had had with Johnny. They seemed skeptical about the invasion being called off. It is possible my information was virgin news to them. I had no way of knowing. I was on the grill, not them. That is one of the chagrins of the secret agent. He rarely knows the result or the actual value of the information he procures. All I could do was to spend the days around the projected invasion date—January 30—glued to the radio and getting each edition of the newspapers as it came out. When Sea Lion failed to materialize, my personal consolation was not nearly so great as my relief.

In actual fact, although I felt confused at the moment, my

interrogators probably were equally at sea. They were but a link in the chain. They would be passing on what they had culled to others. It would be controlled, compared, digested, and added to what was already known.

The interrogation was teaching me the profession. I was becoming aware of techniques, of what I should be looking for, of the questions I should be asking. I began, too, to learn more about the evaluation of my own material. Later, for my own edification, I reexamined the questionnaires. Those given me in Belgrade clearly indicated the intention to invade Britain. The ones I got in Lisbon dealt with the same subject, but I could discern nuances of difference. Questions about armament production and equipment indicated that the Germans were now thinking about a longer war.

A representative of the Foreign Office, Cavendish-Bentinck, took me over for the story of Admiral Canaris's venture in Spain. Again, I wasn't told whether the British knew the story through other channels.

One of the most impressive members of the team I met at the Savoy was J. C. Masterman, ex-dean of Christ College, Oxford, who was brought in to M.I.5 to head the so-called XX Committee. The Twenty Committee, or Double-Cross Committee, as it was variously known, was created to handle the complicated chore of running double agents. One of its purposes, as is reflected by its name, was to double-cross the enemy by feeding it confusing information via its own agents. On my arrival in England, I was assigned to work with the XX Committee, where temporarily I was given the code name "Scout."

J.C. was one of several intellectuals drafted to bring new blood and color to Intelligence. He was not only an educator and historian but also a former Wimbledon tennis player and member of the Olympic hockey team. Cool and calculating, he tempered my impulsiveness, and it was undoubtedly thanks to his guiding rein that I came through unscathed.

After my vetting in the Savoy, the British apparently accepted me into the firm. I now started meeting my new friends in their private homes, clubs, or hangouts. The blitz didn't prevent English social life from carrying on as usual. On the contrary, it was more intensive than usual, undoubtedly the "eat, drink, and be merry" philosophy that prevails in wartime. Except that with the English, the gaiety didn't seem forced. The mood suited my native temperament and practice, but occasionally I unwittingly found myself in company too sedate for my explosive character. That was a mistake I tried not to repeat.

Richard Butler, the aide-de-camp to General Sir David Petrie, head of M.I.5, called shortly before New Year's Eve to transmit an invitation for that weekend at one of the stately homes of England where I had visited before.

"No thanks," I told Butler. "I've been there. Lovely people. Nice is the word for them. The family was nice, the house was nice, ditto for the garden, friends, food, wine. The trouble is, I'm not. I prefer to spend New Year's Eve in the company of a good book or a temperamental popsy."

"In reverse order, I take it," Butler answered understandingly. "I'll pass along your regrets."

A few hours later Dick was back on the phone.

"Another invitation, old boy. Come to White's at six and I'll give you the details." He rang off before I could object.

Dick was waiting for me in the lobby when I arrived a bit resentfully but promptly at six. "Someone who wants to meet you," he said as he escorted me past the porter's desk and into the bar. There he steered me toward an isolated table where a man in mufti was sitting alone. He was thin and fiftyish with dark blond hair and blue eyes.

"Stewart Menzies," Dick introduced us, looking somewhat mischievous, knowing I wouldn't be disappointed by this social engagement.

Menzies, a major-general, was "C," the head of M.I.6.

Contrary to a well-publicized notion, the head of the British Secret Service is always known as "C," not "M." The first commanding officer of the Secret Intelligence Service was Captain Mansfield Cumming, and tradition has maintained the use of his appellation for the office ever since.

"I'd like you to spend the weekend with us," Menzies told me once we had settled the business of drinks and the like. "At my brother Ian's place, Little Bridley, in Surrey. We won't be too many, and we'll have an opportunity to talk."

Menzies was unmarried and, I suppose, did much of his receiving at his brother's home. He also used White's, London's most exclusive men's club, to such an extent that it became known as the second headquarters of Intelligence.

I replied rather formally that I'd be delighted to come for the weekend and, smiling knowingly, C said, "You won't have to worry about popsies. My mother, Lady Hartford, still entertains. She always makes sure there is some glamour around."

"I see Dick gave you a full report," I laughed along with him.

"All my agents do. I want to commend you, by the way, for your reports," he added seriously. "But we'll talk about such things this weekend."

Dick drove me out to Surrey. Little Bridley was a Victorian mansion set in a large park, the lawn perfectly manicured.

From the start, I was captivated by the whole Menzies clan. Directly I was to become a frequent visitor to the Surrey house and eventually the godfather of Ian's first child. Ian was a major in the Transport Division and a Director of Lloyds in civilian life.

Lady Hartford indeed entertained. She conducted me into the drawing room, where several of the other guests were already assembled, and introduced me right off to the most glamorous creature I had set eyes on since arriving in England. "So you are Dusko Popov," was her enigmatic response to our introduction. Her accent was Germanic, her name Gerda Sullivan, and her manner as puzzling as that combination. She had the advantage over me on all counts. Obviously she had heard of me and was anticipating our meeting, but in what way I couldn't tell. I hoped she was being flirtatious but was not at all sure. I definitely was, all weekend, whenever I had the opportunity. She was encouraging, no more. I did learn the why of her accent. Gerda was Austrian. Sullivan was the name of her English husband, whom she had divorced.

"We'll see each other in London?" I suggested to her at one point.

Gerda had huge eyes, very expressive. They swept over me from head to toe. "We'll see a lot of each other in London," was her answer. I felt as though I had been on examination and had just received a passing grade, but there was still an undercurrent that I didn't understand.

Menzies almost literally had to tear me away from Gerda to have the conversation that presumably was the main purpose for inviting me to Surrey.

"I think you will have many opportunities to see Gerda," he said tolerantly.

Menzies took me to a small study. Deep armchairs, a fireplace where the flames were miraculously steady, book-lined walls—it was the traditional and perfect setting. What followed was not commonplace. Even now, many years later, I feel uncomfortable at the way he was able to assess me so clearly after knowing me only a few hours and probably by reading a dossier about me. At times, I felt he was disrobing my character and making me look at it for the first time in my life. And all this was done patiently and dispassionately. I could see why he was the head of the Secret Service, which was in the way of being "master after God." C reported only and directly to the Prime Minister—in this case, Winston Churchill.

"We may regret that you don't belong to M.I.6 any more." Menzies began what was to be a long monologue. "But you are a double agent and, as such, more vulnerable than an ordinary one. Your activity calls for the use of deception and the penetration of the Abwehr. You and your usefulness may live and last only if thoroughly protected and managed by a specialized body. I'm sure that the XX Committee will accomplish that with the utmost efficiency, and they will exploit you to full advantage for their own game. It is an important game, but we mustn't let it reduce the possible crop to a limited field. My department wants to profit by your talents and your circumstantial position as well."

"I don't know about my talents," I said, not out of modesty. I was impelled to honesty by this man. I really did have doubts about my capacity when face to face with an intellect like Menzies'.

"Dusko," he said, looking into the fire like a seer, "one man out of a thousand has the talent to play the fiddle. One out of a hundred thousand has the capacity to be a virtuoso, and one out of a million actually becomes one. My capacity is to assess values and measure them. If I do that properly I have fulfilled half my duty."

Then Menzies proceeded to cut me to bits, delivering his analysis rapidly, without a halt.

"You are honest but without scruples. Your instincts and intuitions are stronger than your intelligence, which is far above average. Your conscience never bothers you, and you are mentally short-sighted and long-sighted at the same time. You are ambitious and ruthless and you can even be cruel. But when you are cruel, it is with an animal cruelty, not a sick cruelty. You like to hit back but you are not in a hurry to do so. When you are frightened, you don't panic. Danger is a stimulant for you. You think more clearly and make better and quicker decisions when pushed by the instinct of self-preservation, than by contemplation."

Now Menzies looked me directly in the eye.

"You have too many devices on your banner for my taste," he said, "but for your job that's ideal." I pondered that later, trying to decide exactly what he meant. Everything else he had said was to the point, whether I recognized myself by his description or not. This remark left room for speculation. It is true, I had been accused politically and socially of standing everywhere from conservative to radical. As far as I was concerned, my banner was that of liberty, but I suppose that can come in many forms, therefore the many devices.

"You have the makings of a very good spy," Menzies continued more specifically, "except that you don't like to obey orders. You had better learn or you will be a very dead spy."

Menzies wasn't a man for melodrama. I told myself I would have to take his advice seriously, even if it made the device on my banner droop.

Now done with dissecting me, Menzies undertook my education as a double agent, making sure, apparently, that there were no holes in my knowledge of the enemy.

"As you may or may not know," he briefed me, "the Abwehr is divided into five sections, or Abteilungs. Abteilung I deals with straight intelligence abroad. It is headed by Colonel Hans Pieckenbrock, a close friend of Admiral Canaris. He is called Piecki by his friends, among whom is your friend, Johann Jebsen."

"Abteilung II deals with sabotage and controls the school of espionage, the Brandenburg Division. It is commanded by Colonel von Freytag-Loringhoven, but the real boss is Walter Schellenberg, a ruthless gentleman-gangster. Abteilung III, counterespionage, is run by Colonel Bentivegni . . . Benti,"

C amended. "Abteilung IV is open intelligence. That means military attachés and military missions abroad, Rear Admiral Leopold Buerkner commanding. The last Abteilung, number V, usually called Abteilung Z, is the most interesting. It is the central administrative section, and it is, as you know, run by the protector of your friend Jebsen, Colonel Oster. Oster is assisted by Hans van Dohnanyi, who is supposed to be a friend of Jebsen's, too. Z holds all the files and coordinates the work of the other divisions.

"Now"—Menzies paused, put a match to his pipe, apparently collecting his thoughts—"to get to the point, we already have a fair amount of information about many officers in the Abwehr, including Canaris, but I want to know much more about everybody who is intimately connected with Canaris and also with Dohnanyi and Oster. I think you could get that information through Jebsen."

"He'd probably know," I agreed.

"It may be helpful if I explain the reasons behind this request. We know that Canaris, Dohnanyi, and Oster are not dyed-in-the-wool Nazis. They are what might be termed loyal officers, or patriotic Germans. In 1938 Churchill had a conversation with Canaris. Unofficially—he wasn't in office then. Churchill came to the opinion that Canaris is a sort of catalyst for the anti-Hitler elements in Germany. That's why I want to know more about the people he attracts. Eventually I may want to resume the conversation that Churchill initiated. In that event, I must be in a position to evaluate the strength of those around Canaris."

I nodded my understanding. Menzies was contemplating a dialogue with Canaris or those close to him with a view to ousting Hitler.

"I am handling this matter myself," Menzies stressed. "All information you pick up is to come directly to me with no intermediary. Ordinarily," he added, "any information I request from you may be given either directly to me or to any of the M.I.6 officers with whom you are in contact."

I considered that and thought it best to ask, "Won't that put me in a rather delicate position with the other branches of the service?"

"Not at all," Menzies assured me. "But if anything awkward ever does arise, I shall iron it out. Actually some of our top people are informed about this matter. And as I mentioned before, if we limit your activity to deception we may lose some capital information. You are too young in the service to realize how a detail may be of importance."

Menzies sipped the whisky-and-soda that he had been neglecting in his preoccupation with his discourse. He set the glass down carefully before continuing.

"In all objectivity—not because of my position—I should tell you, Dusko, that we must win the battle of intelligence if we are to win this war. As things stand now, our airplanes, cannons, battleships, and the like may not be sufficient to defend Britain.

"Well"—Menzies stood up, terminating his monologue—"you'll have a full program for the next few weeks, but see me nevertheless before leaving England. My brother Ian will be glad to receive you any time you want, and he will inform me whenever you are here. I'll take the opportunity to drop in and have a chat."

His hand on my shoulder, Menzies conducted me toward the door.

"One last thing. All M.I.6 representatives abroad will be instructed to give you unlimited assistance, but limit your contacts with them to emergencies only."

5

As C had foreseen, I was kept very busy. It was like preparing a ship for a cruise. The safety of the ship might hang on the smallest detail, and the unspectacular work before departure was more arduous than actual sailing, periods of storm excepted.

My cover story almost raised a diplomatic storm. Yugoslav Ambassador Subbotic had been trying with little success to get the English to grant Navy Certificates for the shipment of goods home. Of course the English were reluctant to grant them, being chary of goods falling into German hands. When I came along the situation changed. It was imperative to issue the Navy Certs so that I could conduct my business. In addition to arranging the Navy Certs, I was doing the buying as well. Some of the goods came from England, the rest from Spain and Portugal, giving me an excuse to travel to those places.

We resolved the problem this way: Yugoslav merchants would be permitted to buy goods provided they were not critical to the war effort and—the real key—under the condition that most were stocked in Egypt. From there they were to be transshipped to Yugoslavia on a monthly requirement basis. That minimized the possibility of resale to Germany or of eventual seizure if Yugoslavia were invaded.

The Yugoslav commercial attaché was very pleased with

the arrangement. It solved a lot of his headaches. We had lunch with the Ambassador, who at first tried to worm out of me the secret of how I had secured the Navy Certs. Naturally, I couldn't tell him. Subbotic became furious. He was a vain man. He had even changed the spelling of his name, using two Bs, a non-Yugoslav form, to distinguish him from a journalist in London of the same name.

"You bribed someone," the Ambassador accused me.

"Come now, Subbotic," I said. "One doesn't bribe the British Admiralty."

He continued to fume and rant, his professional pride very much hurt. Undiplomatically I said, "Stop being an ass." It might not have accomplished that, but it did shut him up. "Please throw me out after lunch," I added to make light of our clash. And continued eating. His cuisine, at least, was excellent.

Every agent has his case officer, the man who "runs" him. In a manner of speaking the case officer is the agent's accountant. Among other things, he keeps track of all details so that there will be no slip-ups, no contradictions that would be giveaways to the enemy. The case officer also is the spy's liaison, backup man, big brother, and father.

Bill Matthews was my case officer. Whoever put the two of us together, probably J. C. Masterman, was a fine psychologist. Bill and I got along famously. He was a Scot, of a family of prominent industrialists, and had a sense of humor rarely surpassed by anyone I ever knew. The same went for his courage.

Bill accompanied me frequently on trips I was obliged to make to gather information for the Germans. The XX Committee had decided that I should actually do this job myself so the Germans couldn't trip me up when they questioned me. Theoretically the concept was sound. In practice it didn't work all that well.

The hitch was my photographic memory. Not everything I saw could be passed on. A board of experts decided what could be told to the Germans. That meant I had to unlearn a good part of what I had seen. I lost more time studying what I had to forget than remembering what I was to report. And there was the risk of something slipping by in a tight interrogation.

We devised another method for my research trips. I would go through all the steps but the last one. Thus, for instance, I was able to describe the exact details of a motor trip I made to locate a fighter airfield that the Germans had requested me to investigate. I went only as far as the immediate vicinity of the field, and then retired to a pub. Later, I was shown photographs, some of them retouched or with portions blacked out, of what I was supposed to have seen.

The airfield in this instance was a dummy. During the Battle of Britain a specialized camouflage division built fake airfields, complete with planes made of paper. Even aerial photographs—which the British took, too—failed to reveal the hoax. The Luftwaffe wasted bombs and planes on such fields every day. If I had approached the field, I would have seen details which shouldn't have been there and which would give German experts the clue to its being a fake. As it was, my trips around England furnished me with excellent small talk and anecdotes to help establish my trustworthiness.

A trip to Edinburgh, accompanied by Bill Matthews as usual, furnished a particularly choice morsel to feed the Germans. We checked into the Caledonian Hotel in the afternoon. I dumped my luggage in my room, took the Leica von Karsthoff had given me, and headed with Bill for the port city of Leith and the Firth of Forth. My target was naval information. The Forth estuary was a major base of the Home Fleet. Bill and I wandered through the area until we found a pub that suited our taste. We settled down to the serious business

of sampling scotch in its native habitat for the time we estimated it would take to sneak some pictures of the naval base.
I was later congratulated by the Germans for my astuteness
and daring in taking these shots.

The police were waiting to question me when we returned
to the hotel several hours later. I didn't have the special permission required of aliens to visit Edinburgh. Fortunately, we
were on Bill's home ground. We convinced the police that I
was in town legitimately to buy a stock of thread at one of
his family mills. I had documents relating to Navy Certs to
back up our tale. The police left with excuses and I had a
genuine documented tale to relate to the Abwehr.

It was Sunday when we left Edinburgh for Glasgow. Among
other things, I was to assess the morale in the British Isles.

"No better place to judge morale than in a bar," Bill decided. "But there's a wee difficulty in this land on Sunday.
The law has it that you can't buy a drink unless you travel
five miles."

The Scots didn't waste time or footage, I discovered. There
was a pub every five miles—to the inch, I could have sworn.
And the local interpretation of that archaic law was, according to Bill, that one had to stop and have a drink every five
miles. I class the last twenty miles of that drive among the
greatest hazards of my war activities.

In the lobby of the Central Hotel in Glasgow, again according to Bill, I delivered an impassioned speech against
Hitler. I had no memory of it.

"You were more anti-Nazi than the chief rabbi of Berlin,"
Bill told me the next morning. "Or else you are the best actor
in the world. But I rather doubt that it was an act with a half-
gallon of whisky in you."

I didn't get the allusion. "Why an act, Bill?"

"Because, you sot, you're an alien double agent and we've
got to keep on taking your pulse. I'm supposed to report

about your feelings. I'm going to tell them you should be serving in an anti-Nazi indoctrination unit."

Bill made the tedium of our long trips more bearable, but I still fretted at my enforced absences from London. I had another collaborator there whose company I found enticing. And it was all in the course of business.

The enigmatic remark that Gerda had made about seeing a lot of each other in London was explained to me by Bill after I got back from Surrey. Bill had stroked his R.A.F. mustache and grinned at me salaciously. He was very English in appearance but Rabelaisian in mores.

"Congratulations. You got yourself the most beautiful social mistress in London."

"What the hell are you talking about?" I asked.

"A social mistress, dear chap, for want of a better term, is a person who undertakes your education in proper society. Stress is on the first word, unfortunately. Gerda Sullivan has agreed to squire you about. Part of your build-up for the chaps in the Tirpitzufer. Very top drawer. Gerda will take you to the best homes in England. You'll meet all the nibs. That will account for many of the gems we hope to plant through you."

"Oh, so I was on inspection. Gerda only takes the jobs she wants."

"Well, she really isn't a member of the firm. Does an odd chore for us now and then."

Gerda did much better at her job than I at mine. She was charming, beautiful, sexy. And intelligent. She dragged me from one party to another, introducing me to everyone worth knowing. All doors were open to her. I acknowledged the introductions but gave these social contacts minimum effort. The only contact I wanted was with Gerda and I was apparently passing another inspection with her. It was an impossible situation. I was operating in a trance, following her

on our rounds like a goggle-eyed fish who sees nothing but
the bait. And she knew it.

Never before in my life had I had such a dominating passion for a woman. I made up my mind to have it out with
her; the situation was verging on the dangerous. I could understand, if not approve, how a man could drive himself to
ruin, sell out, do anything to rid himself of such a consuming
craving. This wasn't sex or love. This was an addiction.

I was to pick Gerda up for lunch. Deliberately I arrived
early at her mews cottage behind Claridge's. I rang the bell
and waited impatiently. It took a long time before Gerda
opened the door. She was dressed in a short terry-cloth robe,
her blond hair still damp and slightly dark around the edges
from her bath.

"Gerda, I must have a serious talk with you," I blurted
out after following her up the narrow steps to her tiny apartment. I had restrained myself forcibly from seizing her sway-
ing hips as we went up the stairs.

Gerda laughed and walked on into the bedroom. I almost
turned and left. What use talking? She knew what I had to
say. I walked into the bedroom. Gerda was lying on the bed.

"Talk, please," she said. Her voice was husky. I had
passed inspection.

We missed lunch. We missed a cocktail party. We missed
the dinner we were supposed to go to. But after that day, my
social difficulties evaporated. Gerda and I became more than
perfect as a team.

I was now properly installed as a businessman in my own
office on the sixth floor of Albany House, a building just off
Piccadilly Circus. The bronze plaque on the door read: TAR-
LAIR LTD.—EXPORT-IMPORT. The TAR was in honor of Colo-
nel T. A. Robertson. We couldn't resist that joke on the
Germans.

Albany House lodged at least fifty different firms. People

were coming and going constantly and my visitors melted into the lot. It was safer to receive visits there from my confreres in Intelligence than for me to go to their offices.

Presiding over Albany House was Susan Barton, a secretarial gem assigned to me by the XX Committee. Even spies must have files and order. Without Susan I would have been lost. She mixed my invisible ink and prepared code messages and the drafts of the letters to be sent to my mail drops. All I had to do was copy in my own hand the material Susan gave me.

We were feeding von Karsthoff only enough information via secret writing to whet his appetite. The bulk of my gleanings were to be transmitted in person, being too voluminous or too important to be sent by letter. That was an excuse—but a valid one, as all excuses had to be—for me to return to Lisbon. Combined with my other excuse—business matters—I would have time and opportunity to accomplish the spying that M.I.6 wanted me to do.

Apart from one other double agent, whose code name was Snow and who later proved unreliable, I was the only one who had actual contact with the Germans. The others were mainly German spies who had been caught and "turned." For the most part they had been landed by U-boats, dropped by parachute, or smuggled in as Allied soldiers during the retreat from Dunkirk after the battle of France. The uncooperative ones usually were executed, the others were "run" from jail or from house arrest. They were the XX Committee's exclusive property, channels to feed double-cross material to the enemy. Their reports were sent back either by secret ink to mail drops or by their own radio sending sets. Most times, a British operator would man the set, imitating to perfection the hand of the agent. This required much practice and skill, since every Morse operator has a different and detectable touch.

The emphasis during this period, at least as far as I was concerned, was on misleading the Germans as to British strength and ability to withstand an invasion. Sea Lion was considered a potential threat, the information I had brought back notwithstanding.

The technique of deception consisted of truth when it was judged that it would do no harm, or when the benefits outweighed the detriments, half-truths which would be misleading, or falsehoods about conditions the Germans couldn't check. Sometimes the lies also would serve to reinforce misinformation the Germans already had.

Among the material which I was to plant with von Karsthoff were documents that I supposedly had put my hands on at the Ministry of Transport while procuring my Navy Certs. These showed that thirty thousand antitank rifles had been distributed to the troops. The documents and the figures were authentic. Our experts considered that it would do no harm to let the Germans know our strength in this sector, particularly since that strength was illusory. In actual fact, the thirty thousand antitank rifles were of little use, since ammunition production for that weapon was deplorably in arrears. Hardly one-fifth of the actual need was available. Ammunition was so scarce that the troops had not even had a chance to practice-fire their guns. Intelligence was filling the gap in industrial production.

I also was to feed them bits and pieces of information which on analysis would tend to confirm what we were fairly sure was an enemy misconception concerning the battle strength of the British Army. The Germans, to our knowledge, estimated that fifteen of the known twenty-seven British divisions were fully equipped and in a perfect state of readiness. Actually, at that moment hardly six divisions were ready to take the field.

In another vein were the opinions and gossip I had supposedly collected as a man about town in London. The idea was to give Hitler what he hoped to hear, namely that certain elements in Britain were prepared to come to terms with him. The Germans believed that the blitz was undermining English morale to the point of collapse and that many politicians thought it was high time to overthrow Churchill and his "clique" and negotiate a peace.

From the way this misinformation was given to me, I have my doubts that Winston Churchill was fully informed about Intelligence's political description of England. Had he known, he probably would have stopped it, perhaps punished its planners. But in espionage the end justifies all means and its practitioners tend to become a suprastate.

Normally the information given me was carefully noted, even to minor details. In this case there were no documents, and the tidbits were fed to me during after-dinner chats. "You may mention," I would be told, this or that. Many politicians lent their names to this in roundabout fashion. Others, I suspect, had theirs used without formal or tacit permission.

As I began to enter the inner core of Intelligence, it became clear to me that the many luncheons, dinners, and weekends I was spending with some of the senior officers were not purely social. They were grooming me, conditioning me mentally, by giving me advice and observing how I absorbed it.

"It may happen," Stewart Menzies told me one weekend, "that at some crucial moment you see your objective clearly. If you are absolutely convinced that you may reach it only by your own methods, then you may ignore the rules and drive ahead. But don't forget, you must be successful. In espionage failures are often fatal."

I understood I was being given carte blanche—a dangerous card, not to be overplayed.

In one regard, however, I was being allowed no freedom

of choice whatsoever. And it was the sorest point of all. I was told officially that under no circumstances could I admit to Johnny that I was an Intelligence officer. Argue as I might that this would handicap me, that I was sure Jebsen knew and approved—more than that, that it was his intention from the start—I couldn't get them to change their directive.

My training progressed in accelerated rhythm. The British were anxious to send me back to the Germans with a load of information just as von Karsthoff, hungry for information, was eagerly awaiting my return.

It was now a question of homework, of memorizing all the material collected for me by the experts of the XX Committee in cooperation with the Army, Navy, and Air Force, the Ministries of War, Production, Civil Defense, and Air. That was a last-minute chore because of another flaw in my photographic memory. I was able to retain everything down to the last comma on a page but only for a limited time, a few weeks. After that it became buried in my subconscious. A thought, a word, might trigger that subconscious and I would remember everything again, but I couldn't provoke the recall voluntarily.

Two nights before I left, a Luftwaffe bombardier delivered one of his large eggs to the Savoy Hotel. It blew off a corner of the building, killing a couple of people and wounding a number of others. I had been at one of those interminable parties and had had an interminable amount to drink. Very sound asleep, I was awakened nevertheless by the explosion. I turned on the light and saw that the room and my bed were covered with fragments of glass from the large mirrors particular to the Savoy. I brushed off the bed haphazardly and was asleep again in seconds only to be awakened again by a well-meaning and considerate American journalist.

"Are you okay?" he asked, shaking me. I sat up, blinking.

"Of course I am. Let me sleep."

"But Popov, let me . . ."

I cut him short. "Bugger off and let me sleep," I growled. And went back to sleep.

Next thing I knew the director of the Savoy was prodding my shoulder. I opened only one eye, not bothering to sit up.

"Rather a busy night, sir," was his opening line.

I grunted.

"Better let a doctor have a look at you. You're bleeding."

I looked into a fragment of mirror that still clung to the wall. My face was cut here and there but I was well anesthetized. The director watched fearfully while I pulled the covers over me again.

"Please, Mr. Popov, uh . . ."

"Look, do I pay my bills?" I inquired.

Startled, he said, "Certainly."

"Then go away and let me sleep."

The few slight scratches that I bore on my face when I arrived later in Lisbon spoke more than a thousand words. I wore them properly bandaged and plastered, and they made my stories of unbearable bombing effects much more credible to the Germans.

Gerda accompanied me to the airport in the Citroën. We held hands in the back seat. The touch of her skin still generated a glow in me but we had no frantic goodbyes and made no futile promises. Like the bombed-out London and Londoners we passed, we were seasoned to wartime. We appreciated the few weeks we had had, looked forward to more if possible, but were aware of the impermanence and instability of life. In a way, the war made relationships much more honest and realistic. Separation and death were all around us. Eternity existed as a dimension in time and space, not in the affairs of men and women.

I did feel tense about leaving England, something like what the troops must feel when moving up to the front line.

I was leaving security for enemy territory, although in no way comparable to going to the trenches. I was going to play a game of wits that I enjoyed in surroundings of great luxury. It was an Alice in Wonderland experience, passing from one world to another, except that in this case both worlds were abnormal. War-torn London to an artificial Lisbon, crowded to the bursting point with refugees and competing secret services superimposed hodgepodge on this city of medieval appearance and archaic mentality.

My attaché case bulged with papers relating to the deals I was to close for the purchase of Portuguese tin and turpentine. During my previous stay in Portugal I had contracted for the goods, contingent on British permission for shipping. I passed British customs as the bona fide representative of a consortium of Yugoslav banks.

6

I was now an old Lisbon hand. There were few people who came back after once having secured passage out. At the Sintra Airport I hopped into one of the antique taxis current in Portugal and made straight for Estoril and the Palacio Hotel. George Black ushered me personally to my old apartment on the third floor overlooking the gardens.

Following the procedure we had worked out beforehand, I went out to call von Karsthoff from a public phone. It was still late afternoon, so I placed the call to his office.

"I'm a friend of the major's cousin from Italy," I identified myself to his secretary. My German code name, Ivan, like my British one (Scout at this time; later it was to be changed), was used only for bureaucratic purposes. It figured in my dossier but never on missions.

Von Karsthoff got on the line himself and replied with the passwords, "A friend of my Italian cousin? You must come to visit. You'll bring some laughter to my house."

"I'd enjoy that very much," I answered. "It's rather urgent. Can we make it for Wednesday?"

"By all means," von Karsthoff agreed.

Normally when I phoned it was understood that the meeting was to be for the following day. If I stipulated it was urgent, that meant I wanted to see von Karsthoff the same day. The hour was fixed by the day of the week mentioned in our conversation. Monday meant 18:10, Tuesday 19:10, Wednesday 20:10, et cetera.

"I shall come by train," I told von Karsthoff, indicating that I was to be picked up in Lisbon at our usual spot on the Avenida da Liberdade. If I said I was taking a taxi, it would mean I wanted to be picked up on the main Lisbon road one mile outside Estoril.

When von Karsthoff wanted to arrange a meeting with me, a more elaborate procedure was used. I would get a phone call at my hotel from a girl giving any name.

"I'm sorry I behaved so stupidly the other night," she would say, and then suggest that we meet at a nightclub later that evening. I would agree, or if I were really busy, would say so and suggest, "Perhaps tomorrow?"

That night or the night after, as agreed upon, I would go to the Estoril Casino. Eventually, von Karsthoff's secretary, Elizabeth, would turn up. She would go to a roulette table, I following, and would play three times, the numbers indicating consecutively the date, hour, and minute of our rendezvous. Then she would play zero or 36. Zero meant the pickup was to take place in Lisbon; 36 meant Estoril at prearranged locations. It was an expensive code. She rarely won. Not only that, I passed on our meeting techniques and identification methods plus car registration numbers and the like to Colonel Jarvis, my local M.I.6 contact. The information was instrumental in tracing other German secret contacts who used the same method.

Colonel Jarvis didn't play turn and turn about. He had a highly developed sense of security, too highly developed for my taste. His code and arrangements changed with every meeting. Our early meetings were brief, usually to exchange messages or pass on some specific information, so I couldn't object to the highly uncomfortable spots he chose, such as the second bench on the left of the entrance to Salazar Park, or the lavatory of a restaurant or bar. Later we sometimes had to have longer sessions, and I expressed my discontent, but to no avail. On a subsequent trip to London, I registered my complaint. I was leading three lives: German agent, British agent, and Yugoslav businessman. I had enough details to take care of without their being complicated by such hocus-pocus. Jarvis was called to London and instructed to agree to my suggestions.

Probably I was being a prima donna. Reasonableness is not a constant companion on a tightrope. Jarvis's caution undoubtedly was justified in a situation where one slip meant downfall. I came to recognize Jarvis's ability, and after that episode went out of my way to show my sympathy and admiration, but I don't believe I managed to eliminate the grudge he bore me for my unprofessional conduct.

Promptly at 20:10, as agreed upon, I turned into the Avenida da Liberdade from the Rua Rossio. Strolling along, I went through the drill of checking to see if I was being tailed. The precaution was mainly window dressing for the Germans since I obviously didn't have to worry about being followed by the English. But it could happen that I would be followed by one of Kramer's men or by others, as happened too, in this maelstrom of special interests.

Liberdade was extremely wide, with sidewalks on each side and a spacious parklike pedestrian walk in the center. It was sparsely illuminated, and at night it was impossible to be observed from the opposite side. I kept a watch on the few other men on the street and the occasional parked car. No one appeared to have any particular interest in me. An automobile of recent vintage drove past me and parked about fifty feet along, leaving its motor running. I didn't recognize it, but Elizabeth and von Karsthoff, one of whom would be picking me up, never drove their own cars to a tref. They were known to every agent around town. Their practice was to borrow a car from some member of the embassy staff.

Walking slowly, I glanced into the parked car. The dim light sufficed to reveal the fine outline of von Karsthoff's profile. I jumped in the back and lay on the seat until we cleared the lights of Lisbon. We drove to one of the several Estoril houses von Karsthoff maintained as an elaborate security precaution. They all had at least one similarity: a garage incorporated into the house so that one could enter unseen. The Germans believed von Karsthoff's homes were under constant observation. Their apprehensions were quite correct.

We dined with Elizabeth, and the conversation covered in broad terms all that I had done and learned in England. We had been on friendly terms before my departure and now we were even closer. I was delighted when Karsthoff suggested I spend the whole of the next day with him at his country house. I would have been less enthusiastic if I had known the ordeal I was to face.

The house lay in the hills outside Estoril on a point affording a view of the sea. I don't know if it was used as an observation post, but the only glimpse I was allowed of the Atlantic was during a very brief respite in a marathon interrogation. If I hadn't been prepared for interrogation in England, I most certainly would have put my foot in it. Not, I believe, that von Karsthoff was trying to entrap me. He was a highly experienced intelligence officer and was methodically drawing the maximum from me.

For every shred of information I gave him von Karsthoff insisted on the source, the time, and the circumstances under which I got it. He probed for every detail, attacked each subject from innumerable angles, seeking additional facts. Frequently I didn't have the answers, his questions demanding a minute precision that we hadn't envisaged in London. I was amazed at the way he was able to tear apart our carefully prepared stories, and I was hard put to fabricate the answers he demanded.

Elizabeth was present throughout, taking down in shorthand every word that passed between us. I knew I had to

keep my story—or rather, stories—straight, so the next day
I reviewed the whole session, committing to memory all the
additions I had invented. It wasn't a useless precaution. In
later sessions, von Karsthoff did hark back to things I had
told him previously.

Like a fine bloodhound put on the trail, von Karsthoff
sensed particular value in Gerda Sullivan and another of my
informants, Dick Metcalfe. Happily, the trail was one we
had laid.

I had described Gerda as a girl I had met at a Yugoslav
Embassy dinner and ascribed much of my political information to her. Von Karsthoff went into her background thoroughly—particularly, I suppose, since she was Austrian.

"Do you think she is in sympathy with the German cause?"
he wanted to know.

"No doubt," I assured him, inventing some conversations
we had had.

"Do you think she would like to work for us?"

"Like to?" I hedged. "Yes, I think she would like to, just
as many other people in England probably would if given
a chance. If nothing else, they'd like to be on the winning
side. But I can't say definitely that she'd be prepared to take
the risk, and I wouldn't want to be the one to approach her.
Gerda is useful to me, she's amenable, she introduces me to
all sorts of influential people, and it's no hardship to take
her to bed, but I don't want my safety to depend on a girl
I sleep with."

Von Karsthoff agreed that sex and security didn't mix.
Actually, it was a delaying tactic I invented on the spur of
the moment because I couldn't risk sounding too confident
of her and I did recruit Gerda as a double agent some time
later on a perfect pretext. Gerda had a photograph of her
father in her apartment. By chance, I looked at it closely
one day and noticed the small medallion on his lapel was

adorned with a swastika. British Intelligence already knew about this blotch on the paternal escutcheon. When I mentioned this to von Karsthoff, he had a check run in Vienna and confirmed for himself that the old man had been a member of the party. This opened the door for Gerda, although she definitely did not share her father's political beliefs.

I had cited Dickie Metcalfe as the source of much of my technical information and as an aid in obtaining the Navy Certs. Again, I credited the introduction to a Yugoslav diplomat friend who had used him as a runner on some minor embassy matters. Dickie was ideal material as a potential German spy. His was the classic case of the gay, irresponsible Army officer. He had a race horse, a racing car, lots of girlfriends, a taste for drink and the high life. Dickie's expenditures eventually exceeded his income, and there were some nasty scandals. He was cashiered from his regiment and earned the reputation of being a disgruntled ex-officer who considered that he had been badly treated. He was also reputed to be constantly in need of money.

What I omitted to tell von Karsthoff was that Dickie had been rehabilitated and was now an intelligence officer working closely with Lord Suffolk of Foreign Office Intelligence. On a mission to the Continent, he was shot down in an aircraft on June 13, 1940, but made his way back to England in six days.

Von Karsthoff rose to the bait of Metcalfe as well, but following instructions from the British, I played it cool. When von Karsthoff asked what Metcalfe thought of the Germans I replied, "I wouldn't know. I never asked him. I couldn't help gathering, though, that he admires the German military machine."

"Try to sound him out a little more profoundly," von Karsthoff suggested, without giving specific instructions to recruit him.

With the help of an excellent champagne that Elizabeth brought in, I reeled off an inspired description of the effects of the bombing and privation in England. The recital was quite contrary to my real impressions, and I ended it with the opinion that the British were fighting with their last gasp.

Von Karsthoff's reply was unexpected. "You are underestimating the British, as are Berlin and Hitler. To me they seem more dangerous than ever. It must have something to do with the fog, their climate. Anyone who manages to live in that climate, to grow and breathe, always has a second wind. But make Berlin believe that." He shook his head.

"So you won't report my findings to Berlin?" I asked, disturbed that our deception was not succeeding.

"I'll report what you have told me, not my opinions. At any rate, that's what they want to hear. They don't want deductions, they want observations."

"Canaris gives his opinions." I fished for information.

"Oh, Canaris." He disposed of him with a wave of his hand. "The admiral is the type of man whose advice is never sought and, when given, is never taken. Listen, Dusko, Germany operates on the Fuhrer principle. With us, only one man really decides. The opinions of the others count only to the degree of their faithfulness to the Fuhrer."

Von Karsthoff's unorthodoxy surprised me. He wasn't the dyed-in-the-wool Nazi I expected, and it came easier to admit to myself I actually liked the man.

"If you have nothing more for me to do here, I should get on to Madrid," I reminded von Karsthoff. I had told him, truthfully, that I had to work my trade deals through the Yugoslav Embassy in Spain, since there was none in Portugal at that time. "I'm in a hurry to wrap things up and get back to London before the British become suspicious about the time I'm spending abroad. I started some negotiations in London to buy tires and some products from the colonies

—tea and coffee for the most part—and I made a point of their being needed urgently, so the British will be expecting me back soon."

I had another reason as well for my haste to reach Madrid. When we saw each other in Rome, Johnny and I had agreed to meet there at the first opportunity. I had sent him a signal through von Karsthoff that I would be in Madrid in a week or two.

"Nothing to keep you here," my spymaster agreed. "You can leave whenever you want. By the way, what hotel will you stay at in Madrid? The Ritz or the Palace?" von Karsthoff asked, naming the two top hotels. No self-respecting traveler would have considered any other.

"I don't know. Why?"

"Oh, it's of no consequence," von Karsthoff answered and then proceeded to tell me things of much consequence. "My equal number in Madrid is a man named Lentz. You may meet him, Jebsen knows him, and besides, he'll be curious about you. He might even try to usurp you from me for fear that you're trespassing on his territory. He has a strong organization in Spain, and the Palace Hotel is almost entirely under his control. The British are strong in the Ritz, although he's infiltrated there, too. You may find it more quiet at the Ritz," Karsthoff hinted.

I knew Johnny would be staying at the Palace. I opted for the Ritz. That would give me a periscope in both hotels. Anyway, they were very close, practically only the Prado Museum gardens separating them.

"What sort of man is Lentz?" I asked von Karsthoff.

"He's a friend of Canaris's, in his fifties, efficient and a good organizer. He's a bit of a pedant, though. You may find that form is more important to him than the objective. But I must say he's running a first-rate spy network in England. Inside the Spanish Embassy. He either has the tacit approval of the government or he's working through the press attaché, I don't know which."

My ears pricked up. This could mean a big haul for M.I.5. It turned out later that Lentz was being taken. There was no spy ring inside the Spanish Embassy. It had been created out of the whole cloth by a clever free-lance agent in Spain who was selling the Abwehr information he made up himself. Later, he came to work for the British under the code name of Garbo.

The mention of working through the embassy struck a sudden chord in my mind. I could play the game as well as Lentz. Taking Menzies at his word, I decided to act on my own initiative. I was sure of my scheme, and the time to strike was now. Requesting approval might delay it fatally.

"That gives me an interesting idea," I told von Karsthoff. "I have some friends at the Yugoslav Embassy in London, and the Yugoslav Ambassador in Madrid is a friend of the family. I might arrange to carry the diplomatic bag from one place to the other and then, with a bit of help from you . . ."

"Name it." Von Karsthoff was eager before even knowing what I'd need.

"Could you procure forgeries of the seals of the Yugoslav embassies in London and Madrid? Two of each? You would keep one set here and I'd have the other in London. Then if I had to transport documents or bulky information, I could break the seals, put my stuff in the bag, and seal it up again. On the other end, I could reverse the procedure." The stunt would enhance my standing with the Germans and help me carry material for the British at the same time.

"Lentz has just the man for the job. Dr. Kuhn. And it'll put you in Lentz's good graces to include him in. He is a touchy man. I'd better be the one to request it though, not you." He turned to his fiancée. "Elizabeth, a telegram to

Berlin. We want to know the size and the form of the seals used by the Yugoslav embassies." Efficient to the core, Elizabeth left the room immediately to code the message.

"You'll have the seals by the time you return from Madrid," von Karsthoff promised. "But tell me, what excuse will you give to your Yugoslav friends for wanting to carry the bag?" As usual, von Karsthoff thought of everything.

"It's to our mutual advantage. They have a shortage of couriers, and I have trouble obtaining visas for Spain and Portugal."

"Very neat," he complimented me.

"About Lentz," I worried. "I shouldn't like to become involved in internal Abwehr jealousies and intrigues. Can you keep him off my back? I don't want him getting the idea that I'm under his jurisdiction."

"Jebsen may do better than I. He can tell his friend Colonel Oster that you prefer to be attached to Lisbon rather than Madrid. But don't mention to Jebsen that I prefer it, too. If it ever got back to Lentz, he'd be sure to put the wrong interpretation on it."

Von Karsthoff then confided to me a top secret development that was to become one of my major scoops. "Very soon we won't need to bother with diplomatic bags or other devices. We'll have a gadget that will facilitate the sending of information. They are developing a method in Berlin to reduce a full page to a film the size of a dot. It will be readable only through a microscope. A mikropunkt, it is called."

"A dot!" I showed I was impressed. "It certainly would be easy to conceal."

"Totally invisible unless you know where it is. It is still in the experimental stage, but as soon as it is ready I shall see that you are among the first to secure its advantage."

7

Ten days in Madrid awaiting Johnny or at least word from him. I had concluded my business transactions and was remaining there only to see him. Lentz hadn't contacted me, which was just as well. I had sensed that von Karsthoff preferred me to steer clear of him. He didn't want Lentz encroaching on his territory.

At last my phone rang and it was Johnny. I threw on my jacket and covered the few hundred yards to the Palace bar in indecent haste for the Spanish capital.

"It's your fault I'm late," Johnny excused himself. "Your reports from London were too good. Piecki was so delighted with them he made me stay while he went over every last detail. He particularly likes the precision of your reports and the positive way you express yourself when you are certain of your facts. The sheer volume impressed him too. It looks like the work of ten men."

Or more, I said to myself.

"Here"—Johnny handed me an envelope—"a bonus with Piecki's compliments."

I slipped the envelope into my breast pocket, not bothering to open it. It contained ten thousand dollars.

"Money isn't what you're after, is it, Dusko?" Johnny looked at me as though he were trying to read my mind.

"Stop X-raying me," I said, feeling uncomfortable. "If you have something eating you, spit it out."

Johnny pretended to ignore my remark, saying, "You're hitting the pinnacle, becoming the Abwehr's top agent. Müntzinger was congratulated for recruiting you, and he's crowing as though he really was the one to find you."

"Well, that's not what's bothering you." I returned to my previous remark, knowing that Johnny was above departmental jealousies and squabbles.

"No," Johnny admitted and looked at me searchingly again. "Dusko, I have no parents, no brothers, just two half-sisters old enough to be my mother. They're completely estranged from me. I have girlfriends till I don't know what to do with them but not one for whom I really care. You're my closest friend—without reservations. If you want to analyze it, you're an ersatz brother and I wish you were a real one."

"I'll have my father adopt you," I jested to relieve Johnny the embarrassment of his seriousness.

"What I'm getting at"—Johnny wasn't being diverted—"is that I'm, let's say, uneasy to have put you in this game. It suits you and you seem to enjoy it but," he took a peanut from the dish on the table, "you can be crushed like that." He opened his hand to show the powdered remains.

"Well, then, let's to the dinner table before it's too late." I put an end to his macabre conversation. "You know the government's latest edict. If they can call time on the Spaniards, this world is coming to an unbearable pass anyway."

"Okay." Johnny looked at his watch. It was near 10 P.M. "The Madrileños are circumventing the final gong, so why not us?"

To try to get Spaniards to bed earlier—and so up earlier—the government had ordered restaurants to close their doors to newcomers after 10 P.M. It was Spanish custom—among the upper classes particularly—to dine at midnight. Executives would show up at the office around noon. But custom is not changed by decree. The Madrileños were turning up at the restaurants a few minutes before ten. Until that hour they were empty. The sudden influx caused slow service. Drinks would be had first, and by the time dinner came it was near midnight and tradition was upheld.

It wasn't easy to get a good meal in Madrid. One could eat properly at only the few luxury hotels and some black market restaurants, but there you would eat excellently.

"Let's go to the Horcher," Johnny suggested, "but watch what you say. It belongs to a German and is under Abwehr control. There is a microphone concealed on almost every table. In the vases."

The Horcher was only a few minutes' walk from the Palace. I think the streets of that posh quarter were so clean because the people were so poor they scavenged everything. A cigarette butt didn't stay long in the gutter. The Horcher had gleaming starched linen, polished silver, and candlelight. We ordered our drinks and settled down for a comfortable wait.

With the concealed microphones in mind, I repeated the spiel I had memorized for von Karsthoff, giving Johnny a gloomy description of England. I figured if the Germans realized who the speaker was, it would reinforce my reputation with them. If they thought it was another source, it would perhaps serve to confirm my report.

Johnny didn't grasp what I was up to and looked seriously worried. A wink and a glance at the vase on our table corrected that. He joined gleefully in the game. We larded our conversation with intimate talk of girls and other things one wouldn't mention if aware of a tap.

On our way back to our hotels, in the seclusion of the Prado Park, Johnny cautioned me about talking in my room or practically anywhere else in Madrid. Lentz—Papa Lentz, as he was called (really Wilhelm Leisner)—had a huge staff.

The German Embassy gave diplomatic cover to some 120 Abwehr officers, and about 400 others were spotted around town in various phony firms and jobs. Among them was a nephew of Admiral Canaris's.

Johnny also gave me the name of a man of another caliber, one who could be trusted. "If you're ever in trouble, contact him at the Embassy," he said. "He will get a message to me without intermediaries."

It was late. We still had a lot of talking to do and no place to do it. I proposed getting a car and going to Toledo the next day. "Lovely drive, beautiful city full of El Grecos and no microphones."

"I'll take care of the car," Johnny offered. "Pick you up at ten."

We glided out the narrow mountain road to Toledo in a magnificent brute of a Hispano-Suiza roadster dating back to the twenties which Johnny had borrowed from a Spanish friend. No bugs in it, motor or otherwise. While Johnny was wrestling with the gears going through town, I was lamenting that I couldn't speak to him forthrightly. To accomplish the task Stewart Menzies had given me, I had to go about it from all four points of the compass. I remarked that a number of Abwehr officers I had met were not Nazis. A certain number seemed positively anti-Nazi, like Jebsen himself.

Johnny said, "Hm," as he wrenched the big wooden steering wheel to get around a horse cart.

"And then there are people like Schacht," I mentioned, "and General von Blomberg. They're both in disgrace, I understand." The ex-Commander in Chief of the Army had been sacked by Hitler on trumped-up moral charges, having married a whore. At the time that didn't hinder the entire Nazi hierarchy from coming to the wedding, but later he was ousted when he tried to oppose Hitler's projected use of the armed forces against Austria and Czechoslovakia.

"There must be many influential people who recognize Hitler's madness and who would want to curb his power and stop this war. They could negotiate with Britain, it seems to me—say, through the Abwehr. With its freedom of movement, the Abwehr would make the ideal instrument." Johnny flicked a glance at me to show that he was listening. "What do you think," I asked, "would something like that be possible?"

Concentrating, he didn't answer right away. He threw his head back, looking at the sky more than the road. After a suspenseful minute he answered.

"A terribly ambitious and naïve idea, 'devoutly to be desired.' My answer is categorically no. A 'no' as big as these mountains. Hitler has no opposition in Germany. It has been either smashed or reduced to complete impotence. German youth has been educated from the cradle to believe in Hitler. To make a successful revolution or *coup d'état,* you need the people on your side. Even that's not enough. You need the army, too, or at least its neutrality. Hitler's opponents are people like myself, drawing-room opposition. We discuss Hitler over a glass of schnapps or a cup of tea. And even many of that clique—the drawing-room opposition—are tainted. They make excuses, find good things to say about National Socialism. In addition, they're not cohesive. They range from Royalist to leftist. They've no organization and they do nothing but talk . . . and that very carefully."

Johnny waved a hand to dismiss them all.

"Dusko," he asked, "is there one example in history of army marshals or generals revolting when victorious? When they are getting the applause, the glory, and the booty? Most of them love Hitler, and those who don't love him admire him. Don't forget, they did the planning of this war and they are winning it for Hitler."

We had reached the river and the gorge opposite Toledo. Johnny steered the Hispano onto the shoulder of the road and stopped.

"Beautiful view," he said, switching off the motor. But it was more than the ramparts of Toledo that he wanted to examine.

"Madly idealistic, your idea," he said, turning to face me, "or whoseever idea it is," he added, shrewdly. "It is totally absurd but so attractive that I won't be able to put it out of my mind. It is worth living or dying for."

He took a long drag on his cigarette, expelled the smoke forcefully, as though giving birth to a fresh thought.

"Nobody can claim that all the German people accepted the Nazi doctrine willingly. If they had, there would have been no Gestapo, no S.S., no S.D. The Nazis 'rendered harmless,' as they say—in other words, murdered—all active opposition. The rest, the passive opposition, lives under the terror of persecution, torture, and concentration camps. Right now it's a waste of time to talk about a change. But if some unforeseeable event or change in the fortunes of war made it possible, it would mean nothing if there were no bridge to cross the river. And I agree, there's no better bridge or more maneuverable instrument than the Abwehr. To use the Abwehr, one would have to know who is who and who thinks what. I shall sound things out and when we next meet, will let you know what there is to be known. Afterwards, if something happens to me, you may pass my findings on to somebody else who wants to chase the rainbow."

I felt both sad and chagrined. My vow of secrecy—which I was sure Johnny had penetrated—prevented me from telling him that there was a rainbow chaser of monumental size, Sir Stewart Menzies, ready to join hands with him.

8

My first open conflict with German counterespionage came about on my return to Lisbon. I noticed that a tall, thin man with distinctive floppy ears, almost rabbit-like, kept appearing wherever I went, in the Casino, the Palacio lobby, the train from the Estoril to Lisbon. His appearance was so distinctive it was difficult to imagine his being employed as a shadow, but I put him to the test anyway.

I walked from the Palacio to the railroad station and bought a ticket for Lisbon. Mr. Floppy Ears, who I could swear hadn't been following me, appeared like a rabbit out of a hat on the platform. For some unaccountable association, I named him Uncle Oscar. The train arrived. I boarded it and took a seat near the door. Uncle Oscar took a seat at the far end of the coach and, as he had always done, hid behind a Portuguese newspaper. Just before the train started, I pulled the oldest trick in the profession. I darted out of the coach. Uncle Oscar had a time elbowing people out of the way, but he followed me. I then reversed the procedure and rushed back into the train almost banging into him on the way. He was fast on his feet and got back into the train, too. Point number one was established. It was no coincidence. He was on my track. I wasn't particularly worried, since I hadn't had any meetings with the British during those days. But I did want to know who was making him hop.

The following evening, I had an appointment with von Karsthoff. My shadow was in the lobby reading his newspaper when I came down from my apartment. I left through the rear exit of the hotel, which was the automobile entrance, and immediately ran around the building to the front pedestrian entrance, next to the park. Uncle Oscar was no longer in the lobby. I proceeded on foot to my meeting place on the road to Lisbon. Walking fast, I soon caught up with the tall, thin shadow. He was going slowly, trying to spot me in the darkness ahead. Since he apparently knew my meeting place, there was little doubt that he was in the service of Abwehr III. Colonel Jarvis knew where I was picked up, too, but I doubted both that he would use such a clumsy man and that he would have me followed.

Leaving Uncle Oscar clear title to the spot on the Lisbon road, I hiked all the way to von Karsthoff's villa. I entered through a neighbor's gate, hitched myself over a high stone wall, and rang the bell at the rear entrance. High heels clicked in response inside the house.

"Elizabeth," I stage-whispered, "don't put on the outside light."

"What happened to you?" she said, opening the door and noting my dusty suit, which she brushed while I recounted my misadventure with Uncle Oscar. It was Elizabeth who had driven out to pick me up, von Karsthoff not being home yet. When I didn't turn up, she'd decided I'd been prevented from coming and she returned home. She didn't know anything about Uncle Oscar nor had she noticed him at the rendezvous point.

"If he's one of our men, I don't know him," von Karsthoff also maintained on his return, "but I'll put out an inquiry on him."

My meeting with von Karsthoff was important. Comments from Berlin on my reports had come through. They wanted still more details. We worked till after midnight, mightily straining my inventiveness. When we were done, von Karsthoff gave me my gold star.

"Admiral Canaris thinks very highly of your work," he said. "He wants us to take particular care of you."

"Slightly superfluous at this point, no?" I bluffed. "If Uncle Oscar isn't your man, he must be British. I think my usefulness is at an end."

"Let's not rush to any conclusions." My spymaster was suspiciously unruffled. "Give me a few days."

Uncle Oscar must have gone on holiday for a few days. He definitely wasn't on my tail. I checked and rechecked because I had a meeting with Colonel Jarvis.

"Not our man," Jarvis confirmed, adding gloomily, "we must be even more careful now. The Germans may change their watchdog."

When I saw von Karsthoff that night, he didn't seem surprised that I hadn't seen Uncle Oscar for a few days, but he avoided comment. He wasn't worried about Uncle Oscar being British, since he gave me a new questionnaire to memorize for my projected trip to England.

At the Casino night club the following evening, Uncle Oscar popped up again. I caught sight of his familiar head at the far end of the room while I was taking a turn around the dance floor with a French girlfriend named Margot. I was extremely annoyed. My date had looked promising. Margot was clinging to me like to a hot water bottle in a cold bed, so I was confident about how the evening would finish, but I had visions of Uncle Oscar at the transom. Margot had been playing the proper "jeune fille" up till that night, so I didn't think she'd appreciate a voyeur.

Exasperated, I was inspired to dubious humor and took vengeance on a poor tipsy girl who had been annoying the whole club. She was one of a party at the table of the Lisbon correspondent of the London *Daily Mail*. Under the illusion that she could sing, she had been breaking our eardrums all evening warbling over the microphone with the dance band.

When the waiter opened a fresh bottle of champagne for us, I took the cork, placed it on his silver tray, and told him to deliver it to the singer with my compliments. Taking me at my word, he presented it to her at the microphone in full view of the audience.

The girl stopped singing but didn't use the cork as implied. She looked in our direction, then charged. Probably misconstruing her tormentor, she picked up Margot's glass with the obvious intention of dashing it, contents and all, in her face. I caught her arm just in time. The glass fell from her hand and I think she was a bit stunned. I turned her around, pointing her toward her table, and with a pat on her rump sent her on her way, saying, "Be a good girl now."

The incident naturally drew the attention of everyone present. The *Daily Mail* reporter rose from his table dramatically and started our way. I noticed he had an arm in a plaster cast.

"You have been insulting my guest," he said pontifically.

"I'm sorry, it was a stupid joke," I admitted. "Please ask the young lady to forgive me."

He wasn't accepting apologies and started to swing a very telegraphed roundhouse blow with his good fist. My reflexes took over. I ducked and responded with a short hook to the jaw. The dance floor was highly polished. He went sliding on his rear end almost all the way across it.

Several people got up from his table, and the atmosphere had all the makings of a barroom brawl. In my dinner jacket pocket I had a sealed envelope containing the German questionnaire and some notes I had made of names and information to pass on to the British. I quickly slipped the envelope into Margot's purse, which was lying on the table.

"Run for it," I told her. "There's a lot of cash and checks in there. Meet me in the hotel lobby."

Margot was frightened. She didn't want to be mixed up in a scandal and so didn't have to be told twice.

The delegation from the *Daily Mail* man's table bore down on me, a squat, powerful-looking character in the lead.

"Are you a Nazi or something?" he said aggressively in a nasal American accent.

"Why?"

" 'Cause you're a fucking coward, hitting a man with a broken arm."

"If you have a broken arm, you don't start fights," I answered with what I thought was much logic.

It wasn't the moment for logic. The squat man was building up his courage to attack, and out of the corner of my eye I saw Uncle Oscar heading for the exit after Margot. He must have seen me put the envelope in her bag.

The squat man started to move in on me. A table was separating us, and I shoved it in his mid-section. He doubled up on it. The girl singer jumped on my back, trying to gouge out my eyes. I had to cartwheel her over my head, and fortunately she thumped into the man, who by that time was trying to get at me. The girl put him off balance, so I was able to plant my left with precision on the side of his jaw. For good measure, I hit him again as he went down. That gave me time to run for it. The *Daily Mail* man's other guests contented themselves with hurling boos and cries of "coward, stay and fight" after me.

I came out of the door running and heard Margot scream from across the park—about a hundred yards—which separates the Palacio from the Casino. I sprinted toward the hotel and made out two figures struggling on the ground. As I neared them I saw that Uncle Oscar was trying to wrestle her purse from her. It spilled open and the contents dumped on the ground. Uncle Oscar grabbed my long white envelope and was scrambling to his feet while I was about ten yards away. I launched my foot at his face. Uncle Oscar went down again, unconscious, spurting blood and teeth but still clutching the envelope. As I was taking it from him, George Black came running up. Black was hardly five foot two, and he was holding a revolver nearly as big as he was. He bent over to look at Uncle Oscar.

"He's not dead," he pronounced coolly, sticking the revolver in his waistband. "I'll take care of this mess, Popov. Take Madame Broche to her room and stay there. If the police come, I'll tell them you hopped into a taxi and went to Lisbon. Don't leave Madame Broche's room until you phone me."

It was noon before I phoned him.

"You can come out now," Black said. "Your man is in the hospital, but the police don't know you sent him there. I told them he was attacked by two ruffians. Odd thing, he confirmed it. He lost several teeth and his nose is . . . well, he's going to snuffle like a bulldog for the rest of his days."

The news made me feel pretty chipper. I had drawn my first Nazi blood. "Thanks," I told Black, "for everything," thinking also of the very comfortable bed into which he had aided me.

The Abwehr III chief, Herr Kramer, assisted at my interview with von Karsthoff a few nights later. I suppose von Karsthoff ordered him to be there. He looked a bit on the defensive while von Karsthoff explained that he hadn't known Kramer had put a man on me until after my complaint.

"I told Herr Kramer not to have you followed any longer, but perhaps he, too, has had orders from Admiral Canaris about taking good care of you," von Karsthoff said, sarcastically. "Uncle Oscar, I'm told, was there purely for your protection. He was checking to see that the British weren't following you. You can go to London reassured. Nobody was. Same for Madrid. I just received a cable confirming that you were not being followed while you were there." By the British, you mean, I thought. The Abwehr man in Madrid was more adept than Uncle Oscar.

"If he was just there for my protection, why did he follow the girl?" I objected. "And why did he grab the envelope?"

Kramer smirked. "He suspected, my dear Popov, that the girl was working for the Gaullists. And maybe she is. He was afraid she would open the envelope. Didn't you ever think of that? Are you so sure you can trust her?"

"More than I can trust an anonymous shadow. I should have been informed I was being protected," I accused.

Kramer shrugged and took his leave.

"I think we need a drink," von Karsthoff sighed when the door closed behind the counterintelligence man. He served me a cognac, and shaking his head regretfully, said, "Germans can be heavy-handed, can't they, Dusko? I'm from Trieste, you know," he explained. "Phoenician background, like yours. That is why we have more finesse, more psychological understanding. The Germans are blunderers. Even when they do the right thing, they often do it the wrong way. Your brush with Uncle Oscar is a minor example. Do you know what happened with the Duke of Windsor?"

I shook my head in response to his question, and he told me his version of the German attempt to kidnap Windsor.

"When the Duke came to Spain after the fall of France," von Karsthoff recounted, "he told some Spanish friends that he wouldn't return to England unless given a very important post and unless the Duchess was recognized as a member of the royal family. He also said that if he had been on the throne, he would have prevented England from entering the war against Germany.

"Hitler took great interest in the story and suggested that

the Duke be kept on hand in Spain. He instigated Windsor's friend, Juan Baigbeder y Atienza, the Spanish Foreign Minister, to approach him and convince him that Germany wants peace with England but that Churchill's clique stands in the way. Hitler wanted the Duke to stand ready to cooperate at the appropriate time and eventually to reassume the throne. The Duchess was to become queen, naturally. Meanwhile, Hitler proposed to offer him fifty million Swiss francs—deposited in Switzerland—so that the Duke could lead a life fit for a king."

"How could he become king again?" I interrupted. "According to the laws of succession, it's impossible. Not after abdicating."

With a laugh von Karsthoff reproached my naïveté. "That is what the Duke replied, too. But when empires are crumbling, Dusko, you don't really think a little infraction of the law counts."

"Of course," I was quick to agree. "I'm starting to think like an Englishman."

"Baigbeder's talks with the Duke went quite well," von Karsthoff continued. "But in the midst of them the Duke came here to Portugal, where he received strict orders from Churchill to proceed to the Bahamas and take up the post of Governor General. Even so we probably would have succeeded in keeping him in Spain or Portugal if Berlin hadn't sent its heavy artillery. Walter Schellenberg from Abwehr II came here with wild plans to kidnap the Duke and frighten him into believing that British Intelligence wants to kill him."

"Schellenberg," I interrupted. "The name rings a bell, but I don't place him exactly."

"Schellenberg is one of my superiors, a rising star in Berlin, a specialist in sabotage and other subtleties like that. You probably read about him in connection with the Venlo incident."

It came back to me in detail. It was in 1940. The Gestapo lured a Major Stevens and a Captain Paine to a small town on the Dutch border supposedly to meet a German general and a group of anti-Nazis anxious to make peace. Schellenberg captured the two Englishmen and claimed to have obtained much important information from them.

"When Schellenberg started meddling, everything went sour," von Karsthoff explained. "And mind you, we had made even more progress by then. We were talking with Primo de Rivera, another friend of Windsor's, and with the Lisbon banker, Spirito Santo, who was his host here. Schellenberg frightened the Duke so much he was persuaded that Intelligence would kill him if he didn't leave for the Bahamas. Schellenberg was pulling tricks like firing shots through the Duke's bedroom window and sending flowers with anonymous messages warning him not to go to the Bahamas. The result of this heavy-handedness was that the Duke said, 'Thanks very much,' promised to keep in touch, and ran off to Nassau. But even when he was leaving, Schellenberg didn't give up. He sent a message saying there was a bomb aboard the ship. It delayed the sailing a few hours."

I wasn't in any position to judge if the story was apocryphal or not, but it was interesting to pass along if only as an indication of the schism in German Intelligence.

Preparatory to my leaving for England again, von Karsthoff examined me like a schoolboy on the questionnaire Uncle Oscar had almost stolen and on the new addresses and code he had given me. Fortunately, I knew them like "Pater Nostrum."

When I complained that the questionnaire was so voluminous—"You'll soon want to know what Churchill had for dinner" was the way I put it—von Karsthoff recommended that I concentrate on what was most important and accessible. Berlin was impressed by the quality of my work, and he ad-

vised me not to spread myself too thin. "Anyway," he suggested, "some of your contacts—which are excellent—might
be disposed to work for us independently. That would take a
lot of the burden off your shoulders. Sound them out. If you
decide you are absolutely sure of them, you can start them
off on their own."

I let myself be persuaded. That was exactly what Masterman and Tar wanted.

9

The bomb shrieked like the one that has your number on it.
A deafening explosion shook Albany House. I expected to
see or rather feel it crumble down on top of us, but it was a
miss, a near miss. Susan Barton was thrown off her chair.
The windows blew in, the flying glass just missing us. Bill
Matthews got up spitting the fine powder and plaster that
covered us all and initiating us to Scottish blasphemy and
cursing. After he had cleared his throat and his sentiments
and we had stood Susan back on her feet, none the worse for
her motorless flight, his concern was for me.

"Poor Dusko," he said, "this would be a hell of a way for
you to go. Too ironic. After skipping in and out of the
viper's nest on the Continent, to buy it in the middle of
London!"

"Hell, don't romanticize," I protested sincerely. "I'm almost
ashamed of spending such a comfortable war in neutral countries. And when I do come back to England, I have the
warmth of being surrounded by friends. What I can't stand
are those damn reports we're doing now. It's the same every
time. Ten or twelve hours a day for over a week, dictating,
answering questions. I'm a bureaucrat, not a spy. And to add
insult to injury, they give me Susan for a secretary," I teased
her. "The great untouchable."

Our more or less flippant reaction to the bombing was

fairly typical of the attitude I found in London this time. Since February, the air raids on the British capital had diminished. In part, that was thanks to bad weather, but the main reason was that Air Marshal Goering had decided to change strategy and tactics for the third time.

At the beginning—in the late summer of 1940—the Luftwaffe concentrated on bombing airports. The idea was to destroy British air power. It nearly succeeded. Many of the fighter bases were partially or completely knocked out. But the Germans didn't persist long enough. Instead Goering promised Hitler to reduce London and the other large English cities to rubble. The new aim was to break the people's spirit. This enabled the RAF to get its second wind, and it came out of the Battle of Britain scathed but undefeated.

Now Goering let up on the cities and started hitting the ports. This new tactic indicated that the Germans were envisaging a long war. Goering was out to starve Britain. The questionnaire I brought over indicated the switch, too. The Germans weren't thinking about an invasion any more. They didn't ask for additional information about ground and beach defenses or the concentration of troops in the southeast. Now they wanted to know about convoys, airplane manufacture, tank and ship construction, and the effects of the submarine blockade.

With the invasion scare over, British morale was on the upsurge, although the U-boat warfare caused great concern. The U-boats were sinking more merchant ships than could be replaced. And the sea represented England's lifeline. Across it came the vital supplies from the Commonwealth and the United States. Psychologically the British were harder hit by the loss of a battleship or a minor naval engagement than by the defeat of France or the Dunkirk debacle.

During my return to England this time I set up Gerda and Dickie as double agents. They differed from most other agents being run by the XX Committee, being of our choosing, not "turned." They were named respectively, Gelatine and Balloon. In line with her father's Nazi party membership, Gerda was supposedly in the business for patriotic reasons. She specialized in using her social contacts to gather political news and secrets and information about new army commanders, nominations, and the like. She was paid only a bonus from time to time and given money for her expenses. Patriotism was not a profitable affair.

Dickie fared much better as a mercenary. As a cashiered officer known as a high liver, Balloon maintained his reputation by constantly requesting more funds from the Abwehr. He got them because his information was exact and regular.

Since I was now running a team with two subagents, British Intelligence saw fit to give me a new code name: Tricycle. Descriptive, I suppose.

According to the unwritten code, male and female agents shouldn't be intimate, so that in time of crisis no emotions are involved. On becoming Gelatine, Gerda half-seriously said, in the midst of an embrace, "I guess we shouldn't be together any more."

"Uh-uh," I mumbled, "have to. It's part of our double-cross of the Germans."

Conscientiously, we continued to break the rules. So did Balloon and Gelatine. Supposedly they weren't aware of each other's existence, thus reducing the risk if one of them were caught. Berlin complimented me for keeping my agents apart.

With the advent of my two new agents, my star went even higher in Abwehr circles. In the several months that I had been operating I had already become well entrenched, the Tirpitzufer praising me as their most important and successful agent in England. Now, I gained even more prestige, and so did von Karsthoff as my spymaster. He probably gained material advantages as well. I also became the favorite son of the Pau da Bandeira, as the Abwehr office in Lisbon was known from the habit of calling such places by their street names. My expenses were running several thousand dollars a month, and I never was as much as asked to account for a farthing.

The paying of espionage agents on enemy soil is one of the big problems of all intelligence services. Somehow, somewhere, cash must be found and supplied to them to keep them operating. Many agents have failed for lack of funds, one German parachutist in England going so far as to commit suicide, not having anywhere to turn. Even the XX Committee couldn't run its "turned" agents if the Abwehr didn't furnish them with money. It would have been a dead giveaway to have them continue.

When Berlin authorized Balloon's appointment as my main subagent in England, von Karsthoff asked me to take a few thousand pounds over for him. I agreed, since it was the only way to start Dickie Metcalfe in his new career. But for the form I objected, insisting that in the future the Abwehr find some other means of paying him. It was dangerous for me to take money to him in England because of the currency regulations. Legally, one could enter England with only a limited amount in British pounds, and all foreign currency had to be changed into pounds. When making the change, the serial numbers of all bills over one pound were noted. I could hardly ask for five hundred pounds, say, in one-pound notes. That in itself would have been suspicious. And if Balloon were caught, the numbered bills in his possession could be traced directly to me.

Von Karsthoff appreciated the dilemma and agreed to look for some other method. He also told me, incidentally, that German spymasters had to get special permission from the Tirpitzufer to advance a large sum to an agent. Berlin didn't trust its spies that much. It was afraid they might pull a disappearing act if they got too much money or, unused to large sums, evoke suspicion by freehanded spending.

Out of this incident, I hatched a plan that would put British Intelligence in the extraordinary position of being the paymaster of German spies in England.

I approached the proposition obliquely, trying it out for size on Bill Matthews.

"Bill," I said to him, "I'm sure that a girl who owes six weeks' rent and has no money can be persuaded more easily to cooperate with a man's amorous proposals if he can back them with hard cash."

Matthews stared at me as though I were going off the deep end. "What girl do you have in mind?"

"No girl. The Abwehr paymaster," I answered as though that made everything quite clear.

"You and your Byzantine ideas." He looked at me with mock grimness. "Have a go at explaining yourself in terms a simple Scot would understand."

"If I had x thousand pounds in London and offered them to von Karsthoff, I'm sure he would jump at them. To pay his agents. Like the girl to pay her rent." I had figured it out so carefully, the analogy looked comprehensible to me.

"So?"

"So I don't have the money and couldn't pretend to have it. We've got to find someone who does and who will accept payment in Lisbon for pounds here. Someone who wants to get his money out of England, say. That's plausible. Maybe he wants to go abroad and can't get permission to take his money out. Or someone who is afraid England is going to lose the war and wants to dump pounds."

"Your girlfriend is starting to make sense," Bill said enthusiastically.

With Tar, we worked out the details of the scheme, which we labeled Plan Midas. We found a rich theatrical agent by the name of Glass, who agreed to cooperate on faith. We never told Mr. Glass exactly what we were up to. All he knew is that we were going to use him as a front. When the time came, we would furnish him with a large sum of pounds, which he was to hand over to the person we designated. In return, a corresponding sum in dollars supposedly would be credited to an account in his name in Lisbon.

We placed our carefully constructed scheme before the XX Committee. The full board sat in judgment and turned it down. Too far-fetched, they said.

Bill's face was long and glum when he told me the news. "But they can't do this," he thumped his hand against the wall. "Why, it's an intelligence officer's dream come true. Imagine controlling the Abwehr paymaster in England!"

The three of us were convinced enough of the validity of our project to return to the attack. We stressed again its benefits to our operation. Off and on, the committee was running thirty to forty captured German spies. The Abwehr was having its usual difficulties paying many of them, and if they weren't paid, the fiction of their working would collapse. The plan also might afford us the possibility of catching any spies who were on the loose. They might be sent to our man to be paid.

Our logic and enthusiasm prevailed. The committee authorized Plan Midas and put up twenty thousand pounds.

On my next visit to Lisbon I mentioned fairly casually while chatting one evening with von Karsthoff that I had come upon an opportunity to make a bit of extra change. I told him about a man I knew wanting to get his money to the States and asked if he knew a bank or exchange agent willing to accept pounds in England. Naturally, I said, my customer would be prepared to lose some money on the exchange rate. As expected, von Karsthoff recognized the possibility this presented to finance our agents in Britain.

"Don't do anything for a few days," he made me promise. "I'm sure I can have a better deal for you than any bank."

Von Karsthoff sent an urgent cable to Berlin. In a few days the top Abwehr paymaster himself, Lieutenant Colonel Toeppen, flew to Lisbon.

"We can do this operation on the spot," Toeppen told me. "Send a message to your man."

I explained that I would have to make the arrangements myself in London. "I will give my man a code word to identify whatever agent you send to his office to pick up the money."

"Very well," Toeppen had to agree, "but you will leave for London soon. Now what is the man's name and address?"

"His name is Charles Sand." I spelled it out for Toeppen to write. "He's a theatrical agent at Haymarket 15, London W.1."

Triumphantly, I returned to London and recounted to the last period my conversation with Toeppen. Suddenly, we realized my memory had played a trick on me. It had substituted a part for the whole, sand being an ingredient of glass. We rushed to Glass's office, changed the name plate on his door, mysteriously told him to answer the phone as Mr. Sand, and put a temporary M.I.5 receptionist on duty at the front desk.

Our alarm and precautions were superfluous. We thought we would have to deal with an agent unknown to us whom we would have to turn. Instead, an agent named Tate, whom we were running, received instructions to fetch the money. A wireless operator, Tate was captured in September 1940 after landing by parachute. The XX Committee considered him so trustworthy he was allowed complete liberty. And the Abwehr appreciated the reports he sent back to Berlin so much they chose him as paymaster.

I was shuttling back and forth to Lisbon these days, and

Johnny was coming in fairly regularly from Berlin, so I saw him on almost every trip. We were collaborating closely, although still without any explicit understanding.

With Johnny's help, I established a very complete list for C of the most important Abwehr people in Berlin and of many others throughout the whole of Germany and Europe. He indicated a startlingly high percentage of anti-Hitler officers in Admiral Canaris's employ. Stewart Menzies showed much appreciation of my report, but some of his aides regarded it skeptically. It was corroborated much later in the purge of the Abwehr after the attempt on Hitler's life on July 20, 1944. More than three-quarters of the Abwehr commanding corps officers were put to death, most without benefit of trial.

Undoubtedly because of his later notoriety, I recall in particular the remark of Kim Philby, who was an M.I.6 specialist on the Iberian peninsula: "Are you trying to apologize for or protect your Abwehr superiors?" he asked me. The opinion of his aides notwithstanding, Menzies evaluated the report as top level and drew up a further list of complementary questions about certain of the higher Abwehr officers. Gradually, I filled in the blank spots on that questionnaire. Menzies's interest in the material we furnished him on the Abwehr was at the root of a remark by one of his subalterns. "C sees me every day," he complained, "but I believe he understands Canaris better."

I also furnished Colonel Jarvis with a list of the main Abwehr officers in Lisbon, including their code names, specialties, and private addresses and did approximately the same for the Madrid office.

Among the German agents whom I ferreted out in Lisbon, one caused me some slight twinge of pain. It was a shock to find him—a man I knew fairly well—working for the Germans. I came on his trail one day when von Karsthoff answered a phone call in my presence from a German diplomat by the name of Baron von Breisky. The Baron had a shrill voice enabling me to hear both ends of the conversation.

"I need some money immediately," I overheard, "to pay my Russian count."

"Immediately!" von Karsthoff huffed. "Your Russian count is in no position to be so exigent. His information is of very little value. Our good money is only serving to buy boots and saddles for his wife. She looks very beautiful winning all those equestrian blue ribbons, but, my dear Baron, we get nothing from the horse's mouth."

A Russian count whose beautiful wife participated in horse shows. It was child's play to trace him. A little checking proved him to be Count Chouvaloff, whom I had met in Dubrovnik, where he and his wife often spent their holidays.

We deliberately allowed the count to go on with his spying, even assisted him, feeding him with misinformation to pass to the Germans.

My quest for more information about the mikropunkt drew from von Karsthoff the answer: "Be patient." Johnny was much more fruitful. With the excuse that he wanted to afford me a maximum of safety and protection, Johnny tried to get hold of a microdot apparatus from Berlin. The process wasn't perfected yet, but he found out something about the theory of it. Photographs, he was told, were taken through a reversed microscope. The technique was developed by a Professor Zapp of the Dresden Institute of Technology. Professor Zapp was satisfied with his optical results and production methods, but he hadn't yet developed the proper sort of negative film. It couldn't cope with the heat generated by the process, and the text became unreadable.

Our deception program was still in the experimental stage, nothing like what it became in 1943 and '44. It consisted largely of passing to the enemy misinformation that could momentarily further the aims of the Navy and the Air Force. A lot of it was information we knew couldn't be verified, and therefore discredited, about production, defenses, and technical matters. To deter gas warfare, I passed a report through Balloon about British readiness, which was calculated to completely discourage such ideas. We also fed the enemy with much political information, which had no direct effect on the war but was aimed at building me up. A double agent in deception is a long-term investment. The strategy is to pay in enough so that he is trusted when the time comes for the big payoff.

The political information, passed for the most part by Gelatine, played its part in psychological warfare against the Oberkommando. We knew that Ribbentrop, the German Minister of Foreign Affairs, nourished a strong hatred for Canaris. The feeling was mutual. Canaris took every opportunity he could to be one up on Ribbentrop in furnishing the Führer with news. Every time one of Gelatine's bulletins scored for Canaris, my prestige with the Abwehr soared.

In certain instances, we didn't know the reasons for an action but, like soldiers, were merely told to implement it, as military jargon has it. Plan Machiavelli was one of those. The Navy wanted the Germans misled about the east coast mine fields. I was to transmit information about fictitious charts to them. I could only surmise that the object was to forbid a section of the coast to the Germans or to waylay them into real mine fields elsewhere.

Colonel Robertson and Lieutenant Commander Ewen Montagu, the naval member of Committee XX, were coaching me. I knew something about charts and naval matters—every boy from Dubrovnik is a part-time sailor—but even so, memorizing a naval chart was proving to be impossible.

Tar stared at one of the bogus charts tacked on the office wall and shook his head despairingly. "Can't be done, not

even by a bloody wonder like you." It was a mass of numbers indicating depths and of crosses pinpointing the mine
fields. "Tell you what"—Tar came up with a sudden idea—
"we'll put a pretty bow around them and you can take them
to Lisbon. Why not?"

We all three looked at each other. "Why not?" Montagu
and I echoed. The solution was so simple. Then it hit me
that it was too simple. The whole idea from the start was too
simple.

"How the devil am I supposed to have put my hands on
these charts in the first place?" I objected. "They're top secret. Did I sandpaper my fingertips and crack the Admiralty
safe or am I sleeping with the Fleet Commander's wife?"

There was a moment's respectful silence. One doesn't sacrifice a Fleet Commander's wife lightly. Montagu puffed
away at his pipe, his handsome face contorted in thought.

"I have it," he said at last. "An English barrister, a naval
reserve officer who happens to be a Jew, is scared stiff that
the Germans will win the war. He's heard horrible tales
about concentration camps and death ovens and wants to
take out some insurance. Dusko becomes friendly with the
man, who senses that their opinions about the outcome of
the war coincide. When he hears that you go to Lisbon often,
he asks you if you would consent to pass these charts to the
Germans in some way or other, in return for which he wants
a letter from a high German authority guaranteeing him
protection when England falls. Of course, they'll want to see
the charts before handing over the letter, so you'll have to
hold out the promise of more charts later on as insurance.
How does that sound to you?"

"Possible," Tar pronounced. "Given what the Germans
are doing to the Jews, there is a certain logic in it, a logic
they anyway might well buy."

"It sounds improbable enough so that I don't think anyone will believe it was manufactured," I agreed. "The usual invented story is always so neat. There's one thing though, we'll need a real identity for the traitor. Someone they can check on."

"Sorry, I thought you understood," Montagu said quietly. "His name is Ewen Montagu."

I did pass the charts to von Karsthoff, who accepted the story of Montagu's cowardice at face value. But the Tirpitzufer refused to give Montagu the letter. I suspect he knew they would and had no intention of continuing the game in the first place. I never did learn if the Germans discovered the charts were phony, but at any rate, the affair didn't blow up in my face.

10

Events in Yugoslavia were threatening to endanger my position with the Germans. On March 27, a group of patriotic Yugoslav officers overthrew the Regent, Prince Paul, for signing a pact with Hitler the day before. The *coup d'état* received enthusiastic support from the overwhelming majority of the population, which was strongly pro-Allied. It also threw Hitler into one of his renowned rages. He postponed all other operations, including Operation Barbarossa (the invasion of the U.S.S.R.), and ordered Operation Punishment, the destruction of Yugoslavia, militarily and as a nation. The operation was unmerciful. For three days and nights the Luftwaffe bombed Belgrade without cease. Helped by Romanian, Hungarian, and Bulgarian troops, the German Army brought the ill-prepared Yugoslavs to surrender in twelve days. Hitler's wrathful decision delayed the campaign against Russia, and his generals later complained with bitterness that it prevented them from gaining a blitzkrieg victory over Russia in the fall of 1941.

In the early days of April, while all this was happening, I was in Madrid. My nerves were on edge. I had no news of my family, and the press was thundering stories about Nazi victories.

In the heated atmosphere of a bullfight one Sunday afternoon, I lost my control. The bull had stumbled three times after charging, and a Spaniard sitting in back of me jeered,

"He's collapsing like Yugoslavia." I swung around and slapped him, shouting, "Puerco." The insult was more serious than the slap, and the man looked ready to kill me.

"Puerco," I repeated. "Soy Yugoslav."

He was really a decent chap and couldn't apologize enough when he learned the reason for my outburst.

Reading the signs, I saw that the Abwehr would question my loyalty. Not only was my country no longer neutral, it had dared to stand up to the Führer. If I had to undergo an inquisition, I wanted to be able to choose my inquisitor. I rushed to Lisbon to avoid falling into the hands of Papa Lentz.

Von Karsthoff barely allowed time for the usual civilities before he got to the question of Yugoslavia. My apprehension had been right. I tried to beg the question with a few cynical and superficial remarks about the stupid and suicidal behavior of the Yugoslav government and people. It was too facile an attempt.

"Popov"—von Karsthoff gave me one of those direct-to-the-eye looks—"are you a Serb or a Croat?"

Practically all Serbs were pro-Allied. A number of Croats sympathized with the Ustachi fascist movement, which was promoting Croatian independence under Hitler's aegis.

"You're from Trieste, you should know the answer to that." I begged the question, launching into a history of our mutual province, Dalmatia. "My city, Ragusa, or Dubrovnik, as it is now known, was the bright star of Dalmatia. It was allowed by the Pope to trade with the infidel Turks, and that way it remained free and became rich and independent. It was a republic for over eight hundred years. A powerful republic. It possessed one of the mightiest fleets in the Mediterranean to protect its trade. Ragusa never had territorial ambitions, nor did it allow any country to dominate it either, even nominally. Until Napoleon. He was the first one to occupy Ragusa. He made it a French duchy. Then after the

Congress of Vienna, we became English for a short period, then Austrian. World War I made us Yugoslav, but the Italians always claimed we were part of Italy—and now we are."

Von Karsthoff held up his hand to stop my flow. "Thank you for that brief and clear historical treatise." He was forced to laugh. "But it doesn't answer my question. Are you a Serb or a Croat?"

Really, he was trying to help me. All he wanted was a statement that I was a Croat, something he could tell Berlin. It would have been an easy solution, but what von Karsthoff didn't appreciate was that it wouldn't resist the slightest investigation in Dubrovnik. Anybody there would have said it is impossible for a Popov to be an Ustachi.

"I was about to answer your question when you interrupted me," I complained. "There are families in Ragusa in which it happens that one brother is a Serb and the other a Croat. But the true Ragusans are neither one nor the other. They are Ragusans, that's all.

"I don't know what is going to happen to my old city when this war ends, but I can assure you if I am alive I shall devote my life to seeing that it is neither Serbian nor Croat, but Ragusan."

"I see," von Karsthoff said simply, evidently impressed by the tone of sincerity with which I had delivered my polemic. He was relieved, too. I had supplied him with an argument for Berlin. He was not going to lose his top agent because some ignoramuses there didn't know the history and mentality of Dalmatia and Ragusa.

Such actually was the case. I heard later that he wrote a fifteen-page report explaining to the Tirpitizufer my indifference to all Yugoslavia, Serbs and Croats included.

The occupation of Yugoslavia ended the business pretext I was using as my cover. No goods would be permitted to go to my occupied country any more, and I wouldn't have the excuse to travel to and from England. I discussed the problem with both von Karsthoff and Johnny. Von Karsthoff promised to see what solution he could find, which sounded a bit negative to me, particularly since the loyalty question still hovered above my head. I fell back on Johnny, asking him to raise the question of renewed cover with his friends in Berlin, Colonel Oster and Colonel Pieckenbrock. The reply from Berlin was prompt and startling. It also wiped away any doubts about the Tirpitzufer's confidence in me.

A Colonel Maurer, in charge of the Abwehr I in the West, was dispatched to Lisbon and met with me in von Karsthoff's country home.

"What do you think your position will be?" Maurer began by asking me. I doubted that he had come from Berlin just to find out my opinion, but I gave him a straight answer.

"I can only surmise. I suppose the Yugoslav government-in-exile will start operating from London like all the others. Like the Poles, the Dutch, and all the rest of them, they'll probably create some sort of token army and take their orders from Churchill. I'll have to go along with them so as not to put myself in an awkward position. I'm a reserve lieutenant. I might find myself in the Yugoslav Army. Or I might be drafted into an administrative service in one of the ministries."

"Ah," Maurer pounced, "could you use some influence? Could you get yourself into a ministry?"

"I think I could go right to the top," I answered, seeing what he was driving at. "I know General Duson Simovich fairly well." Simovich had started the *coup d'état* in Belgrade and was now Prime Minister. "His son Boris and I studied law together in Belgrade. I used to go to their home in Zemum rather often."

"Good." Maurer was getting the answers he wanted. "Do

you think you could swing a job or a mission in the United States?"

"Don't you think I could continue in England?" I countered. "Or do you think my usefulness there is at an end?"

"On the contrary. We are very impressed by what you accomplished in England. You are a first-class agent and a good organizer. You formed a little net of your own, which is functioning to our satisfaction. But you can't be in two places at once, and we have more important plans for you in the United States."

Taking the opportunity to acquire some information, I interrupted to ask, "Don't tell me that in the States, where you have several million Germans—many of whom, I'm told, are patriotic to the Fatherland—you are short of agents?"

Von Karsthoff undertook to answer, possibly because my question was slightly impertinent and he was used to my ways. "That's just the trouble. We have too many. Our V-men flourished there like mushrooms after the rain. There are enough of them to form a division. But they behave like boy scouts, gossip, have picnics, and I wouldn't be astonished if they soon form an official organization and hand out publicity releases."

"They don't need one," Maurer said sarcastically. "They are all members of the German-American Bund. That goddamned bund. They're all sitting ducks for American counter-espionage if it comes to war. J. Edgar Hoover has files on all of them. He picks them up by the dozens like whores on the Reeperbahn. For political Wassermanns. It makes good propaganda against us, those scandals. The English warmongers will use them yet to push America into the war against us."

I didn't see any point in becoming involved in a situation that the Americans already had in hand, so I told him rather snottily, "Don't count on me to go discipline your amateur spies. I'm neither a policeman nor a schoolteacher."

"You misunderstand." Von Karsthoff sought to soothe me. "Nobody wants you to do that. You are too valuable to us to mix you up with those oxen. What has happened is that the Führer is very angry because of the scandals caused by the FBI arrests. He put Admiral Canaris on the carpet for it, even though he has very little to do with what happens in the United States. So now the Admiral wants to create absolutely new outposts with no links to the bund."

"Shouldn't that be the job for someone from the central organization in Berlin?" I questioned.

Maurer and von Karsthoff exchanged an abashed glance and Maurer continued the explanation. "We did send someone. Our specialist for U.S. affairs, Major von der Osten, but he had bad luck. He was there only a few days when he was run down and killed in Times Square by one of those crazy American cab drivers. Poor von der Osten," he sighed, "he died like a civilian in a hospital. Never even regained consciousness. He was a good man, he didn't have any identification on him, and everything would have been alright if it weren't for the stupid American agent he had contacted. He provoked suspicion by going to retrieve von der Osten's belongings from his hotel room. He got away, but someone alerted the FBI and they found some papers among von der Osten's things that led them to a few of our other men."

"So." I sized up the situation. "If I'm correct, the Tirpitzufer would like to rebuild its entire organization in the States."

"More than that, Ivan," Maurer said, calling me by my code name, which they did from time to time. "We would like to start again from zero and organize something solid. As things go now, the Abwehr and Admiral Canaris are the targets of much criticism. You can imagine what Ribbentrop and the Foreign Office are saying. They are making things hell for us, using us as an excuse for their failures. They say we are destroying their efforts to keep America out of the war."

Maurer was visibly upset. He knocked back a cognac in one gulp and shook his head as it went down to soothe his rumbling stomach.

"And do you expect me alone to replace the vast organization over there?"

"No, no," von Karsthoff intervened. "Nobody expects anything as ambitious as that. But look what you did in England all by yourself, practically without any help or advice from us, and in such a short time."

If you only knew what help I had, I thought, while von Karsthoff went on with his eulogy.

"You have a perfectly organized cell operating there. Each member works independently as he should and ignores the existence of the others. If one falls, the others can continue. You only have to do the same thing in the States on a slightly larger scale. After a while, when everything is going properly, they can do the work and you'll just have to give them directions and control them."

"A good spy does not necessarily make a good spymaster," I put in cautiously, not being at all sure the English would agree to this project. I preferred not to commit myself.

"We have full confidence in you." Von Karsthoff overruled my hesitancy.

I said thanks and added, "Let me see first if I can talk myself into a job to take me to America. You can imagine I don't want to go into the Yugoslav Army, so I'll do my best."

The game was tempting. The mission the Germans wanted

me to undertake was extraordinary. It would put us in control of the enemy's American espionage organization so that when the United States entered the war—as we all felt inevitable—it would have one leg up. For the moment perhaps the FBI had matters under control and was netting all existing German spies, but that was creating a vacuum which the Abwehr was bound to fill. What better than to have our own men sent in?

On a personal level, the idea of going to the States was appealing, too. As it was to so many other Europeans, America represented to me the land that offered absolutely everything to a young man with ambition.

The sole drawback was Johnny. He had been at my side in practically every undertaking. His support from a distance of five thousand miles could hardly be as effective. If ever I longed to discuss matters with him, this was the time, but he was away on a mysterious mission in southern Italy. Even von Karsthoff didn't know what he was doing there. Johnny had sent me several messages, one mentioning that he could not come to Lisbon until June. The others gave me news of my family. They had come through the twelve days of blitzkrieg without harm, and now Johnny had taken them under his protection.

I went back to London to see the reaction there. British Intelligence ruminated for a few days and finally decided that it would be in the interest of all if I went to the States. From the British point of view, it was vital that German spies in the States not be given the chance to reveal ship departures and data on arms and supplies going to England. The Battle of the Atlantic was the primary front, and losses to U-boats were devastatingly high.

"We shall probably ask you to come back in the not distant future," Tar told me, relating the combined decision of M.I.5 and M.I.6. "For the moment we can spare you. Our deception campaign is still embryonic, and perhaps it may even be better to keep you under wraps for that, keep you from being blown, and save you for when we really need you. But for god's sake, don't go and blow yourself in the States. You needn't worry about this end," he added consolingly. "Balloon and Gelatine will fill the gap."

"I'm glad to know I'm not indispensable," I said a bit wryly, "but I'm going to be capricious and put one condition on my going to the States."

"Going to be," Tar laughed. "My dear old Tricycle, you are and always have been but we all love you for it. Puts a bit of color in the organization. Now tell me, what's your condition?"

"That I'm to remain an officer of the Intelligence Service. I can be on loan to the FBI or the State Department of any U.S. intelligence outfit you want, I don't care which, but I want our firm to have the last word on everything concerning me."

"Not to worry." Tar winked. "We're not letting you out of our sweaty hands. The FBI will be running you, but you'll go to New York as our man. You'll report to our representative there, Colonel Ellis. Administratively, you'll be under William Stephenson in Washington. He's our chief coordinator in the States. Okay?"

"Very much so."

Stevenson, the British Ambassador to the Yugoslav government-in-exile, set up an appointment for us to see General Simovich, the new Prime Minister, about arranging my cover. Tar, Stevenson, and I were ushered into the Prime Minister's office, and the Ambassador undertook to act as our spokesman.

"The Foreign Office, the War Office, and Mr. Popov personally are asking you to help them, and I came along to express His Majesty's Government's thanks and support,"

Stevenson said formally. "Mr. Popov is engaged in an anti-German activity classified above top secret. I personally know nothing about the nature of that activity, but if you wish, Colonel Robertson will explain it to you."

Simovich was more General than politician and not inclined to diplomatic circumlocutions. He said that that wouldn't be necessary and came around from behind his desk to hug me. He was still the way I had seen him last in my student days, gray-haired, tall, and slim.

"Dusko, I'm happy you are doing something really useful," he said simply. "We all must pull together to vanquish that monster Hitler. Say what you need. If it is in my power it will be done."

Tar explained for me. I needed an appointment in the United States that would serve as a cover for my other activities, a job that would leave me free and independent of supervision. We explored a few possible slots in the diplomatic field, none of which were suitable. Finally Simovich was inspired to create the post of Delegate of the Yugoslav Ministry of Information for the United States and the rest of America to coordinate propaganda efforts.

The post wasn't as far-fetched as it sounds. There were about one million people of Yugoslav descent in America, and I actually did make speeches before some of them in addition to organizing aid and understanding for the Yugoslav cause. Nor was it unusual to be given a job. The Yugoslavs who managed to flee were converging on London. The Ministries, in need of civil servants, were only too glad to employ them. Before they arrived, there were more ministers around than workers.

I spent the next few weeks supposedly supervising and instructing Gelatine and Balloon, preparing them to operate independently. Also to impress my German friends, I collected a variety of information calculated to draw a round of applause and a good send-off to the States. I procured answers, artfully arranged, to their questions about the construction of five King George class battleships, electronically controlled land mines, and other new arms. In my own hand I copied some beautifully deceptive sketches of new Vickers Armstrong plants at Weybridge and near Crayford and a precise map of imaginary underground factories producing parts for Wellington aircraft. We hoped this would lead the Germans to plow some empty fields with their bombs and raze some attractive but uninhabited woods.

The news from the front around this time was overshadowed by the sensational flight of Deputy Führer Rudolph Hess to Scotland in a Messerschmidt fighter plane. At the time and long afterward, there was much speculation about the reason for Hess's coming to England. A day or two after it happened, I was dining with Major Masterman at the United University Club off Trafalgar Square. Brendan Bracken, who had just come from supervising the interrogation of Hess, joined us for coffee. Bracken was a close collaborator of Churchill. Later that year, he became Minister of Information. He had been spending the weekend with the Prime Minister at Ditchley when the Duke of Hamilton arrived to announce Hess's landing.

Bracken dismissed the prevalent theory that Hess was insane, saying that he didn't show any visible signs of mental disturbance and was behaving calmly and with dignity. Hess claimed to be privy to the Führer's intimate thoughts. Without doubt, he was one of Hitler's closest friends. According to Hess, Bracken said, Hitler admired Britain and despised the rest of the world, particularly the Bolsheviks. Hess said he knew that Hitler was ready to negotiate peace with Britain and was willing to offer terms that would mean hardly any loss to the British. Hitler supposedly wanted the return of former German colonies, the evacuation of Iran by the British, and acceptance of peace with Italy. Hitler also wanted a free hand in Europe.

"And Russia?" Masterman asked.

"The only thing he said about Russia," Bracken answered, "was that Germany had certain demands against Russia that must be satisfied.

"If you believe Hess," Bracken said, "Hitler is almost a humanitarian. He told us how much Hitler suffers because of the blitz, the women and children killed. He believes the blitz and the U-boat blockade will destroy British industry and the large cities and that the British will have to surrender or starve to death.

"Hess had the effrontery to tell us that Hitler would not negotiate with Churchill or the present cabinet. Hess says he knows there are what he called 'peace movements' and that if they were aware of Hitler's intentions they would contact him—Hess, that is—and oust the present government."

I couldn't help wondering how much our planted reports of low British morale might have influenced Hess—and even Hitler. It would be interesting, I speculated, if British Intelligence had unwittingly inspired the Hess incident.

11

Although all was ready for my departure—the FBI, I was told, eagerly awaiting my arrival—I postponed it from week to week, feeling I must see Johnny before putting the Atlantic between us. There was too much at stake, both in the American venture and in what I had set up already, to leave without a last consultation.

At last a telegram arrived, coded as a business message, to inform me that Johnny was in Lisbon. I booked my seat on the KLM plane and scurried about completing the chores that needed doing at the last minute. On June 22, two days before I went to Lisbon, Germany attacked Russia. There was jubilation in England. We weren't fighting alone any more.

When I met Johnny he was as high-spirited as I was but, astonishingly, so were the other Germans. They were celebrating the incredible German advances and the seeming rout of the Red Army, expecting a victory as rapid as those in France and the Balkan countries. In that atmosphere the explanations by the military experts that Russia was absorbing the first German attack and would fight in depth failed to console me. I was in a fit of depression, probably the unrecognized strain of the past year contributing to it.

One afternoon that week when I had to kill two hours, I walked into a movie in Lisbon, thinking it would divert me from the worries and apprehensions I was experiencing. The first thing I saw on the screen was a German newsreel, tanks on the Eastern front crushing everything in front of them, airplanes flattening towns and villages, hundreds of dead bodies in the ditches of roads, along which marched columns miles long of Russian prisoners of war.

I was overcome by a feeling of my own puniness in contrast to that military behemoth. For the first time, I was having the psychological DTs, the occupational disease of spies. I was alone without comrades in arms. I could practically feel the German tanks on the screen rolling over me. My shirt and forehead were soaked in sweat. I rushed out of the cinema into the fresh air and sun. It was a deep trauma. When I'm worried I still can't go to the cinema.

A double whisky and a walk calmed me. That, and meeting the only friend I had in Lisbon. Johnny had the answer to my nightmare. "Do you think," he asked, "that Hitler is a better general than Napoleon?"

"Hardly," I replied.

"Then stop worrying. If Napoleon didn't break Russia, Hitler won't either."

Immediately on meeting Johnny I had gotten from him the story of his mysterious mission in Italy. Mysterious because for the moment, we didn't know what was behind it. As often happens in intelligence, I got the piece to complete the puzzle shortly afterward. It gave my journey to America greater urgency and was, I thought, the major intelligence coup of the war.

On a secluded observation point of the Boca do Inferno cliffs overlooking the Atlantic outside Cascais, Johnny gave me the details of his special mission to Italy. The breakers thundered in underneath, and not a person was in sight to disturb us.

"Peculiar," Johnny mused. "The mission was for the Japanese."

"In the south of Italy?"

"At Taranto. Major naval base there."

"I remember, that's where the British fleet attacked and put half the Italian Navy out of action. But what have the Japanese to do with Taranto? And with you?"

"I'll start at the beginning," Johnny offered. "The Japanese Foreign Minister, chap named Yosuke Matsuoka, came to Berlin at the end of March. He had a bevy of navy and army brass with him to hash out the military aspects of the Tripartite Pact. Seems that some months before coming, the Japanese put in a request for the Abwehr to get them the details about Taranto. The Abwehr does the odd job for their intelligence boys, you know. Places they can't go. Too easy to spot slanty eyes and yellow epidermis. Not very Aryan, our allies." Johnny couldn't resist a dig at the Nazis.

"Well, the Abwehr didn't furnish them with much. Matsuoka repeated the request when he got to Berlin, and Ribbentrop rose up on his toothpick legs and started screaming at Canaris to do something. I got nominated for the job because somebody probably figured my name would lend prestige. The Abwehr people in the Far East work under the cover of two trading firms belonging to the family: Jebsen & Co. in Shanghai and Jebsen & Jebsen of Hamburg, which has offices all over that part of the world. The Japanese first made their request through contacts in those firms."

"So that's where nepotism got you," I teased. "Were the Italians cooperative with their great German ally?"

"Up to a point. They were very much on the defensive, trying to justify themselves. Blamed the whole thing on surprise, which, of course, is no excuse in war. Especially not for a strongly fortified port."

Looking at the unobstructed, limitless view of the sea, I reflected on how difficult a surprise attack would be. "But why are the Japanese so interested in Taranto?"

"Why? Because it shows how one successful attack may annihilate a large part of an enemy fleet. Cunningham, the British Admiral, sneaked his aircraft carrier, the *Illustrious,* to about a hundred and seventy miles from Taranto. Then he put out two waves of bombers, twelve the first time, nine the second. They dropped a potpourri of torpedoes, bombs, and flares, which proved very effective. The Japanese wanted every last detail: the effectiveness of the nets protecting the anchored ships, damage done to the dockyards, the petrol installations, the workshops. Everything. Now if they're planning something similar, they've got a yardstick to go by."

"It would be hell if they really attacked in strength," I figured worriedly. "Cunningham didn't use much, nineteen planes in all. Supposing someone put up hundreds?" I was wondering about the vulnerability of the British Navy. "Do you think the Japanese are coming into the war, Johnny?"

"Hitler is pushing them to come in, but the pro-war clique in Japan is facing strong opposition, they say. And then they also disagree with Berlin as to whom to attack. Hitler wants them to go up against British outposts like Singapore and Malaya. The main object of the Japanese is fuel, and that means the Dutch East Indies. But in that area they'd have the United States to contend with."

"Then we can sleep calmly." I expressed my confidence in the States. "They'll never take on the United States. It would be suicide."

Johnny plucked a blade of grass and chewed on it thoughtfully, as he replied, "Don't be too sure. Under certain circumstances they might. Hitler doesn't want the Japanese to attack the Americans, but he'd still prefer them to be kept busy in the Pacific rather than have them here in Europe.

"I got an expert opinion on the situation from an old friend, Baron Gronau, last week. Gronau was in Taranto with me, also for prestige. He's the German Air Attaché in

Tokyo and was one of our aces in the First World War. Also he's an intimate friend of Goering's. Gronau says the Japanese will be forced into the war if Roosevelt keeps insisting that they evacuate China and Indo-China and above all if he declares an oil embargo against them. The Japanese Navy has about eighteen months' reserves of oil. Gronau says the logistics are that they'll have to strike before the reserves drop below twelve months."

"So the question is where."

Johnny nodded his agreement, his face somber. "If my calculated opinion interests you," he said, "the Japanese will attack the United States." Then he dismissed it all with a wave of his hand to tell me the good news he had. "Your family is together in Dubrovnik and I think I'll be able to keep them safe. The Italians may be moving in there, and I put a word in with them while I was in Taranto. As for the Ustachi, they haven't managed to do anything in Dubrovnik yet. They've been damn bloody with the Serbs everywhere else—not that that's stopping that brother of yours, Ivo. He's thinking of moving back to Belgrade."

It was what one expected of Ivo. I had had other news of him. Ivo was medical officer with an army unit in Montenegro on the Albanian border when the Yugoslavs capitulated. He left his outfit and walked back home, stopping at a friend's on the way to borrow civilian clothing. In the confusion after the surrender, nobody bothered him and he escaped being taken as a prisoner of war. I also heard that one wing of our house in Belgrade was destroyed by a bomb that fell on a neighboring building, the Royal Automobile Club. Luckily, nobody was there. The family had left for Dubrovnik earlier.

12

The Germans found my appointment as Delegate of the Yugoslav Ministry of Information ideal for their purposes. I could justify my presence anywhere in the United States where there were Yugoslavs, and since there were over a million of my expatriate countrymen, that meant just about everywhere, in any factory or dockyard. My official standing also would give me automatic entry into Washington political circles.

"How exactly am I to organize a spy network in the States?" I asked von Karsthoff at the start of our preparations for the American venture.

Von Karsthoff confounded me by answering, "Organize nothing." My furrowed forehead spoke for me and he explained, "We don't want an organization per se. We had that and it collapsed because there were too many links between agents. Do as you did in England. Make your own contacts and when you find someone likely, rely on your own judgment. If you are absolutely sure of a man, you have the authority to appoint him as a subagent. Run each agent separately and concentrate on quality, not quantity. A compact reliable group will do better than a horde of amateurs like we had. And above all, Ivan"—von Karsthoff's voice registered sincere concern—"don't risk your life or your position. If you have the slightest doubt about anyone, let him drop."

For once, the inevitable wait for a seat on the Pan-American Clipper to New York was fortunate. My official position with the Yugoslavs was not sufficiently important to warrant an immediate priority, and for obvious reasons, British or American influence could not be used. Thanks to the wait I received the most important information of World War II in the fanciest and most sought-after wrapper.

Von Karsthoff was in a particularly jovial mood when I arrived at his villa that morning. He was in the garden, seated under an old pine tree, which protected him from the midsummer sun. A manila folder lay on the bench next to him. A smile as dazzling as the sun spread over his face as he greeted me with a hearty, "Hello, Dusko, I've got something for you." He pulled a familiar-looking sheaf of papers from the folder and extended it to me. A questionnaire.

"Not another," I groaned, looking at the top of the sheet. The first paragraph was headed "Naval Information." I glanced at the second paragraph. It concerned the assembly of troops for overseas transport from the U.S. and Canada.

"Back to school again," I feigned disgust. "Okay, Herr Professor, I'll start memorizing."

"No, no." Von Karsthoff took the questionnaire away, preventing me from reading more for the moment. "No more memorization. Come." He led me back into the villa and into his study. On an antique peasant table, oiled black with age, stood a gleaming microscope.

"Have a look." Von Karsthoff motioned me to the instrument. I peered through it, fiddled with a dial to adjust it for my vision. I was seeing the first page of the questionnaire von Karsthoff had taken from me. He took me by the arm, pulling me away from the table.

"It's the mikropunkt. You are the first agent to get it. Here, I'll show you how it works."

He extracted the glass slide from the microscope and

handed it to me. Mounted on it was what looked like a speck of dirt. Von Karsthoff was like a child—or a father—with a new set of electric trains. He opened a small white cardboard pillbox, like a magician doing a trick, and showed me the contents, several small dots about the size of those over an *i*, similar to the one on the slide.

"Here's what you do," he explained. "You take one of these, they're really little pieces of film, and with a tiny drop of collodion, you stick it on anything you want. Any old scrap of paper, your luggage, on your skin if you want.

"Elizabeth," von Karsthoff called to his secretary-cum-girlfriend, who was typing in her little office off the study, "bring us some champagne. Three glasses. You must toast this with us. This little dot will revolutionize our espionage system. Do you realize the immense possibilities it offers?"

I realized it only too well. You could conceal a volume the size of the Bible in your personal belongings and carry it undetected through any control. I picked one of the dots out of the box with tweezers and placed it on the back of my hand. It wasn't even a good-sized freckle.

"What about the apparatus to make them?" I asked. "When do I get one? That would really offer possibilities. Why, Ludovico, I could send you even the most detailed blueprints."

"Patience," von Karsthoff said. Elizabeth came in with the champagne and he twirled the bottle in the ice bucket. "You are the first agent to get the dots, and I promise you'll be the first to get the apparatus. I hope maybe by the end of the year. Our scientists are working overtime to simplify the production method."

Meticulously wrapping a napkin around the frosted bottle, von Karsthoff poured three glasses and proposed, "Here's to your success, Dusko. Yours and the Abwehr's."

We drank and I promised to put the microdots to the best

of use. A question of interpretation, I thought to myself. Discreetly, Elizabeth went back to her typing as soon as she finished her glass. And we went back to work. I didn't have to memorize the questionnaire but I had to study and discuss it. Picking up the list of questions I glanced at it while still sipping my second glass of champagne. This time I read further. The second heading was Hawaii. The Tirpitzufer was asking for information about ammunition dumps and mine depots on the Isle of Oahu, where Pearl Harbor is located. Tirpitzufer, my foot, I swore to myself. This linked up with Taranto. Here was the answer to the question Johnny and I were wondering about. This was the Japanese target.

"What's this about the Isle of Oahu," I asked von Karsthoff. "I'm sure we're not planning a campaign right now in the Pacific, so it must be for our Asian ally, no? Same thing as Jebsen was working on."

"So one would presume," he replied.

"Hawaii is a bit off my beat, unless I can pick something up in Washington."

"No, I have specific instructions about that. You are to go to Hawaii . . . and as soon as possible."

I nodded and murmured, "Very well." The picture was developing nicely. The Tirpitzufer—or the Japanese—weren't asking an academic question. There was some urgency about it. The action wasn't for tomorrow but it was for soon. According to Baron Gronau it would be before the Japanese fleet reached the one-year point in fuel reserves. Not difficult at all to figure out.

"You'll have to find an excuse for going there," von Karsthoff remarked. "Maybe medical. The climate is good. You can pretend to catch the grippe as soon as you arrive in New York."

"Or he can run off on an amorous escapade," put in Eliza-

Dusko Popov
as a young man.

Dusko Popov
today.

Sir John C. Masterman, head of
the Double-Cross Committee.

Colonel T. A. Robertson—"Tar"—
head of M.I.5 Double-Cross Section.

Sir Stewart Menzies, the man called "C,"
head of the British Secret Service.

The Honorable Ewen Montagu,
then naval representative to
the Double-Cross Committee.

Dickie Metcalfe,
code name "Balloon,"
British Intelligence officer
in the Tricycle net.

BRITISH SECRET SERVICE TRANSLATION
OF THE GERMAN QUESTIONNAIRE WHICH
TRICYCLE TOOK TO AMERICA

Naval Information.—Reports on enemy shipments (material food-stuffs—combination of convoys, if possible with names of ships and speeds).

Assembly of troops for oversea transport in U.S.A. and Canada. Strength—number of ships—ports of assembly—reports on ship building (naval and merchant ships)—wharves (dockyards)—state and private owned wharves—new works—list of ships being built or resp. having been ordered—times of building.

Reports regarding U.S.A. strong points of all descriptions especially in Florida—organisation of strong points for fast boats (E-boats) and their depot ships—coastal defence—organisation districts.

Hawaii.—Ammunition dumps and mine depots.

1. Details about naval ammunition and mine depot on the Isle of Kushua [sic] (Pearl Harbour). If possible sketch.

2. Naval ammunition depot Lualuelei. Exact position? Is there a railway line (junction)?

3. The total ammunition reserve of the army is supposed to be in the rock of the Crater Aliamanu. Position?

4. Is the Crater Punchbowl (Honolulu) being used as ammunition dump? If not, are there other military works?

Aerodromes.

.1. *Aerodrome Lukefield.*—Details (sketch if possible) regarding the situation of the hangars (number?), workshops, bomb depots, and petrol depots. Are there underground petrol installations?—Exact position of the seaplane station? Occupation?

2. *Naval air arm strong point Kaneche.*—Exact report regarding position, number of hangars, depots, and workshops (sketch). Occupation?

3. *Army aerodromes Wicham Field and Wheeler Field.*—Exact position? Reports regarding number of hangars, depots and work-shops. Underground installations? (Sketch.)

4. *Rodger's Airport.*—In case of war, will this place be taken over by the army or the navy? What preparations have been made? Number of hangars? Are there landing possibilities for seaplanes?

5. *Airport of the Panamerican Airways.*—Exact position? (If possible sketch.) Is this airport possibly identical with Rodger's Airport or a part thereof? (A wireless station of the Panamerican Airways is on the Peninsula Mohapuu.)

Naval Strong Point Pearl Harbour.

1. Exact details and sketch about the situation of the state wharf, of the pier installations, workshops, petrol installations, situations of dry dock No. 1 and of the new dry dock which is being built.

2. Details about the submarine station (plan of situation). What land installations are in existence?

3. Where is the station for mine search formations [Minensuchver-baende]? How far has the dredger work progressed at the entrance and in the east and southeast lock? Depths of water?

4. Number of anchorages [Liegeplaetze]?

5. Is there a floating dock in Pearl Harbour or is the transfer of such a dock to this place intended?

Special tasks.—Reports about torpedo protection nets newly introduced in the British and U.S.A. navy. How far are they already in existence in the merchant and naval fleet? Use during voyage? Average speed reduction when in use. Details of construction and others.

1. Urgently required are exact details about the armoured strengths

of American armoured cars, especially of the types which have lately been delivered from the U.S.A. to the Middle East. Also all other reports on armoured cars and the composition of armoured (tank) formations are of greatest interest.

2. Required are the Tables of Organisation (TO) of the American infantry divisions and their individual units (infantry regiments, artillery "Abteilung," and so forth) as well as of the American armoured divisions and their individual units (armoured tank regiments, reconnaissance section, and so forth). These TO are lists showing strength, which are published by the American War Department and are of a confidential nature.

3. How is the new light armoured car (tank)? Which type is going to be finally introduced? Weight? Armament? Armour?

1. Position of British participations and credits in U.S.A. in June 1940. What are England's payment obligations from orders since the coming into force of the Lend Lease Bill? What payments has England made to U.S.A. since the outbreak of war for goods supplied, for establishment of works, for the production of war material, and for the building of new or for the enlargement of existing wharves?

2. Amount of state expenditure in the budget years 1939/40, 1940/41, 1941/42, 1942/43 altogether and in particular for the army and the rearmament.

3. Financing of the armament programme of the U.S.A. through taxes, loans and tax credit coupons. Participation of the Refico and the companies founded by it (Metal Reserve Corp., Rubber Reserve Corp., Defence Plant Corp., Defence Supplies Corp., Defence Housing Corp.) in the financing of the rearmament.

4. Increase of state debt and possibilities to cover this debt.

All reports on American air rearmament are of greatest importance. The answers to the following questions are of special urgency:

I. How large is—
    (a) the total monthly production of aeroplanes?
    (b) the monthly production of bombers [Kampfflugzeuge]?
    (c)   "   "   "   " fighter planes?
    (d)   "   "   "   " training planes
    [Schulflugzeuge]?
    (e)   "   "   "   " civil aeroplanes
    [Zivilflugzeuge]?

II. How many and which of these aeroplanes were supplied to the British Empire, that is to say—
    (a) to Great Britain?
    (b) to Canada
    (c) to Africa?
    (d) to the Near East?
    (e) to the Far East and Australia?

III. How many U.S.A. pilots finish their training monthly?

IV. How many U.S.A. pilots are entering the R.A.F.?

Reports on Canadian Air Force are of great value.

All information about number and type (pattern) of front aeroplanes [Frontflugzeuge]. Quality, numbers and position of the echellons [Staffein] are of great interest. Of special importance is to get details about the current air training plan in Canada, that is to say: place and capacity of individual schools and if possible also their numbers. According to reports received every type of school (beginners'— advanced—and observer school) is numbered, beginning with 1.

Simone Simon

At Locust Valley,
Long Island, house during
American assignment.

The author outside his office on his Cote d'Azur estate, former summer palace of the Bishops of Grasse.

beth, who had just returned to the study. "Then he won't have to pretend," she added mischievously.

"We'll leave the manner to our ingenious Ivan," von Karsthoff told his fiancée. I wasn't sure if he was annoyed or not. Addressing me, he added, "Jebsen probably told you how anxious Admiral Canaris is to get rapid results on this particular subject. Any way at all will do . . . carte blanche . . . just get there."

I communicated the news of the impending attack on Pearl Harbor to Lisbon M.I.6 posthaste. They got on to London, and I was instructed to carry my information personally to the United States, since I was leaving in a few days. Apparently, they thought it preferable that I be the bearer of the tidings, since the Americans might want to question me at length to extract the last bit of juice.

Berlin was sparing nothing to ensure the success of my mission. The German expert for the United States flew to Lisbon to help in my education. He was a diesel engineer who had traveled all over the United States, but for my money, he should have stuck to engines. Rather pedantic, he ticked off a list of do's and don'ts in the States which struck me as elementary. Some of them I rather doubted were correct. Like take your hat off in an elevator if a woman enters but don't do so if in a business elevator. I never wore a hat—also a must, according to him—so I didn't have to observe this quaint lack of chivalry. I was also informed not to wear black shoes, since Americans didn't favor them, and to wield my knife and fork in conformity with the American manner. It all seemed and was superbly superfluous, since, as even my mentor admitted, I was openly and obviously a newcomer to the States and wouldn't be expected to be familiar with American ways. And even if I needed to adopt a disguise, my engineer friend suggested I borrow a Yugoslav or Middle European Jewish name. He also told me how to get what suffices for identity papers in the States by purchasing and getting title to a secondhand car under an assumed name, using a temporary hotel address. The same went for a driver's license, which he explained also was sufficient for normal police checks or post office identification. Very different from the official identity cards required in Europe. Actually, I never had recourse to any of the American expert's tricks and ignored his tips on etiquette and conduct as well.

I'm told that Ian Fleming said he based his character James Bond to some degree on me and my experiences. Could be. More to the point, I rather doubt that a Bond in the flesh would have survived more than forty-eight hours as an espionage agent. Fleming and I did rub shoulders in Lisbon, and a few days before I took the clipper for the States he did follow me about. Perhaps he developed what happened that night into a Bond adventure.

When the Germans got a signal from Tate that he had received the twenty thousand pounds from Mr. Sand, good to their word, they handed me the equivalent in dollars minus a fair commission. A few intermediaries in the Abwehr assuredly greased their own palms in the transaction, but who cared? Supposedly, I was to transfer the money—approximately eighty thousand dollars—to Sand's account in New York. Actually, I was to hand it over to M.I.6, but since the transaction took place in the evening, I was stuck with the money until I could make the necessary contact and arrangements the following day. Probably Ian Fleming got wind of the deal. I came down from my apartment to the lobby of the Palacio Hotel, the packet of bills in the breast pocket of my evening jacket. I preferred to carry the money with me rather than call attention to it by depositing it in the hotel safe. I noticed Fleming in the lobby but thought nothing more about it. Then I went to a café for a drink before dinner, and there was Fleming skulking about outside. At dinner he appeared in the same restaurant. My senses were aroused, and I noticed that he followed me thereafter as I walked in deliberately leisurely fashion through the gardens leading to the Casino. To have an M.I.6 man on my tail at this point was amusing because I knew it was the money, not me, that he was safeguarding. Besides, I was reasonably sure Fleming was operating on his own without instructions. British Intelligence had enough confidence to entrust me with eighty thousand dollars. The secrets I carried in my head were worth much more.

We strolled through the halls of the Casino, my shadow and I, observing the play at the different tables. I paused at a baccarat table. A favorite bête noire of mine was playing there, an insignificant-looking but wealthy Lithuanian named Bloch, who attempted to compensate for his tiny stature by arrogant play. When holding the bank he would never set a limit, as was customary. Instead, he'd announce haughtily, "Banque ouverte," meaning the other players could bet as much as they wished. It was ostentatious and annoying, and not to me alone. Others had remarked the same thing.

I don't know what devil was behind me, perhaps Fleming or the knowledge that he was there, but when Bloch announced "Banque ouverte," and the croupier said, "Les Messieurs debouts peuvent jouer," in my coolest manner I announced, "Fifty thousand dollars." Dipping my hand into my breast pocket I extracted the sheaf of bills and started counting the sum out on the green felt covering of the table. Even for the Estoril Casino in the fever of the war, it was a lot of money. The chatter stopped. Somehow the wager communicated itself to the other tables in the room, and all became silent. I glanced at Fleming. His face was the green of bile.

Obviously the Lithuanian didn't have that sort of money on him. He squirmed in his chair in embarrassment.

"I suppose," I addressed the chief croupier, "that the Casino is backing this man's bet, since you didn't object to his 'Banque ouverte.' "

"The Casino never backs any player's stake, sir," the croupier answered as I knew he would.

Pretending irritation, I swept the money off the table and, putting it back in my pocket, said, "I trust you'll call this to the attention of the management and that in the future such irresponsible play will be prohibited. It is a disgrace and an annoyance to the serious players."

Fleming was recouping his *sang-froid*. He had a smile of amusement on his face. I'm sure he had seen through and was appreciating my comedy. And the Lithuanian was cured. Friends told me that he never again pronounced the words "Banque ouverte" in the Estoril Casino.

13

On August 10, I boarded the Pan American Boeing 314 flying boat at the Cabo Ruiva dock in the Tagus estuary for the flight to New York. I had another appreciable sum of money in my pocket: forty thousand dollars given me the day before by von Karsthoff plus twelve thousand of my own and eight belonging to the Bailoni bank in Belgrade. The latter had been for the purchase of goods, which now could not be delivered. Instead of returning it to them in occupied Yugoslavia, the Bailonis, who were old friends, had asked that I hold on to it.

In 1941, forty thousand dollars was a truly huge sum, and the fact that the Germans were willing to advance so much at one time was an indication of their confidence in me and of what I might accomplish in the States. When I needed more funds, I was to get them through a bogus Portuguese firm under German control. Supposedly the money would come from the sale in Spain of tin I had bought for Yugoslavia but which was not shipped because of her entry into the war.

The big flying boat took off in the early afternoon. Its elegance and comfort were a reminder of prewar days. Dinner was served at a refueling stop in the Azores, beautifully prepared fish fresh from the Atlantic. While we dined, the stewards made up comfortable berths, and we slept our way across the ocean to Bermuda. There, a British Intelligence Officer, John Pepper, tall and distinguished, as befitted the surroundings, joined me for the hop to New York.

"I'm just a sort of flying nursemaid," Pepper joked. "Protocol, you know. I'll introduce you to our liaison officer with the FBI and to the FBI man who will be in charge of you. And as my first chore," he said, getting up from his seat, "I'll introduce you to the great American institution of dry martinis." He went to the Clipper bar and returned with two frosted glasses.

"You really needn't bother," I thanked him. "Very kind of you, but I can manage my own introductions."

"Never, never reveal that to anyone. Bermuda is deathly since the war. I use every pretext to go to New York."

Pepper was amusing company and valuable despite his protests of uselessness. Since he would be passed through Immigration and Customs easier than I, I handed him my briefcase. It was stuffed with the German questionnaire in its original, the microdots, secret ink, addresses of mail drops in Portugal and South America, and some notes of my own.

"It might save unnecessary explanations," I explained needlessly. "Be better, in fact, if you just hand it all over to the Americans."

Pepper shook his head. "Chain of command, old son. I'll give it to Colonel Ellis—Dick Ellis, our man in New York— and he'll see that Foxworth gets it. Foxworth is chief of the FBI for New York. The FBI will be waiting for you at the airport, by the way. I'll pick you up right outside Customs to do the introductions."

At the Port Washington seaplane base, Pepper and I went through the pretense of ignoring one another. It took me close to an hour to get through the formalities of Immigration. Then a stranger approached me, saying, "Will you follow me, Mr. Popov?" He got me through Customs immediately and passed me on to another man, who guided me to a parked car. In the back of the car sat a man I took to be Clark Gable.

"Let me introduce myself," he said as I slid in beside him. "My name is Charles Lehman. I'm an officer of the FBI and I am to take care of you. Sorry for all the cloak-and-dagger business. Usual precautions, you understand. In case someone was watching for you."

I refrained from telling him it would have been more discreet to have allowed me to take a cab to my hotel. Instead I remarked that we had lost Pepper. That didn't seem to bother Lehman.

We drove through Queens and into Manhattan, I, engrossed with my first view of New York. Lehman gave me instructions to meet Foxworth the next day. "I'll ring you," he said, "when Mr. Foxworth is ready to see you. We'll meet in the lobby of Rockefeller Center. It is only a few blocks away from your hotel. Don't talk to me, just follow me."

He dropped me at the Waldorf Astoria, saying, "Have a rest."

A cold shower replaced the recommended rest, and a club sandwich ordered from room service restored me. I was anxious to see New York. Out of habit, before going out I locked my suitcases away in the closet, marking their exact positions with faint pencil lines and placing a hair between the two sides of one of them before closing it.

I walked out of the Waldorf and down Park Avenue. Nowhere in the world was there a feeling of so much wealth and abundance. Walking aimlessly, absorbing the feel of the city, I was impressed by its vitality. At the first bank I encountered, I opened a checking account with a small sum of money by merely signing two cards. The absence of red tape was a pleasure.

Broadway. The automotive district. I gazed in the show-room windows and was taken by a red Buick coupe with a sliding sunroof, which was a novelty then. In ten minutes, I had bought the car and had been guaranteed delivery, registration included, the following day. I wouldn't even have to come for it. The salesman promised to leave the car, keys, and papers in the hotel garage. Again, the ease and speed of the transaction impressed me.

The atmosphere pleased me. People didn't go around complicating life. Business was conducted in a proper business-like manner. More than to any country outside my own, I was drawn to the States.

Lightheaded with the perfume of this completely different and new society, I returned to my room at the Waldorf Astoria early to be ready for the promising adventure of the following day. I rationalized what seemed to be my cool reception. There was undoubtedly a valid reason for it.

Mechanically I unlocked the closet door and knelt to verify the position of my suitcases. They were no longer in line with the faint pencil marks. The hair I had placed between the sides of my large gladstone was no longer there. A hotel valet? The German-American Bund? The FBI? Nothing was missing. That discounted a thieving employee. Berlin had gone to such pains to keep me untainted by its faltering American organization that I doubted they would have assigned anyone to check on me. The FBI? Perhaps yes, in an excess of caution and zeal. Calling it part of the game, I refused to be disturbed.

As I had hoped, Lehman phoned in the morning, not losing too much time. He told me to meet him at eleven. I walked slowly to Rockefeller Center, running a check on a possible tail.

Immediately on entering the building, I spotted Lehman scanning the directory on the wall. He gave no sign of having noticed me, but he had. He walked back to a bank of elevators. I followed and entered the same car as he did. At the twenty-ninth floor he got out. So did I. We made a circle of the corridors and wound up back at the same bank of elevators. He touched the Up button but let the first elevator pass. Lehman pressed the button again. When the elevator doors slid open, the solitary man in the cage gave him an almost imperceptible nod. We got in, and Lehman allowed himself to smile at both of us, but still didn't speak.

We shot up nonstop to the forty-fourth floor, where I was double-marched through the reception room, down a short corridor, through a secretary's office, and into a large room where a medium-sized man of about fifty stood, apparently waiting for me. He looked more like a successful lawyer than a regional chief of the FBI.

He gave me the perfunctory "Glad to meet you" and got down to business right away. "I received the material you sent via Colonel Ellis," he said. "I'll be sending it on to Washington as soon as we have your amplifications on it."

I refrained from asking why it hadn't gone yet. If the Americans were to counter a Japanese attack, every twenty-four hours would count. It takes time to move armies and the mountains of materiel they consume. Much as I had come to admire the efficiency of American business, I was in the process of deciding that bureaucracy was the same the world over.

Foxworth took the file I had given to Pepper out of a desk drawer and started to extract some papers from it. "These must be in here by error," he said, holding out some old bills, telegrams, and letters of mine. "They're personal."

"No error," I told him. "They contain a new and very ingenious secret method of communication that the Germans have invented."

"Oh, a new code?"

"Something like that. Have your experts look at it. I'd like to know if they can detect it once their attention is drawn to it."

"Mike is in the building," Lehman put in. "He may be interested in having a try."

"Mike is one of our decoding experts from Washington," Foxworth explained. "Call him in, Charles, please."

I showed the expert called Mike the typewritten copy of the questionnaire. It was five pages long. Then I handed him the bills, telegrams, and letters.

"All the text of this questionnaire is contained in these papers," I told Mike. "To simplify your task I'll tell you right now that there is nothing in secret ink, so don't waste your time with developers."

He looked a bit puzzled and went out without a word, already studying the papers. Equally anxious, but about the content rather than the form, I turned to Foxworth, saying, "Now, what can I explain to you about that information?"

"Well"—Foxworth weighed his words—"it all looks too precise, too complete, to be believed. The questionnaire plus the other information you brought spell out in detail exactly where. when, how, and by whom we are to be attacked. If anything, it sounds like a trap."

"Not when you know the sources—particularly the main source—and the background. The main source is Johann Jebsen," I answered, explaining precisely Johnny's history, position, reliability, and relationship. "I can be categorical about Jebsen. He would have warned me of a trap, no matter what.

"The second source is Baron Gronau. I don't think you can question his qualifications as an expert on Japan. If his information is exact, there's no reason to doubt his conclusions. You can expect an attack on Pearl Harbor before the end of this year unless the negotiations with the Japanese produce a definite result."

I couldn't read anything in Foxworth's face. I might have been discussing the price of cabbages, but I knew that he was absorbing everything I said. He impressed me as being highly intelligent.

"The third source, of course, is the questionnaire. If that is a trap, then it means my whole mission to the United States is window dressing. And that is just not possible. The rest of my mission is too important to the Germans. They wouldn't sacrifice it and me with it. Sooner or later you'd learn that you'd been had and I would be blown."

Foxworth was giving me a very penetrating look, and I could see him trying to evaluate my importance. Was I a pawn to be traded off?

I answered his unasked question. "As for me, you've had, I know, a report from the British. With all due modesty, the Abwehr considers me its top agent and has absolute faith in me. My assignment in the United States testifies to that. A spy network here is of primary importance, and for the moment they have nothing, or next to nothing."

"That may be," Foxworth answered candidly, "but I wouldn't know. All arrangements for your coming to the United States were made directly between London and Washington."

"Well then, with whom am I going to organize my mission? I was told you would be running me."

"Probably, since I understand you are making New York your headquarters, but I'll have to get specific instructions directly from Mr. Hoover."

At this point, Mike came back into the office looking as frustrated as I felt I must.

"I can't make head or tail of this," he complained. "There

are twice as many letters in the decoded text than in all the papers that you gave me. Normally it's the other way around. Are you sure there is something in these papers?"

I instructed him to fetch a microscope. When he came back I took up one of the telegrams and explained about the microdot on it.

Mike looked at the telegram closely and shook his head, failing to find the dot. The others examined it as well and couldn't make it out either. I had to show them how to spot it by angling the paper under a strong light until a reflection caught the minuscule point of collodion. Then I mounted the dot on a slide, and they took turns peering interestedly through the microscope.

"Fascinating," Foxworth said. "I'll tell you what I'll do. I'll take this to Washington myself. I'm sure Mr. Hoover will be very amused. And while I'm there I can get instructions about you."

"And in the meantime?" I asked. "I should start collecting information and organizing my spy net."

"Oh," Foxworth replied vaguely, "get yourself settled here in New York first."

My interview was at an end. There was no choice but to wait until Foxworth's return from Washington. Lehman escorted me to the elevator. "Are you going to stay on at the Waldorf, Dusko?" he asked. With the American informality that I liked, we were on a first-name basis already.

"No, I think I'll take an apartment, Charlie. Might as well if I am going to be working from here."

Good idea," he said, and it wasn't until a few weeks later that I realized his question was not idle chatter but implied criticism of my staying at one of New York's best hotels.

With the help of a real estate agent, I selected a penthouse apartment on the corner of Park Avenue and Sixty-first Street.

The building had just been constructed, and the few altera-
tions that I requested were promised within a week. The day
after renting the apartment, I consulted a firm of interior
decorators and chose my furnishings, and they also were
promised in a week. My spirits lifted and I became even more
enthusiastic about American efficiency.

14

Now that I was settling down to life in the States, I started to see to my social life. Among those I contacted was an old flame for whom I had always maintained a very special spot in my heart. We had gone together in Paris before the war, and she was now in the States, having been called to Hollywood. She was the French movie actress, Simone Simon. Simone was working on a film in California, so except for the few times when she came to New York, we didn't see much of each other during my early days there. Later, when her hectic career permitted, we did manage to resume for a while the close friendship we had known in France. My association with Simone, too, aroused Mr. Hoover's ire.

While waiting for my new quarters to be ready and for the go-ahead from Foxworth, I decided to pay my respects to the Yugoslav Ambassador. I called Lehman to tell him I was going to Washington and hopefully asked him if I might report to FBI headquarters and perhaps receive instructions first hand. He couldn't answer on his own initiative, so he promised to call back.

"You are not to approach headquarters," was the reply he had for me. "Instructions will be given to you in New York on your return."

I went, I returned, I moved into the new apartment, I was settled in New York. Lehman came to see me. I took him on a tour of inspection. The penthouse was on the twenty-second floor, almost above the noise of the city. It consisted of a large living room, a study, a bedroom, and a good-sized balcony running all around it. He made no immediate comment but asked instead, "What did you do with the sixty thousand dollars you brought from Lisbon?"

I showed him the small safe I had had built into the study. "Except the five thousand I put in a checking account, it's all there."

"Could you let me have the cash for a few days?" he asked. "The numbers on the notes may have a tale to tell." I opened the safe and gave him all but a few hundred dollars, which I kept out for immediate expenses.

He sat down at my desk to count the money, insisting on giving me a receipt. I poured him a drink, and as he sipped it his eye roved over the room. Finally he commented, "I don't think Mr. Hoover will approve of all this . . . of all this plush layout."

From boyhood on, I was used to considering my private life exclusively my own affair, so I answered, "It's of no consequence whether he likes it or not. I trust he will judge me by my work and by the results. And speaking of work, there's something we should take care of right away." I wasn't giving him an opportunity to return to the subject that was no concern of his, nor of his chief. And I did have pressing matters to settle. Lehman gave me one of those pursed-lip Gable glances of understanding.

"I'll do what I can," he hedged.

"It's nothing that requires a conference. I have to communicate with von Karsthoff, that's all. I'll need the invisible ink John Pepper delivered to you. And can you prepare the cover text of a letter—something banal, as though it came from a merchant sailor? You know how to do that sort of thing better than I."

"What about what you're going to write in secret ink? We'll have to know what you're saying."

"I've got to give them my address and telephone number in case they want to contact me, and advise them that I am making arrangements to go to Hawaii, perhaps next week. That's the first thing on my agenda. They are very eager for me to go, as you know."

"I saw the questionnaire," Lehman commented dryly.

"But you didn't hear the verbal instructions. Their advice was that I find a good excuse, and look, Charlie, I don't want to shock the founding fathers and Puritans, but the excuse they suggested was a girl. It seems I have the reputation of being a playboy and taking a girl on a trip fits my cover. Like this apartment." I couldn't refrain from placing a barb.

"And are you a playboy, Dusko?"

"I don't like labels, Charlie," I answered levelly. "Playboy is a silly word. I do what every man does or would do if he had the opportunity. The only difference is I'm not hypocritical. I don't attempt to hide it."

"Christ, Dusko, I'm not criticizing you," Charlie said. "I'm doing my job. Who is the girl? We'll have to know."

"Name is Terry Brown, English, beautiful, if you need that for your records. She came over here to get away from the blitz. She is rich but couldn't take much money out because of the currency regulations, so she makes a living as a fashion and photographic model. All she knows is that we're off for a week's frolic in the sun, and that suits her down to her manicured toenails. Okay?"

"Well"—Lehman massaged his cleft chin—"I have no instructions, but go ahead and make the preparations anyway. I'll let you know as soon as I get the go-ahead."

A week passed before I had news from Lehman. He called to tell me to meet him in one of the large hotels near Pennsylvania Station. That was the arrangement we now had for our rendezvous. The FBI thought it was too dangerous for him to come to my flat or for me to visit their offices. Charles would take a room in one of the big transient hotels around Thirty-fourth Street and ring me to give me the room number and the time of the meeting. My instructions were never to take a taxi directly to the hotel. I was to change cabs once or twice, and also go into a movie house and then out again immediately. When I first got those instructions, I thought the FBI must have learned that the Germans had someone on my tail. It turned out, though, that those were the usual FBI precautions.

As soon as I entered the hotel room Lehman told me without any preliminaries, "The trip to Hawaii is off."

"Oh no," I said, stunned. "I've got to go there. Don't you realize that?"

It was still unthinkable to me that we wouldn't lead the Germans down the garden path. I tried to convince Lehman, or rather the FBI through him. "If the Germans find out I never went to Hawaii, it will cause a stink from here to Berlin. They'll never trust me again. I can't send them anything without going there."

Lehman shrugged, and the realization filtered through to me that the FBI wasn't planning to send any information about Pearl Harbor.

"How about sending something else? On another subject. Anything to string them along."

Poor Lehman was really at a loss. We knew each other well enough now to be friends, and he was the sort of man to like me if only because I was trying to do my job. "Mr. Hoover will be here in New York in two weeks," he said lamely, "and will see you then."

"Two weeks?"

He shrugged again. "I asked Mr. Foxworth about giving you information, but he is at a loss, too. There must be a hitch somewhere between your people, the British Security Coordination, I mean, and our office in Washington. They'll have to sort it out between them. There is nothing we can do about it in New York. Just relax, take it easy for a couple of weeks," he advised me shamefacedly.

I threw him a glance that said just about everything and walked out of the room.

If I had to take it easy for a couple of weeks, I wasn't going to sit like a petitioner in New York waiting for my audience with J. Edgar Hoover. Pretending that I had some business matters that required me to stay within easy communication of New York, I proposed to Terry that we go to Florida instead of Hawaii. Sun is sun, and she hadn't had a holiday in over a year. Her happiness and enthusiasm were contagious. We hopped into the Buick and two days later were lying on the sand in Miami in the hot September sun.

While on the beach the day after our arrival, my attention was drawn to a man who stuck out like an Eskimo at a nudist colony. He was standing in the middle of the beach fully dressed, including hat and tie. He was waving at someone imperatively. I looked around me to see the object of his gestures and realized he was signaling to me. Terry was half asleep. I asked her to excuse me and followed the man, who fitted my conception of an American gangster, to the beach bar. There, someone looking like his half-brother was sitting on a stool, his fist enveloping a glass of beer.

"Sorry to disturb you, Mr. Popov," said the beer drinker, "but you are registered in this hotel as man and wife with a girl you're not married to."

House detectives, I thought. I'd heard stories about such situations. I was facing perfunctory puritanism or a shakedown.

"I don't know a better method of sharing a bedroom with

a girl," I took the humorous approach. "I'm sure things can be cleared up. Let me go fetch my wallet."

"Nothing can be arranged that way," said the specter from the beach, and they both produced FBI identification cards. Still an innocent, I was relieved and told them, "I have some friends who are colleagues of yours in New York. Would you care to give them a ring? They may straighten this out."

"We are here on orders from Washington," they informed me, "to warn you that you are breaking the Mann Act. The Mann Act, Mr. Popov, makes it a federal offense to cross a state line with a girl for immoral purposes, in case you don't know. Our orders are to have you send that girl away immediately or we will have to act."

"And supposing I refuse?"

"Washington isn't kidding, Mr. Popov. We have orders to take you in. It will cost you a minimum of a year and a day in prison."

"Okay." I held my temper. "I'll take her back to New York. We'll leave tomorrow."

"No," the one at the bar ordered, "you'll put her on a plane today and return alone. Otherwise you'll be breaking the Mann Act several times before getting to New York."

Terry didn't believe my story about hotel detectives and the Mann Act. Her eyes filled with tears when I said I would have to put her on the plane immediately. She never spoke to me again. I'm sure she thought I wanted to get rid of her for some nefarious purpose. I regret that I hadn't the sense to have told a good lie and spared her feelings.

During the lonely two-day drive back to New York, I rehearsed what I would tell Foxworth, Hoover, and the whole FBI. But the only one I could see was Lehman, and I couldn't release my fury on him. He was too abashed. All he would say was, "Sort it out with the Boss." Another ten days passed before I got a chance to do that. Foxworth phoned to say that I was to come to his office at once.

J. Edgar Hoover encountered me. I use the word advisedly. There was no introduction, no preliminaries, no politesse. I walked into Foxworth's office, and there was Hoover sitting behind the desk looking like a sledgehammer in search of an anvil. Foxworth, dispossessed, was sitting silently in an armchair alongside.

"Sit down, Popov," Hoover yelped at me, and the expression of disgust on his face indicated that I was the equivalent of a fresh dog turd which had had the audacity of placing itself beneath his polished brogans. I bit my tongue and sat in the chair across the desk from him. Now, if ever, was the time for diplomacy.

"I'm running the cleanest police organization in the world," Hoover ranted. "You come here from nowhere and within six weeks install yourself in a Park Avenue penthouse, chase film stars, break a serious law, and try to corrupt my officers. I'm telling you right now I won't stand for it." He pounded the desk with his fist as though to nail the words into my brain.

"I don't think," I said quietly, "that a choirboy could perform my job, but if I've caused trouble, I pray you, forgive me."

Hoover turned to look at Foxworth, his face grim, not quite able to judge if I was serious or pulling his leg. From over his shoulder he gave me a long, penetrating look, turned away again, saying not to me but to Foxworth, "He may leave now."

I lit a cigarette and settled back in my chair. The moment had come to make my play.

I gave it to him straight. "Mr. Hoover, my apologies were purely an exhibition of manners meant to take the edge off your unjustified remarks."

Hoover turned purple and choked out, "What do you mean?"

"I did not come to the United States to break the law or to corrupt your organization. I came here to help with the war effort. I brought a serious warning indicating exactly where, when, how, and by whom your country is going to be attacked. I brought to you on a silver platter the newest and most dangerous intelligence weapon designed by the enemy, something your agents have been trying to unearth for over a year and failed at. It could have done much harm if not discovered in its initial stage. But mainly, I came to help organize an enemy agent system in your country, which would be under your control and your orders. I think that is quite a lot to start with."

"I can catch spies without your or anybody else's help," Hoover barked. "What have you done since you came here?"

"Nothing but wait for instructions, which never came," I answered.

Hoover breathed in deeply and noisily. It seemed to calm him. "What kind of a bogus spy are you?" he said accusingly. "None of their agents have contacted you since you arrived, as far as we know."

For a moment I was shaken. Was it possible that no one had explained to Hoover the Abwehr's purpose in sending me to the States? Or if it had been explained, could he have not understood? In either event, I was faced with the problem of explaining to that impatient and irritable man something that should have been clear to him from the beginning. I tried.

"In the last few months, you have successfully broken up the existing German information organization in the United States. Obviously, they have to replace it with a new organization. I am the one, or one of the persons, who was entrusted with that task. I am not to contact any of their old agents now or in the future, and none of them knows of my existence. I am to build an organization of my own. To stay on in the job, I must produce results; that means information and new agents. Up to now I've been permitted to do exactly nothing."

"You're like all double agents," Hoover interrupted me. "You're begging for information to sell to your German friends so you can make a lot of money and be a playboy."

The man wasn't even listening. He was nursing his preconceived phobias. I felt like exploding but continued to try to make him see reason. "I'm not a spy who turned playboy. I'm a man who always lived well who happened to become a spy. The Germans believe, just as you do, that I work for them for opportunistic motives. They expect me to live the way I always have, and if just to please you I accept a lower standard, they'll become suspicious. But please believe me, if it helped our common cause, I would be willing to live on bread and water in the worst slum you could find.

"As for the information you say I'm begging from you, the object is obvious. You cannot expect a crop if you don't put in the seed. You cannot deceive the enemy if you don't . . ." A braying laugh from Hoover stopped me. He turned to Foxworth and said, "That man is trying to teach me my job." Foxworth didn't reply, his face was twisted into what could be taken for a smile, if you wanted, or a grimace.

I recognized the futility of it all. "I don't think anyone could teach you anything," I told the FBI chief, and walked toward the door.

"Good riddance," he screamed after me.

There goes the ballgame, I thought to myself in American argot as I walked home. I felt more horror than disgust, and my morale hadn't been so low since Dunkirk. Hoover was handing the Germans a victory of incalculable proportions.

I rang Colonel Ellis to report on the fiasco with Hoover and to prepare a strategic retreat. He asked for a day or two to see what went wrong and to seek advice from William

Stephenson, head of British Security Coordination. Stephenson, Ellis said, was the only man in British Intelligence who could handle Hoover, perhaps because he was Canadian and Hoover was less xenophobic with him than with a European. I roamed my apartment like the caged animal I had become. Leaving seemed the only solution. I told Ellis as much when we met for lunch two days later.

"Hoover is a very difficult man," Ellis understated diplomatically, "but you have to understand that he rescued the FBI from the corruption into which it had fallen during the Harding administration. That was in 1924, but I think he is still obsessed with the idea that it may have a relapse. He is very mistrustful of anyone who tries to mix in his affairs."

"Colonel Ellis," I protested, "those are apologies for the man. They don't do any good. They don't change the facts. And the facts are that he is obstructing some very important work."

"I know, I know," Ellis lamented. "He's a heavy-handed policeman, and we've had a lot of failures in our dealings with him. Still, the man's not unintelligent and he is honest."

"From where I sit," I said, "he would be more suited to Hitler's team than ours. And to all intents and purposes that's where he is."

"Dusko!" the Colonel rebuked me.

"Sorry, that's the way I see it. There's no use my sitting around New York any more. Let's try to get me back to London with the least amount of damage."

Ellis shook his head sadly and said, "You are at an impasse, Dusko. You can't go back to London. Not yet. Your sudden return would ruin your reputation with the Germans, but what's more, it would compromise many of Masterman's plans and perhaps some people."

"But if I stay here and do nothing," I objected, "I'll be finished with the Germans anyway."

"True. But it would only be you. And," he said rubbing

his chin thoughtfully, "I'm not sure that this episode has to end so badly."

"Episode!" I exploded. "You call that scene the other day an episode. It was last-act curtain."

"No, we must give Stephenson a chance. He may fix matters. It's been known to happen. You see, Hoover pulls tantrums like that every day, sometimes with his best friends."

"Is he really the best America can offer to run an intelligence service?"

"For the moment, he is the only thing it has to offer. His is the only organization that exists. Mind you, if the United States enters the war, as looks likely, something better and more efficient undoubtedly will come along. But America is still uncommitted, and Hoover probably thought you were warmongering. Most times that is what he thinks of all of us."

I waved my hand at him wearily. "Please, no more excuses."

"All right, no more excuses. But you hold tight awhile. Give Stephenson a chance. He has connections."

I learned sometime later that the "quiet Canadian," as Stephenson was known, had entry to President Roosevelt whenever he wished.

I returned to my vigil. It wasn't a lonely one, and but for the contretemps with Hoover, I was enjoying New York and was still impressed with the United States.

Lehman contacted me as though nothing had happened. "I'd like your help," he said when we met as usual in a Pennsylvania Station hotel. "You are a friend of Samuel Finkelstein, aren't you"

"You're pretty well informed, Charlie." I smiled. "But I'm not his friend. He's an acquaintance. We met in Lisbon."

"He is in New York now, living in a hotel uptown. Could you meet him, as though by accident, and renew your friendship? I mean, acquaintanceship. We have good reason to believe he is a German agent. Perhaps they blackmailed him into becoming one, but we would like to know for sure."

I knew about Finkelstein. M.I.6 in Lisbon had warned me that he had been seen going into the Pau da Bandeira several times. We were convinced the poor chap was a blackmail victim.

"Sorry, can't help, Charlie," I said. "I couldn't testify for you as a witness without lousing up my position. Finkelstein is small fish at best, so it would hardly pay to jeopardize everything. I mean in England. I'm already screwed up here, or didn't you know?"

"You won't be asked to testify," Lehman promised. "And it would help. Help you."

"You mean it would make your boss cooperative?"

"Yes, perhaps." Lehman turned on his photogenic smile.

"Then by all means," I agreed. "Mr. Finkelstein and I will renew our friendship."

Charlie mapped out his plan. I was to run into Finkelstein accidentally and invite him to my place for a drink. The FBI would plant a microphone in my study controlled by a switch I could throw to put us on the air whenever I wanted the FBI to listen in. I was to exchange confidences with Finkelstein and encourage him to talk about himself. The FBI would take care of the rest. I gave Lehman a key to my apartment and arranged to be away one afternoon while some FBI technicians bugged the place.

The plan worked well, except that Finkelstein didn't reveal any confidences. I invited him up again a few days later, again with no results. "Try some more," Charlie insisted, "we must get that sonofabitch."

I tried but Finkelstein didn't talk. Anyway, probably he had nothing to say. A short time later he volunteered for, and was accepted by, the Army Air Corps and served honorably throughout the war.

Successful or not, the FBI paid off for my cooperation.

Lehman transmitted to me some minor information—nothing very hot—about airplane and tank production and some budget figures for 1941 and 1942 relating to rearmament. It was at least something to pass on to the Abwehr and gave me some hope that Colonel Ellis was right. Perhaps all the bridges weren't blown, and we could still work with the FBI.

One idle afternoon, I looked a bit too closely at the bug the FBI had installed in my study. I traced the wire running from the switch with which I was supposed to be able to turn it on and off at will. The wire ran under the inlaid carpeting. I followed it but after a few yards, lost the trace. There seemed to be no more wire. I tore up the carpeting. The wire led nowhere, the switch was a dummy. The FBI could listen in whenever it pleased. Not only that, I continued my investigation and found that my living room and bedroom were bugged as well.

Fuming, my first impulse was to tear out all the wires and wrap them around Lehman's neck. Then reason prevailed. I thought of the efforts British Intelligence had made to mend my clash with Hoover. Obviously the FBI still didn't trust me, but we had made some slight progress nevertheless. Still, I wasn't going to live in a bugged apartment. I not only believe in the privacy of the individual, I practice it. I enveloped the microphones in the living room and the bedroom with four inches of cotton wadding. That put the ball in the other court, and the reaction came in forty-eight hours.

Lehman called to ask me to meet him at 1400 hours. I agreed, but warned him I might be a bit late because I had a luncheon appointment. The appointment was bogus. At noon sharp, I left the house, making a point of asking the doorman to get me a taxi only after I came downstairs, in order to give anyone who might be watching ample time to spot me standing in front of the building. I boarded the cab, made sure we weren't being followed, and after a few blocks told the driver to return to the service entrance of my house on Sixty-first Street. I took the service elevator up to my flat and installed myself quietly in the living room. From where I sat, a mirror reflected a view of the entrance hall and the front door.

At about twelve thirty I heard a key being fitted into the lock and saw the door opening slowly. I coughed a few times. The door closed silently, but despite the rugs in the corridor I could hear the hurried steps of two men going toward the staircase.

I kept my appointment with Lehman. He had nothing to say to me that couldn't have been said over the phone.

"Come on, Charlie," I chided him, "you didn't get me down here to pass the time of day. Let's put our cards on the table. You want to know why the microphones in my bedroom and living room are dead." He opened his mouth as though to protest but couldn't find the words. I waved him to silence. "Wait, I'll tell you why. I packed them with cotton. And I tumbled to that phony switch you had installed, too. And I shall change my lock too, now that you have a key."

"Goddamn it, Dusko," Charlie flustered, very irritated, too honest to deny the facts and too loyal to criticize his organization.

"Don't say anything, Charlie." I relieved him of the onus. "There's no point and I'm not holding it against you. I'll take it up with your boss."

Before seeing Foxworth, I conferred with Colonel Ellis, to whom I told the whole humiliating tale. He could do nothing but confess his impotence.

"Any intervention from us would do more harm than good," Ellis estimated. "Hoover is very jealous about any interference with his organization, especially from the British."

"So we are back where we started from," I complained grimly. "Hoover would rather pillory me than let me help him. Does he really expect to catch spies with a policy like that? And to catch them before they do any harm?"

Ellis shrugged downheartedly. "I'm sure he expects to get every last one of them. I can only recommend to you that you try to persuade Foxworth to intervene. Perhaps if he makes a strong enough case to Hoover . . ."

Foxworth opened our interview by saying, "Lehman told me everything."

"I expected he would," I answered. "But I didn't come here to complain on a personal level."

Foxworth looked relieved. So was I, because he looked receptive as well. Not that I doubted his sincerity or integrity. Or his intelligence. He had all those qualities, as did Lehman, but I didn't know to what point he jumped when Hoover cracked the whip.

I delivered what I intended as my peroration. "Mr. Foxworth, correct me if I'm wrong, it is my understanding from British Intelligence that your organization was consulted about my coming and was in full agreement."

"I believe that was the case," Foxworth replied, judiciously.

"Well, since I arrived here, two months have elapsed and nothing has been accomplished. I know that as a person I'm not Mr. Hoover's cup of tea. I'm just one of those Balkan savages." I couldn't avoid the sarcasm. "I'm suspect. I joined the fight even before my country got into the war. A premature antifascist, I think I've heard it called. Now I want to fight even more, now that my country, my family, my friends are involved. In addition I'm a sybarite, a playboy, a no-good bastard, if you wish. But I'm also the person the Abwehr sent here, and you've got to work with me. If I fail, you're going to have another Abwehr man here, and he won't be a British Intelligence agent. He won't be on your side.

"Don't you think the question of Mr. Hoover's taste and my personality should be secondary? All I'm asking is that you let me get on with my work. Under your orders. You're aware of what I did in England. I can accomplish the same thing here. That's what I've been sent to do," I almost pleaded with him. "The Germans are practically making you a present of their espionage system in the United States and you're rejecting it. My God, man, what more do you want?"

Foxworth looked at me with composure. He was not angered, nor to my relief did he try to justify what had happened. He asked what I had been hoping for: "What action do you propose?"

"Not one but hundreds," I answered. "In England, British Intelligence formed a special committee to run a team of double-cross agents such as I mean to recruit. The committee is composed of representatives of all the various intelligence services: Army, Navy, Air Force, Foreign Office, Civil Defense. Backing them up are a lot of executive officers and staff members, experts on everything that might be concerned. They select and filter the information that is to be passed to the enemy. Everything is coordinated so that nothing gets through which would be harmful to anyone or in conflict with the deception plans of any of the other services. You can see I'm not suggesting a one-man show with myself as the man. This is a tremendous undertaking that requires the cooperation of everyone."

"I know," Foxworth said. There was a note of discouragement in his voice. "That's the trouble. Theoretically, the FBI is concerned only with counterespionage in the United States. Believe me, Mr. Hoover is doing a marvelous job of that, but he is limiting his intelligence activities to that alone.

I'm not sure that he is eager to allow other services to mix in our work. However, I'll say this, the aim you propose is worth having a go at."

His slight encouragement sufficed to make me return to my theme with enthusiasm.

"Of course it is. Look, the main object of counterintelligence is to thwart the enemy's agents. If you can do that by creating double agents, it is even better than catching them. Otherwise, every time you catch a spy the Germans will send over a substitute. If we form a net of, say, ten to fifteen FBI officers posing as Abwehr men, the problem is solved once and for all. There'll be no more new spies or very few. And if I'm allowed to put through this scheme I can almost guarantee catching those few. Through my contacts in the Abwehr we reached the point in England of knowing an agent's identity before he arrived. It will work the same way here. And in addition to all this, we'll be handing the Nazis a load of phony information."

In my eagerness to put my point across, I was leaning halfway over Foxworth's desk and brushed some papers onto the floor. "I guess I'm being carried away by myself," I laughed. Foxworth did too.

"All right," he said, "let's see if we can make a start. The first thing a spymaster should have is a proper communications system. Supposing we set up a short-wave radio sender for you? How would you go about doing that if you were a real German spy?"

It seemed to me the first thing a spymaster should have is spies, but I held my tongue.

"The Abwehr didn't give me any instructions about radio," I said, considering the problem carefully. "I was given a book code and invisible ink for communication, that's all. But . . . I think if I informed the Abwehr that I've found a trustworthy operator who could build a transmitter, I could get an okay."

"That's the way we'll start, then. We put the last transmitter the Nazis had out of action. It's quite likely they're itching to have a new one. I think the scheme will appeal to the big boss."

Suddenly, I saw through Foxworth's generous offer. The tip-off was the "appeal to the big boss." The Abwehr wasn't all that anxious to have a transmitter. If they were, they would have instructed me to set one up. It was obviously Hoover's idea, and I could imagine his reasoning: if the Germans had a transmitter they would notify their spies to use it, and the FBI would haul them in like fish in a net. I knew it wouldn't operate that way, but I could never convince Hoover of that. The Abwehr wouldn't send any spies to use the transmitter because they didn't want me compromised by the existing organization. However, I decided to play along; perhaps this little puff of wind would start the ship moving.

"On second thought," I told Foxworth, "I think I'll present the Abwehr with a *fait accompli*. I won't write to ask for permission. I'll write saying that I have the possibility of setting up a transmitter and am going to Rio de Janeiro to get full technical and operating instructions from headquarters there. It would be impossible for me to go to Lisbon for instructions anyway—I wouldn't have a good cover for it—but I can go to South America as part of my job for the Yugoslav Ministry of Information. I know it will be okay with the Germans if I go to Rio to consult Alfredo."

Alfredo was the code name for the Abwehr's top agent in Latin America. He was well established in Brazil as director for South America of the AEG, the Algemeine Elektrizitets Gesellschaft, a major German electrical manufacturer. Alfredo operated a powerful transmitter, code-named Bolivar, and much of the traffic for the Americas was funneled through him.

Foxworth had no objection to my going to Rio but wanted to know what I would do there for the Yugoslavs.

My cover, I explained, would be the thousands of Yugoslav immigrants in Brazil. The government-in-exile was campaigning to recruit the able-bodied young men there for the army it was forming in Cairo. It was offering twenty-one dollars a month, the pay rate of the American G.I., and that was an attractive sum to my poor fellow countrymen, mainly Dalmatians who had been duped into going to Brazil in the lean years after the First World War. They had been given contracts by Brazilian ranch owners promising them fifty to a hundred acres of rich land to be paid for by four or five years' labor. After starting to work on the isolated plantations, they discovered that they were indentured for life. Their employers—among them the local police chiefs, mayors, and judges—ran company stores, where they were obliged to purchase at high prices. Just to stay alive, the Yugoslavs had to spend more for food and clothing than they earned. Each year found them deeper in debt. The only solution was to run away. Most of them did, ending up in the industrial centers, mainly in São Paulo, only to find conditions at times worse. Jobs, when and if they could be found, were paying fifty cents a day. Soldiering for twenty-one dollars a month and a chance to return home eventually would certainly appeal to many of them, and I hoped for a good crop of recruits.

That was my cover for taking the trip. I also needed a cover for the Germans, something to justify the months spent in the States. I couldn't arrive in Rio, where communication was easy, without some information for the Abwehr. I asked Lehman to see what he could do about procuring it. He busied himself in Washington, and I thought that at last the gears were moving. When he produced the material I was to take to Rio I was flabbergasted. I could have clipped the same thing out of one week's newspapers. There was no use arguing with him, he was a messenger boy.

I went to the New York Times building on Forty-third Street and leafed through the editions of the last six weeks. I selected about ten times the material that the FBI had given me; facts and figures about production, troop training, marine construction, and the like. Exercising my imagination, I trimmed and dressed these findings and dreamed up sources to whom they could be attributed.

15

Rio was three days from New York via Pan American Airways. First night, Miami of bitter memories; second, Belém, in the Brazilian state of Para, where the main offbeat tourist attraction was a still-functioning slave market. Men, girls, and young boys, penned in wooden cages, for sale at a few dollars a head, a reminder of the concentration camps on the other side of the Atlantic that I hadn't expected to see here. The third night, the glitter and glamour of Rio and the Copacabana Palace Hotel by way of contrast.

The AEG offices were large, smart, and modern. I walked in unannounced and asked for Alfredo. "Ludovico sent me," I told the carefully groomed man who came out to greet me. "My name is Ivan."

"I was expecting you." Alfredo put his arm around my shoulder and conducted me to his private office. His welcome was warm. My star had not yet completely fallen with the Germans.

I gave Alfredo the information I had brought along and a poor excuse to go with it. I told him I had sent the main crop directly to Lisbon and hoped I wouldn't be caught up in the lie.

"Unfortunately," I added, "my cover job with the Yugoslavs takes up too much of my time. I hope they will give me a few assistants soon, though, so I can free myself for our work. The way things are, it is taking more time than I thought to establish a secure net of agents."

"Oh, I am sure Berlin understands your problems," he said encouragingly. "But from what I hear you did spoil them by the wonderful job you did in England."

"England isn't America," I said, for want of anything better.

That anodyne set him off on a bunch of clichés about how Germany was going to conquer Russia this year, England the next, and bring the United States to terms bloodlessly because the Americans were soft.

Since that was the mentality of Herr Alfredo, I decided to win his friendship by a complementary series of oft-told fables. I recounted stories about the strength and influence of the America First movement and of widespread dissatisfaction in the States caused by the sentences against German agents. "People wonder why British agents don't get the same treatment," I said righteously.

"Yes," Alfredo intoned, "we have many friends in the United States."

"Too many for my sort of work," I answered. "I like to swim in clear waters entirely surrounded by enemies. Then yon can spot your friends easier. In the United States, one never knows if one is dealing with an *agent provocateur*. In England, it was easy."

Alfredo was a caricature of a Nazi, yet exactly the type I had observed on this side of the Atlantic. The little comedy I played for him worked and put me in his confidence.

"Would you mind helping me solve some minor problems," he asked, "some information I need from the States? I would like the answers directly. I think I can sort them out better than they can in that big mill on the Tirpitzufer."

"Gladly," I told him, "just add them to the new question-naire that Ludovico sent you for me. You can put them on microdots, can't you?" I fished.

"Of course," he boasted, and showing me six or seven typewritten pages said, "You don't think I'd ask you to memorize all that."

"I was promised a machine to produce microdots, too." I simulated envy. "Do you have any idea when I'll get one?"

Alfredo approved of zeal. "I'll help you get one," he promised. "It is partially a question of transport, and I can solve that. Know-how is also a big problem. Berlin will prob-ably do for you what they did for me. They sent me both the material and the experts. I shall try to make similar arrange-ments for you. They can send the material to me, and I will forward it to Canada."

"Isn't that rather roundabout?"

"No, the transport from home to here is easy and I have the means to send things to Canada. A cotton exporter here is in my pay. One can hide a lot in a bale of cotton. The shipment will go with a Portuguese captain who is also under my control. So is the shipping agent in Canada. I can get it to you anywhere in Canada, although Montreal or Quebec would be preferable. From there you'll have to pick it up and get it into the States. That should be relatively easy for you, no?"

"I'm sure I can handle it," I answered, figuring that was the least I could ask from the FBI.

Like the efficient business executive he was, Alfredo started making notes, listing exactly what we would have to do. "It will save us a lot of unnecessary communications and maybe misunderstandings if we figure out everything now," he ex-plained. "So here is how we shall operate. The material will take a good month to reach Canada after leaving here. My Portuguese Captain runs a tramp steamer and puts into many ports. I'll send you a radio signal through Bolivar when he weighs anchor. It will say that I have handed the money to a bald-headed doctor. Exactly thirty days after getting this message, go to Quebec and check in at the Château Frontenac. Now," Alfredo pointed his gold pen at me, "once you are in the hotel, pretend that you are ill. A grippe or something that you can recuperate from fast. Wait for the bald-headed doctor to call on you. This is one doctor who comes without being summoned. His prescription will tell you exactly where to pick up the apparatus, and he will give you any other details you need to know. Is that all clear?"

"Very clear."

"Good." He started making notes again. "Now, about the information you need for the radio transmitter: wave length, identification signals, radio code and signals for communication with Hamburg and Bolivar, listening and sending times and . . . oh, I'll have it all put on a microdot for you."

My sojourn in Brazil stretched to three weeks. Aside from seeing Alfredo, which I did several times, I had to take care of the recruiting for which I had ostensibly come. There was no faking when it came to a cover. I saw various officials, organized a program, and went around making speeches. On the side, I enjoyed Rio, maintaining my reputation as a bon vivant, a part of the job that was never difficult.

Alfredo's private questionnaire, the answers to which I was to give him exclusively, deceived me. It looked as though the Germans had downgraded me to commercial espionage. The questions were, among other things, about uranium, and I hadn't the faintest clue what use that obscure ore was to be put to. If Alfredo knew, he gave no indication of it. Nothing in his attitude even hinted at the race for the atomic bomb. Alfredo gave me a list of three firms and the names of their representatives who had been combing South America for uranium mines. He wanted to know how they processed the ore, to what degree of purity, by which method, the quantity they processed, and the amount they had in stock.

At one of our meetings, I mentioned to Alfredo that I might want to buy some semiprecious stones to take back to the States with me. They were part of the window dressing of my voyage, presents I would give to friends. The next time we met, Alfredo had at his office a Señor Carlos Almadero, a Brazilian stone trader.

"Señor Popov may want to go into the business of importing gems to the States," Alfredo announced to Almadero. And to me, too. It was the first I knew of such business aspirations. "He will only take a few samples now but will write to you if he needs more. Please serve him properly."

Almadero spread out a vast collection of stones for me to choose from and promised to fill whatever needs I had.

"There," Alfredo said with satisfaction when the gem merchant left, "now you have the perfect mail drop. You can write to Almadero in secret ink or using microdots when you get them. He is a kind of partner of mine and letters to him will reach me directly."

Alfredo was a remarkably efficient spymaster, coping with and profiting by every situation. The only thing he didn't know was that I reported everything about him to the regional FBI officer who contacted me in Rio.

My business in Rio at an end, I faced the return to New York with much misgiving. I would be able to accomplish nothing there until the arrival of the Portuguese skipper. Even the setting up of the radio transmitter would be no concern of mine, since the FBI would be doing it. No, I would simply be returning to the harassment of the FBI, and the thought gave me the shivers. I canceled my plane reservation and booked passage on a ship. Two weeks of relaxation, I rationalized, would make me better prepared to face that hornet's nest.

Among the passengers on the ship was the entire Colonel de Basil Ballet company, returning from a South American tour. On our stop at Trinidad I was set to explore the island with a ballerina named Dora. We stood by the rail watching the pilot boat approach and planning our day. A short, extremely freckled man with thin reddish hair, very British, climbed up the ladder from the pilot boat and a few minutes later approached us and asked discreetly if he might have a few words with me.

"I'm Major Wren, I'll show you my credentials later," he said when we were alone. "Will you spend the day with me?" It was a polite way of phrasing an order. He noticed me glance back at Dora and assured me humorously, "No need to worry about her, she won't have any trouble finding something better than you."

"I wasn't concerned about her," I answered. "Look what sort of a substitute I'm getting." He took my joke, if joke it was, good naturedly, told me to call him Freckles, and whisked me off to his house overlooking the harbor.

Wren was head of the M.I.6 office in Trinidad. He had been advised of my coming and requested to get a full account of my doings in Rio. I recounted the story over an excellent Creole lunch, and while we were drinking our coffee he called in his secretary, to whom he dictated it all in the form of a cable to London. I sat by and feasted my eyes on the secretary. She was in the tradition of London headquarters, long-legged and brainy but also sensationally beautiful. She returned my glances with a knowing smile.

"I'll have to run down to the office to code this," Wren said when he had finished dictating. "It will take a couple of hours, but I'll leave you Jane, here, as compensation for your ballerina." I didn't protest.

"Sorry about the ballerina," Jane said when the Major left, although she really wasn't.

"I'm not. Not now."

"Tell me," Jane's eyes twinkled, "do you pursue girls because you are a secret agent or are you a secret agent because you pursue girls?"

"Only when they are impertinent," was the enigmatic answer I found for Jane.

Jane was great compensation. If anything, she overcompensated. Or we did.

Freckles took his time about encoding the telegram. When he finally came back, he introduced me to another Trinidad delight: Planter's Punch. He was pouring me into his car to take me to the ship when a jeep drew up alongside. A corporal jumped out, very Buckingham-Palace-guard for this climate, saluted, and stood at attention. "Urgent telegram, sir."

Freckles read it and handed it to me. It was already decoded. It read: "Tricycle is not to give Portuguese captain's name to the FBI."

I stopped floating, the Planter's Punches lost their wallop, I was back with my bête noire, the FBI.

"Christ," I exploded, "how the hell do they think I'm going to manage that? I played it all open and above board with the FBI man in Rio. Told him everything about Alfredo and what we were planning."

"But you didn't tell him the captain's name?"

"No, I didn't know it then, but it's on one of those microdots."

"Which one? Do you know?"

"No, Alfredo pasted them on. If we have time before the ship leaves, we can look at them. Get hold of a microscope."

"Relax," Freckles waved his hand. "The ship can't leave until I give permission."

We drove down to the docks and boarded the ship. While I went to the cabin to get out the papers that had the dots on them, Freckles initiated a covering action, a search of the crew's quarters, and gave instructions for some of the sailors to be questioned. The captain wasn't happy about the delay, but he showed no impatience. Controls of this type were not unusual.

Freckles left the search in the hands of his subordinates and came to join me in my cabin. He had sent someone to scout up a microscope, and we had time for a drink before it arrived. After reflection, I was feeling much relieved by the incident. London was obviously having the same trouble with Mr. Hoover as I was. At least I wouldn't be an outcast. I confided as much to Freckles.

He tugged at an eyebrow reflectively. "If I can read the signs right, London considers your Portuguese captain to be their game, since the field of action is going to be Canada. They'll want him to lead them to the other people involved in this operation. If by any chance he lands in the States first and Hoover gets his hands on him, goodbye all. Hoover will clap him in jail and we'll never get anyone else."

"He probably will."

"Probably," Freckles snorted. "Haven't you noticed that that man deliberately ignores all the rules of the intelligence game, particularly the one of discretion. He never keeps anything quiet. When he's successful, I mean. He's the biggest publicity hound in existence. Whether he is catching a gangster or a spy, he makes sure it hits the front page. If it's not front-page material, he's not interested. I'd say that he turned thumbs down on your mission because it has to be carried out in secrecy and anonymity."

There was a knock at the door. Freckles opened it and took delivery of a microscope, which he set on the low table where our drinks stood. While I prepared a microdot, Freckles looked on with interest. It was the first time he had seen one.

Fortunately for the ship's schedule, the second microdot I mounted was about the Portuguese captain. I studied it for a while, made some mental notes, and then turned the microscope, the dot with it, over to Freckles. We went out on deck, where Freckles called off the interrogations and gave the officer of the watch permission for the ship to depart.

Gesturing with the microscope which he held in his hand, Freckles turned to me with concern as he headed down the gangway. "Watch that type Hoover, Tricycle, me boy. Take it from an old warhorse out here under the banana leaves, he can be dangerous. He'll bugger you up just like he would this operation."

We were three days' sailing from New York. Rumors were circulating around the ship that the Japanese had attacked United States shipping. Some passengers claimed to have heard the bulletin on the radio news. The day was Sunday, December 7, 1941. A few hours after the first rumor, the ship's loudspeaker announced that all passengers were to assemble in the first-class lounge.

His face very grave, the Captain waited until everyone appeared and imposed silence on us by a simple nod of his head. In a funereal voice, he announced that the Japanese Navy had attacked Pearl Harbor. "We have no details," he added, promising to give us the news the moment it reached him. He then turned us over to one of his officers, who warned us that since the United States was at war, we might be attacked by a German submarine at any moment. Lifeboat drill took place immediately afterward. The seriousness of the moment could be read on everyone's face. Except mine.

It was the news I had been awaiting. I couldn't say anything to relieve the tension of my fellow passengers, but I was sure the American fleet had scored a great victory over the Japanese. I was very, very proud that I had been able to give the warning to the Americans four months in advance.

What a reception the Japanese must have had! I paced the deck, no, not paced it, I floated above it exultantly. It was nasty for the Americans to be involved in the war, but it was the saving of the world. Now there was no doubt that we would win.

Then the news started trickling in. Involuntarily, I shook my head till my brain felt as though it were coming unstuck. The bulletins simply were not believable. The Japanese had scored a surprise attack on Pearl Harbor. How, I asked myself, how? We knew they were coming. We knew how they were going to come. Exactly like at Taranto. And that's how they came, combined torpedo and dive-bomber attacks, exactly as employed by Admiral Cunningham against the Italians. Except that the Japanese planes hardly should have gotten off the deck.

More news. The battleships *West Virginia* and *California* had been sunk at their moorings. At their moorings, I moaned. They couldn't have been at their moorings. They had to be steaming to attack the Japanese fleet. Then it was the *Arizona*. Blown up. Every other battleship and unit of the fleet heavily damaged. This was Orson Welles, I thought, remembering his famous scare broadcast. I couldn't credit what I was hearing. Somewhere, somehow, there had to be an explanation. In one and a half hours the mastery of the Pacific had passed from American to Japanese hands.

16

Charles Lehman came to meet me at the dock. He had me through Immigration and Customs as easily as through a saloon door but not fast enough for me. I was burning to get him alone. Lehman would know what happened, what had gone wrong.

"Charlie, what happened?" I asked the first moment I could.

He looked at me, not understanding. He didn't realize what I meant.

"Pearl Harbor, Charlie. Why?"

"Oh," he caught on at last. "I guess we were had. Those double-faced Japs, negotiating in Washington right up to the last minute while their fleet was sailing to attack." He went on with a very complicated description of the interdepartmental work of the FBI, its relationship with the armed forces, their dependence on the President, and the President's on the Senate.

I listened somewhat dazed, waiting for him to make sense, waiting for an answer. It never came.

"Charlie, what the hell are you saying? You're talking to me, Charlie, not the *New York Times*. To me, Tricycle, Dusko Popov, the guy who came here in August and told you the Japanese were going to attack at Pearl Harbor before the

end of the year. I even told you how. Taranto, Charlie,
Taranto. Now, what happened?"

"Take it easy, Dusko, don't get so excited."

"Sorry, Charlie." I calmed down a bit. "Do I sound like a
madman? I haven't slept for three nights. I've been trying to
figure this thing out."

"Things can go wrong," Charlie intoned slowly. "I do my
job. Mine is not to question why."

I let it drop. Charlie wasn't the one with the answers. I
turned over my material to him: the microdots and my notes.

"I'll look this over and ring you this evening," Charlie
said, "to tell you when to come to the office and dictate your
report." Then incredibly, he added, "We're in the war now,
you know. We shall have to start working seriously."

I answered, "From your mouth to the ears of Allah."

"Whose ears?" asked Charlie, not getting the allusion.

"Mr. Hoover's."

"But what name did you call him first?"

"Skip it, Charlie. I wasn't calling him names. It was an old
Arab proverb. I meant that I hope all of us get down to
business."

"Um," he grunted, perhaps not too pleased that I should
invoke the name of his lord in what he considered vain. Or
perhaps I'm doing him an injustice. It was difficult to tell the
attitude of Hoover's minions at times.

In response to an SOS from Colonel Ellis to London,
Ewen Montagu also was awaiting me in New York on my
return from Rio. Ellis had signaled the FBI's failure to supply me with information for the Abwehr. Intelligence, fearful
that this might cause me to be blown, dispatched Montagu,
one of its top trouble shooters, to the scene. His assignment
was to furnish me with Stateside information for the Abwehr,
which he was to collect from British and Canadian sources.

Montagu arrived in New York just a couple of days before Pearl Harbor. By the time he came to see me, a few days after that event, he told me optimistically that the situation had changed. J. Edgar Hoover had told our man in Washington, Bill Stephenson, that now with the United States in the war, he would cooperate with me fully. Montagu had had the same reaction from other American sources.

Unfortunately the assurances later proved false, but they did have the effect of obviating Montagu's mission.

Momentarily encouraged, I dictated my report on Rio and then went over it minutely with Foxworth and his assistants. They didn't seem any more aware than I of the importance of the questions about uranium. On the contrary, the impending delivery of the microdot apparatus aroused much interest in them. As British Intelligence foresaw, Foxworth asked me if I couldn't get more details about the Portuguese captain who would be transporting the equipment to Canada.

"Perhaps I can when he arrives," I lied, hoping that the storm might pass by then and the British would give me permission to talk.

Noting the radio information I had brought, Foxworth told me that they would start setting up the transmitter. "It will operate from Long Island," he informed me, "and will be ready to send by the second week in January."

"Splendid," I said, wondering why it would take so long. "Can I do anything to help?"

"I don't see what," he dismissed me. "Go have a merry Christmas and a happy New Year."

I didn't go that easily. While I had Foxworth alone I wanted to get an explanation for the Pearl Harbor debacle. Perhaps the chief of the New York office would be more informed or more revelatory than his underling. Diplomatically this time, I broached the subject of the Japanese attack.

"It surely united the whole country." I repeated what I had heard and read everywhere. "The Americans are standing like one man."

"We react that way in a crisis." Foxworth reiterated the standard concept of every people.

"It's a healthy reaction," I answered banally. "I suppose one should do all one can to encourage high morale, but between us, what happened?"

"What do you mean?" Foxworth asked sharply.

"Exactly what you think I mean." There was no other way but to call him to order, to stop the pretense. "Did everyone have a lapse of memory? A convenient lapse of memory? I brought you the warning four months ago. It would appear that nothing was done about it. Everyone was caught with his pants down in Pearl Harbor. Why? Why, Mr. Foxworth? Didn't you expect me to ask? Do you think I can just go blithely about my way without wondering? It has been on my mind day and night. I've been expecting someone to have the perspicacity to explain."

Foxworth looked directly into my eyes, but it wasn't out of frankness. It was a duel.

"It shouldn't be on your mind, Popov. You are a soldier. You don't ask questions. Do your job and let others do theirs." And then he added what sounded like a menace, although I prefer to believe I misinterpreted it. I had come to like and have a certain respect for Foxworth. "You had better learn," he said, "to walk in step with us."

My eyes bored back into his. "First I have to walk in step with myself, Mr. Foxworth." I never believed in the merit of the good soldier, blindly obedient. For one thing, I saw too much of that in Germany.

We sustained our duel of the eyes as if he were trying to decide whether to be friend or foe. At last, the skin around his eyes crinkled, and I saw that they were smiling.

"Forget all that, Dusko," he said in a kindly tone. "Searching for truth beyond your reach may be dangerous. It may stir up an idea in Mr. Hoover's head."

I registered his advice without a word, just nodding noncommittally as I got up to leave.

"Mr. Hoover is a very virtuous man," he said enigmatically as he accompanied me to the door. I didn't tell him what I thought of that philosophic drivel: it smacked of bigotry.

I never did get an answer to the enigma of Pearl Harbor. Over the years, I have studied the question, tried to draw conclusions, heard all sorts of speculation and conjectures. There have been official inquiries and courts-martial, but nowhere have I ever read or heard mention of the documented evidence I brought to the United States of the Japanese plans to attack Pearl Harbor.

For my own intellectual curiosity, if nothing else, I've had to draw conclusions. For a while, there was what I believe to be a canard circulating that President Roosevelt deliberately allowed the attack to take place so as to draw the United States into the war. This rumor was based on the disclosure that there had been some other evidence that the Japanese were planning an attack. The other evidence, however, was not specific at all and merely tended to bolster a possibility that everyone knew existed. I have had to discount the Roosevelt theory on the basis of pure logic. Granted even that Roosevelt might have welcomed an attack as a means of coercing the American people to unity in a war he was sure must come sooner or later, he still could have accomplished the same result by alerting his armed forces to the eventuality. Short of capitulation to the Japanese demands, there was no possibility of stopping their aggression. So attack they would. And the United States armed forces could have been waiting for them. The reaction of the American people would have been the same. They were attacked: they would defend themselves. There was no need to have a defeat to accomplish this. No need to sacrifice the American Pacific fleet and thousands of soldiers, sailors, and civilians on December 7. No need to have placed the Japanese in a position to conquer half of the Pacific. Not in the wildest fantasy would this be indicated. Nor could a man in Roosevelt's position ever consider such an action. Not the day but the man would go down in infamy. Aside even from questions of logic and morality, President Roosevelt could never have envisaged such an immortality.

Another supposition as to what went wrong comes from Sir John Masterman. He expounds it in his book, *The Double-Cross System*, published in December 1972. Masterman's book made the first public mention of my activities during the war and of the deception tactics employed against the enemy. He managed to get all that material declassified. Previous to that, we were bound to silence by the Official Secrets Act.

Masterman wrote:

. . . Tricycle's questionnaire for America . . . contained a sombre but unregarded warning of the subsequent attack on Pearl Harbor. Tricycle had established himself as a leading and highly placed agent in England and had made two more visits to Lisbon, the first in January and the second in March and April 1941. So much was he trusted that it was arranged that he should go to America (at the behest of the Germans) in order to start a large-scale espionage network for them there. He accordingly left England on 26 June, stayed for some time en route in Lisbon, and finally departed for America on 10 August carrying with him his questionnaire concealed under a series of full stops. On 19 August we received copies of the questionnaire from M.I.6 and this questionnaire was read to the Twenty Committee and translations were sent to service members. It will be remembered that the full stops were photographed and enlarged by the F.B.I. in America, who were therefore in possession of all the information contained in the questionnaire.

After giving this background, Masterman goes on to state:

Obviously it was for the Americans to make their appreciation and to draw their deductions from the questionnaire rather than for us to do so. Nonetheless, with our fuller knowledge of the case and of the man, we ought to have stressed its importance more than we did. With the greater experience of a few more years' work, we should certainly have risked a snub and pointed out to our friends in the United States what the significance of the document might be; but in 1941 we were still a little chary of expressing opinions and a little mistrustful of our own judgement. The lesson is, no doubt, that once an agent is firmly established, any questionnaire given to him has a much greater and more immediate intelligence value than that usually attributed to it.

Masterman's mea culpa is interesting chiefly because it demonstrates the lack of cooperation and trust between British Intelligence and the FBI. The British were afraid of a "snub," or in other words, of being told to go mind their own business.

I cannot accept Masterman's analysis because, with or without the British underlining my importance as an agent and the importance of the questionnaire, the evidence was there for all to see. Masterman's comment, it must be taken into account, was made in a book intended primarily as a text for intelligence organizations. His object, I believe, was to stress a point, to tell his readers that nothing must be left undone, nothing left to chance. Even in the most obvious cases, everything should be spelled out, is what Masterman is saying, in effect. I cannot argue with him there, but it seems to me an oversimplification to blame what happened on the FBI's inability to evaluate a questionnaire and a man. Certainly, an organization such as the FBI should have been capable of this. Besides that, the questionnaire was not the only basis available for its judgment. When I received the questionnaire from the Germans, I communicated it to M.I.6 in Lisbon. It would have been possible to forward it to the Americans immediately rather than to await my departure. It was the decision of M.I.6 to send it with me because I could supply additional information to confirm the questionnaire. I could tell them of Jebsen's contact with the Japanese delegation to Berlin, of his trip to Taranto, of Baron Gronau's findings and evaluation. I was the man who had assembled all this information, and I would be on the spot to be interrogated by the Americans. They could rip my story apart and satisfy themselves about the most minute details.

Instead, what happened? J. Edgar Hoover waited for weeks before seeing me, and then almost threw me out of his presence after thirty seconds.

If for some abstruse reason the FBI was not competent, certainly others, to whom the information should have gone, were. Intelligence reports normally are sent to the other services and to the President himself. Roosevelt, for one, was an accomplished statesman and politician and former Assistant Secretary of the Navy, certainly no neophyte at evaluation of all sorts. And even were this information undervalued, out of prudence it could not have been completely discounted. It was too vital. At the very least, it would have provoked an alert in Pearl Harbor.

Thus, the other supposition one can form is that it never became known, that this information never reached the Army or the Navy or the President, that it never went beyond the autocratic J. Edgar Hoover. I've had to ask myself, Could Hoover have pigeonholed the information? Could he have "lost" it in an administrative shuffle?

If so, the action demands an explanation. From my own observation, Mr. Hoover was paranoiac in his relationship with everyone outside his own realm. Within the government of the United States he had carved out a kingdom that was inviolable. No President dared depose him. The law called for retirement? The law was waived for him. Perhaps behind the walls of his kingdom he was blind to all else. If it did not concern him, he would have no part of it. Perhaps. A profound explanation is beyond my competence. Some historian, some psychologist, someday may unravel the reasons.

I can only attest to his irrational behavior.

A culminating incident occurred after the war. I was living in New York, doing some legal work. I got a phone call from a Brazilian acquaintance whom I had known in Belgrade, the former Brazilian Ambassador to Yugoslavia, Alvis de Sousa. I had last seen him during my stay in Rio. His greeting was far from cordial. Why, he wanted to know, had I involved him in unwanted publicity? I had to calm him down before discovering what had happened.

An article written by Hoover for the *Reader's Digest* of April 1946 carried as an illustration a reproduction of a telephone memo from Minister de Sousa, on which a microdot was concealed. The name of the recipient was not on the memo, only a hotel room number and the date. De Sousa looked through his diary and found he had left the message for me.

I procured a copy of the *Reader's Digest* and found in it an article entitled "The Enemy's Masterpiece of Espionage," bearing the byline J. Edgar Hoover, Director, Federal Bureau of Investigation. Hoover was claiming the credit for breaking the secret of the microdot by the capture of a spy. He didn't mention me by name but wove into his fiction some facts about me.

One day in August 1941 [the date of my arrival in New York] we met a youngish traveler from the Balkans [Hoover wrote] on his arrival in the United States. We knew he was the playboy son of a millionaire. There was reason to believe he was a German agent. With meticulous care, we examined his possessions—from toothbrush to shoes; his clothes, his papers. While a laboratory agent was holding an envelope so that the light slanted obliquely across its surface, he saw a sudden tiny gleam. A dot had reflected the light. A dot—a punctuation period on the front of an envelope; a black particle no bigger than a fly speck.

With infinite care, the agent touched the point of a needle under the rim of the black circle and pried the thing loose. It was a bit of alien matter that had been driven into the fiber of the paper, where it looked like a typewritten period. Under the microscope it was magnified 200 times. And then we could see that it was an image on a film of a full-sized typewritten letter, a spy letter with blood-chilling text.

Hoover then proceeded to quote what was the text of the questionnaire—which, if memory serves, I had handed over to the FBI, not in August 1941 but later that year in December after my trip to Brazil.

We now knew that the Balkan playboy had orders to investigate not only our atomic energy project but also to report on monthly production of planes, how many were delivered to Great Britain, Canada, Australia and how many American pilots were being trained. Under questioning, he was bland, affable and, seeing that we knew about the dots, he began to gush information.

Curiously, Mr. Hoover never says what happened to this spy from the Balkans. He never mentions him being prosecuted, jailed, or hanged.

The article goes on to say:

I doubt if we can ever disclose the method by which we were able to spot and intercept hundreds of microdot messages written in South America. [Obviously he cannot disclose the method—I was it.] On one spy we found what seemed an innocent telephone message on a crumpled memo form from a hotel switchboard. But the printing of that blank contained two periods which when enlarged contained several messages. . . .

This was the memo form reproduced in the article. Hoover credited it to another of his "captured" spies, but Minister de Sousa had no doubt that it was me. I promised him I would do something about it.

A confrontation with Hoover was indicated. I telephoned Hoover only to be told he was not available. I left my name and phone number, asked that he call me back that day, and settled down to wait. Hoover never did call. I phoned again, and when I couldn't get Hoover on the phone, I flew to Washington.

At FBI headquarters on Ninth and Pennsylvania, a receptionist took my name and showed me into a waiting room adorned with trophies of the FBI's famous cases. Among them I discovered some of my microdots.

A man who identified himself as an assistant to the FBI chief finally came out to interview me. When I explained that I wanted to see his boss about the *Reader's Digest* article, he told me Hoover would not see me. Up till that point, I had been stating my case calmly. Now I started becoming angry.

"You go tell Mr. Hoover he'll see me right away or I'll hold a press conference. If he wants the whole world to know about his lying, I'll be glad to oblige."

Mr. Hoover decided he had time to see me after all.

"Popov, I'll have you kicked out of this country," he shouted the moment I entered the office. "You think you can come here and . . ."

"Stop ranting, Mr. Hoover, it doesn't impress me," I interrupted him, furious but coldly so. "You can have me thrown out of the United States, I don't doubt that. But you can't stop me from exposing your lies."

His bluff called, Hoover calmed down and suggested in a conciliatory tone that we try to arrange things. I wasn't out for revenge and told him as much. All I wanted was to avoid embarrassment for my Latin American friend. Truth to tell, it would have been a delicate matter—and embarrassing for me as well—to have exposed Hoover. I was bound to silence by the British Official Secrets Act.

"I'll tell you what I'll do," Hoover bargained, "I'll get in touch with *Reader's Digest* and see if I can't stop publication of the article in their Spanish and Portuguese editions."

I agreed to the compromise, since that would avoid even more annoying publicity for Sousa. I presume it was arranged. I was so disgusted I never bothered to check, but I heard no more about it from Sousa.

I walked away from the FBI building with a knot in my stomach. The interview with that irrational, ranting man lent credence to my suspicion that here was the person responsible for the disaster of Pearl Harbor. The man had a sinister character. Here was no simple being carried away by bouts or raving. In the same breath he was capable of cool bargaining and of making a deal to cover his shabby lying. He hadn't even the conscience of a normal person. He acted as though it were his divine right to fabricate whatever tale he pleased, to hoodwink the public at will. He never gave a thought to apologizing, even to trying to justify himself. He was merely outraged at being caught out.

Quite likely the admirers and supporters of J. Edgar

Hoover are going to be up in arms. I have opened the Pandora's box of speculation about a man who is a hero to many. I dare pose a question that may reflect on his honor and glory, his competence and fitness. There may be some who will cry shame at my daring to speak harshly about a dead man. I am not at all concerned about such hypocrisy. The evil that a man does lives after him.

The supporters of Hoover need only produce the evidence that should exist in the archives to clear his name forever. It cannot be claimed at this date that the files must be kept secret. Not now, not since the British Official Secrets Act was waived in regard to these revelations. The responsibility for the debacle at Pearl Harbor should be determined. This is not to say categorically that man profits by the lessons of history—but he should have the opportunity to try.

17

After Foxworth's admonition not to search for the truth, I was completely disoriented. Not only was I fed up, I didn't know where to turn or how to proceed. I drifted through New York for a few days, purposeless, unemployed. One afternoon, seeking a few hours of oblivion, I entered a movie house showing a Sonja Henie film on Sun Valley. The beauty of the clean white snow and mountains overcame me. I had to escape the morass that was swallowing me. That same evening, I telephoned to book a room in Sun Valley Lodge.

To make sure the decks were clear, I called Lehman before leaving, giving him my address. "Don't break your leg," he said, cheerfully. My answer was rather sour. "Better that than to sit doing nothing."

In Sun Valley, one wouldn't know there was a war on unless one bothered to read a newspaper. It was a merry mixture of golden youth, Hollywood film stars, and high society. And girls. No day passed without someone throwing a party. I was caught up in the whirl but very unhappy about it. I was too intimately involved in the war. My family was in occupied territory, my friends were under the bombs in London, Johnny's neck was in the noose of an Abwehr uniform, and I could only rust in America at the whim of a despotic bureaucrat.

I skied from early morning to dark, telling myself that at

least I was keeping fit, trying to blunt the keen edge of my impatience by physical fatigue. It didn't work. My nights passed in a blur of alcohol and sex. It was easier to grin in company than to sob alone in New York.

I was very relieved when one day in early January I heard Lehman's rough voice on the phone. "Can you come to New York?"

"When do you want me there?" I jumped at the summons.

"Right away."

"Tomorrow afternoon at the latest," I promised.

I was in New York that same evening. Lehman came to see me in my apartment, enthusiastic.

"We are starting to transmit to the Germans tomorrow."

"Great." My enthusiasm matched his. "I hope you are sending enough material to compensate for my long silence. We shall have to rebuild their confidence in me."

"I certainly hope so, too," Charlie answered. "Here's what they are sending." He showed me two pages of coded material.

Not understanding, I asked, "Well, what's in it?"

"I don't know. They gave it to me this way, coded."

I swallowed hard. "Maybe we can sort it out tomorrow. What time do you pick me up?"

"What for? No point in your coming, Dusko," Charlie said uncomfortably. "We can manage without you."

I didn't hold back my anger any more. "Spit it out, Charlie. What's the score?"

"Hell, Dusko," he ground his teeth. "Strict orders from Washington. You are not to come near the transmitting station ever. Or to contact the operator."

"But the operator is one of your men, isn't he?"

"Yes, but that doesn't change anything."

"Charlie, I'm not arguing with you," I told him calmly.

"All I want you to do is to transmit my reaction and my objections. Okay?"

"Okay," he assented, throwing himself into an armchair.

"Now, just imagine the next time I meet the Germans they ask me about the information I sent, or about the operator. I won't have the answers. You know what that means: finished, curtains. Goddamn it, Charlie, Washington is putting a bullet in the back of my neck. And at the same time, they are destroying whatever you may build here and what's already been accomplished in England. Don't they realize that?"

"I'll repeat what you've told me," was all Charlie would say.

"Supposing the Germans ask something personal," I insisted. "How will you answer without my help?"

"Washington is sure you'll cooperate. You can't let things go bust. Your whole family is in Yugoslavia."

That was it. I recalled another of my grandfather's sayings: "When your friends and enemies agree about you, the situation becomes really dangerous."

"Good luck, Charlie." I bade him farewell.

He picked up his hat. "See you tomorrow night."

"No you won't. I'll be in Sun Valley tomorrow night. You can try to ring me."

My suitcases still weren't unpacked. I only had to buckle them up to take the escape route again the next morning.

I ran but I didn't escape. Sun Valley was a failure, the snow and the mountains no magic cure. The luxury and the idleness palled. Whatever I did, I couldn't stop brooding about the failure of my mission.

I returned to New York, to an equally futile atmosphere. I was allowed to do next to nothing. In desperation, I turned with a vengeance to the pleasures that New York has to offer.

Simone Simon had finished the film she was making in

Hollywood and had returned to the east coast. Not by accident, she took an apartment on the seventh floor of the building in which I lived. We became regular fixtures in the fashionable restaurants, an item of inventory in El Morocco and the Stork Club. We made the fashionable parties and the opening nights. When that was no longer a palliative, I tried becoming the country gentleman. I rented a house on the Gold Coast of Long Island, in Locust Valley across from the Piping Rock Club, and bought a hundred or so books that I had always wanted to get around to reading. I read them all but found no answer there either.

Dick Ellis, to whom I turned intermittently, had no remedy to offer either. He rejected my pleas that we implore the help of an influential political figure who might intervene from above. "It may provoke a scandal," he judged, "and could ruin the double-cross organization in London."

My extravagant escapism melted away the forty thousand dollars the Germans had given me, and I was digging into my own reserves by midspring. Soon, I was reduced to asking Charlie to radio the Germans an urgent SOS for funds. Perhaps the FBI thought they might capture a messenger that way, because for once my request was granted. According to Charlie's story, he had had to put up a fight for me in Washington; Hoover deeming me impertinent. I think my deduction closer to the truth.

The Germans ignored my request. That was a tip-off as to the quality of the information they were getting. Never before had I been refused funds.

Toward the end of spring, Charlie came to Locust Valley, a now unaccustomed smile on his face. "It came, Dusko, the message. They radioed: 'Funds for you handed over to the hairless doctor.'"

"That calls for champagne." I led Charlie into the house. "We'll have the microdot apparatus in a month."

"By the way, who is the hairless doctor?" Charlie asked as he held out his glass to the flowing bottle.

"You know who he is, the man who'll be meeting me in Quebec."

"His name, I mean."

"Don't know. No one ever told me."

Two days later, Charlie was back. "Hoover wants a name pinned on the hairless doctor. Come on, Dusko," he cajoled me, "try to remember."

"Blindfold me. Maybe I can pin a tail on the donkey," I said furiously. "I told you once I didn't know."

"We've got to know," Charlie persisted. "We sent a message to Germany suggesting that the hairless doctor come to New York."

I actually moaned, "Oh, no," and then told him fiercely, "You really are trying to fuck things up, aren't you? Why didn't you consult me before pulling a stunt like that?"

"Why should anyone consult you?" I had provoked the usually calm Charlie into hostility. "You have nothing to say here."

"Charlie, Charlie," I said wearily, "this little game is getting tiresome. And it's too transparent. Look, I know everything I say is going to go right back to your superiors and that's fine. That's just the way I want it. All you're interested in is to put the handcuffs on this hairless doctor to show how efficient the FBI is at catching spies. For the good of all of us, I hope the Germans don't fall for your game."

Charlie looked at me peculiarly and admitted, "So far they haven't. Their answer was to repeat the first message."

"Well," I breathed a sigh of relief, "good for them. And better for us. Charlie, if we play this right, we've got the Germans in our pocket. The microdot will be the easiest and the safest way for them to send any sort of complicated material—like maps, plans, formulas—out of the country. If I have the equipment, the Germans may send some of their other agents to us. Then is the time to pick them up and to turn them in, if possible. But if you arrest the doctor, that ends everything. Can't you get them to understand that?"

"I don't shape the bureau's policy, Dusko," Charlie said hopelessly.

Despite their persistent sabotage, I decided to make a last stab at forcing the FBI's hand. In the next month I would have to find out definitely if the FBI was going to cooperate or not. If they wouldn't, I would have to apply leverage from Canada once I picked up the microdot apparatus. I would refuse to return unless Hoover agreed to start a double-cross operation and allowed me to send material to re-establish myself with the Abwehr.

Should Hoover refuse, I planned to remain in Canada and operate from there. The scope would be limited but better than nothing. To do so, of course, would require inventing a reason that the Abwehr would find credible.

I kept my plans to myself, not discussing them with the British. I feared they would feel obliged to reveal them to the Americans out of an exaggerated sense of fair play. But I was confident that once I presented them with a *fait accompli,* they would be only too happy to accept. It was like working in enemy territory except that at the bottom of my heart I always expected the FBI to come to its senses and agree. With this in mind, I hatched a somewhat complicated method of bringing the microdot equipment to the States from Canada. As always, it had to be done as if I were an authentic German spy. My cover for the trip, of course, was my work with the Yugoslav Ministry of Information.

Simone and I had returned to the city from Locust Valley for a few days. We happened not to be spending the afternoon together, so Simone came up to the penthouse for an

apéritif before going out to dinner. She had her mother living
in the seventh floor apartment, and my place was our headquarters. Not that Madame Simon interfered. She was gay
and as beautiful as her daughter, and they were constantly
taken for sisters.

As she always did, Simone arrived bouncing with high
spirits and mine soared to meet hers. It was not possible to
be depressed with Simone around.

"Where to tonight, darling?" she asked after giving me a
warm hug and a warmer kiss. We had made the same rounds
of the fashionable East Side spots too often and I knew Simone was getting restless.

"Let's explore the Village for a change. We'll smell out a
good restaurant and then Café Society Downtown has a new
show."

"Magnificent." Simone was enthusiastic about everything.
She curled up on the oversized couch, almost purring, drinking the champagne I had poured her. She held the glass in
the palms of both hands and her huge eyes twinkled at me
from over the rim.

"How about getting away for a while for a real change?"
I proposed.

"You, my darling Dusko, have something up your sleeve."
Simone was hard to fool. She accepted without a word my
job with the Yugoslav government, but she confided to me
many years later that she always suspected me of some mysterious carryings on.

"I should go to Canada on business one of these days soon.
I'll only have to see a few people and maybe make a speech
or two. You could accept that invitation to appear at the
French Play Festival in Quebec for the war-bond drive. That
will get us both off the hook, and we can mix a lot of pleasure
into a little business. What say?"

Of course she agreed. Simone was the most agreeable girl in the world. She even organized the trip into a party, corraling Jean Pierre Aumont and a few other French actors in the States at the time to accompany us. It wasn't really a coincidence that Simone was invited to Quebec just when I had to go there. She was invited almost everywhere, everywhere there was a war-bond drive.

Like most film stars, Simone traveled with mountains of baggage, and the customs men tended not to subject her to a search. For German consumption I planned to sneak the microdot equipment through with her stuff. Alfredo had warned me that it would be too voluminous for the ordinary traveler's luggage. I had no qualms about using Simone, knowing I'd have her blind approval. Anyway, there was no risk involved. The FBI would be standing by at the border, and a wink would pass her through even if the inspector was immune to her charms.

The green light from Washington for my trip was taking time. Since she had to rehearse, Simone was forced to take the train for Quebec without me, leaving me looking more than a little foolish.

"I'll join you later," I promised, inventing a pressing diplomatic engagement. She didn't raise a fuss. It wasn't her way, and it is possible she was suspecting around this time that I was an agent, but not a free one. It's hard to be close to someone and not develop a second sense about them.

Putting off my departure from day to day, calling Charlie repeatedly to inquire if instructions had come from Washington, my nerves were at the surface of my skin. This was carrying things too far. Finally with only a few days left to go to deadline, I told Charlie that I was leaving for Quebec.

"Be patient another day or two," he advised me.

I pretended to view the matter casually. "Oh, Charlie,

there's really nothing Washington has to arrange. I think I can just take off. If there are any special instructions, you can get them to me through your man in Quebec or you can give them to the British. I'll be in constant touch with them."

"Okay," Charles conceded. "What train are you taking?"

"I'm driving. It'll be easier to cover my traces on the return trip if I'm followed by German agents."

"Well, okay." Charlie was very reluctant. "Good luck."

Early the next morning I threw my bags in the Buick and headed north, traveling fast. There were few cars on the road because of gas rationing. Thanks to my semidiplomatic status, I had an unlimited allowance, an X card.

In the late afternoon, I reached the Canadian border.

"Passport," the Immigration officer demanded.

I handed it through the car window. He glanced through it and then at me. "Wait a minute." He went into the office and returned with his superior.

"Got your income-tax declaration?" this one demanded.

"Tax declaration? What for?"

"All foreigners leaving the country must file a tax declaration."

"I'm just going out for a few days to visit some friends. I'll be back in less than a week."

"Doesn't make any difference," he said, pulling his cap down on his forehead to emphasize the point.

"Okay, let me have one. I'll fill it in."

"You should've thought of that before. It's got to be signed and stamped by the New York Internal Revenue office."

He turned his back on me and walked away. The Immigration man returned my passport and I turned the car around and drove to a motel I had noticed a few miles down the road. From there I phoned Lehman and told him my troubles. He sounded genuinely surprised. I gave him the benefit of the doubt. Perhaps he was as ignorant of the law as I was. I hadn't presented an income-tax return when I went to South America, and no one had asked for it.

"You must have an FBI representative somewhere in this area," I suggested. "Can't you get him to fix things?"

"I'll call you back," said Charlie, laconic as usual.

I ordered a coffee and told the waitress I was expecting a call. It came in a half hour.

"Sorry, Dusko," Charlie began, and I couldn't believe him. "No way of bypassing that tax-return formality. Washington says you are to come back to New York."

"What?" I screamed, thrown entirely off balance. "You're pulling my leg, Charlie."

"No, Dusko, those are my orders."

"Goddamn it, Charlie, there's a war on," I said using the popular refrain of those days. "Don't they know it in Washington? This is insane. You know what is at stake."

"Sorry, Dusko."

"Sorry are you? And Washington is sorry too." I let loose with a stream of the strongest invective culled and translated from the half-dozen languages I speak. Charlie only said, "Sorry, Dusko" again.

After getting that off my chest I said, "Now listen, please, Charlie, you get back to Washington and talk some sense into them. I'll wait here."

I ordered dinner, toyed with it, drank more coffee, the call never came. I phoned the office. Charlie wasn't there and the duty officer said he didn't know where he was. I went to the bar and took the only remedy available.

No one ever offered an explanation, an excuse, an apology. Charlie did say a few weeks later, "If the Germans need it badly enough, they'll bring that equipment to the U.S. Then we'll catch them." Apparently that was Hoover's reasoning. Was it because he didn't want to organize a double-cross system? Or was it because he cared only about making head-lines by catching another spy, and if he couldn't do it, the hell with everything?

Reviewing the situation, I feared that I might have given away my intentions by some of my preparations. I had paid most of my outstanding bills and transferred a fair amount of money to Canada. But even if Hoover guessed that I might be planning to stay in Canada, how could he have sacrificed such an important mission? Surely he didn't think the bald-headed doctor would be captured when he turned up at the Château Frontenac to see me. Before blundering into the hotel, he would be bound to check first to make sure I was there. The fact is, nothing more was ever heard of the bald-headed doctor. Or of the microdot apparatus.

I drove back to New York at probably the slowest pace ever recorded. I would have had ample opportunity to appreciate the beautiful scenery of upper New York State, the Hudson River valley, but I didn't see a thing except the ribbon of road leading to a dead end. I was like a mechanical toy that had been wound up and directed against a wall. I continued to function, moving futilely against the wall, not even making a scratch on it.

My first duty was to call Colonel Ellis. We met and I told him the sad story.

"Get me out of here, Colonel," I pleaded. "Send an SOS to London. You've got to convince them."

"I'll try," he promised. "I'll recommend your withdrawal in the strongest terms possible." Ellis was as aghast as I was at Hoover's transparent artifice and utter disregard for the exigencies of the war.

For undoubtedly valid reasons, London replied, "Wait." It was a long wait. My relations with the FBI deteriorated to zero. They never consulted me, had any work for me to do, or told me what, if anything, they were doing in my name. Out of actual necessity and incidentally to keep up appearances, I did have to request that they send a message to Germany asking for more funds. The message was never answered, and that ended the radio transmissions. Not having the money to pay my supposed operator, there was no alternative but to close down the transmitter. The FBI had to agree to that. I suspect they did so readily enough, since they weren't catching any spies with the poor bait they were offering.

If ever I lived a profligate life, it was during this period. Dispirited and without direction, I drifted between the penthouse and Locust Valley, partaking of all the fruits of country and city living but not really savoring either. Simone had forgiven me the Canadian stand-up. When she wasn't occupied, I spent my time with her. When she was away or busy, there were others, many others. Mr. Hoover wouldn't have approved. My personal funds were giving out, and I faced running into debt. It may be a black mark in my book, but reducing expenditures was foreign to my upbringing and temperament. I couldn't see that it would get me anywhere except into further depression.

At the end of the summer, a few long months after my desperate petition to London, help finally came in the form of Ian Wilson, a new member of M.I.5. Wilson was a lawyer, a member of a well-known firm that had many connections in the States. He was a tall, distinguished Scot, skilled in negotiations, patient, calm, and wise. He was sent to see what might be salvaged of the wreck of my mission.

Wilson and I spent endless sessions assessing and analyzing the situation in regard to both the Germans and the FBI. Wilson also got other viewpoints and estimates from his varied contacts.

"It's a bad show," he finally pronounced in his faultless

Oxford accent. "I've put out feelers and it is quite definite: the FBI will not go along with us. And there is no reason for you to nurture a guilt complex. I strongly doubt that basically their stand is in any way influenced by your personality. They simply want to go it on their own, in their own way, right or wrong. Strong indications of xenophobia, I should say."

I had regretfully come to that conclusion months ago, but I was glad to have it official. Now perhaps I could get on to something else.

"Right," I said much relieved. "Now what about the Germans? Will London allow me to pick up with them again?"

"You'd be a damn fool to play with them again."

Wilson's remark was strictly according to the code. One was expected to demur and play the fool.

"Come on now, Wilson," I chided him. "I'm not playing the hero. The game happens to suit me. And if I don't do it then I'll either have to go into the Yugoslav forces in Cairo— and that would be a bloody bore—or I'll join the RAF, and that's dicier than Intelligence." I'd been taking flying lessons on Long Island and already had my pilot's license.

"That is debatable, particularly in your case. The Abwehr will clip your wings if they catch you out in a lie. But that's all beside the point. What we have to determine is whether you'll endanger other people and the deception program."

While this decision was being debated, Freckles Wren arrived in New York from the Caribbean. He was en route to Madrid to take up the post of head of M.I.6 there. Freckles tipped the scales in my favor.

"It would be smashing if Popov could work with us," he told Wilson. "I'm sure we can sort things out. Dusko, your friends in the Abwehr wield a lot of influence. Couldn't they smooth matters out for you?"

"It would be worth a try."

"Ian, what say you?" Freckles questioned.

Wilson weighed his words before answering. "If it were simply a matter of the Abwehr pardoning him for not doing his job in the States, I wouldn't hesitate. Influence might well turn the trick. And I do know that M.I.5 would be happy to have their Tricycle operating again. Ditto M.I.6. They'd like their man in Lisbon. But we have one big imponderable: we don't know what the FBI put over the radio transmitter. Some bright lad in the Tirpitzufer might pose one question too many and trip you up."

"Put it up to London," I suggested.

Ian tapped a cigarette on his battered silver case. He put it between his lips slowly, struck a match and looked at me. The match burned to his fingers and he dropped it, still looking at me. "Very well," he came to a decision, "I think I can speak for headquarters. If you are willing to take the risk, I'm sure they won't refuse to take the chance, too."

"Well, that's settled then," Freckles said heartily. "Bring on the white elephants." Seeing the puzzled expression on my face he explained. "A favorite parlor trick of mine. Say you get in a tight situation and don't know how to explain. And imagine you could suddenly conjure a white elephant into the drawing room. Everyone's attention would be drawn to it, and they'd forget the embarrassing question. Right?"

"I suppose so, but how do I conjure up the elephant?"

He tapped his head. "Out of your mind, dear chap, out of your mind. You'd better go over equipped like a maharaja or don't go to Lisbon."

Fortunately, I didn't have to pay overweight on elephants when I boarded the Clipper. I had a stable full. I also had some choice morsels of information to pass to the Germans, a luxury I hadn't been afforded in ages. I got them in New York, but they came, of course, from the British.

The British also bailed me out of New York financially. In addition to paying my debts, I had to pay American income tax on my declared salary from the Yugoslav Ministry of Information—declared but never accepted. I later repaid the British when the Germans reimbursed me for my American expenses.

18

The October sun was warm in Lisbon. The Tagus sparkled. I felt alive again seeing it as the Boeing glided in. I was back in the game again.

My reaction disturbed me in a way. I was enjoying the game, the duel of wits, the aura of undefined danger. Yet that wasn't the reason I was there. I had a fierce hatred of Hitler and the Nazis to begin with, more so with my family and country under their oppression. Yet I could still take pleasure in this fight. It should have been a grim duty, but it wasn't, and none of us in the game felt that way about it. Probably that was one of the requisites of a good intelligence agent.

No one on the German side was expecting me in Lisbon. Before doing anything else, I went to the main post office and sent a telegram to Johnny at the Hotel Adlon in Berlin asking him to come to Portugal without delay. Then I picked up my baggage, hopped into one of Lisbon's antique taxis, and drove to the Estoril, confident that there would be an apartment for me in the Palacio despite the shortage of rooms. George Black, the ubiquitous director, was on the steps as the taxi pulled up. He gave me a very broad smile and a suite overlooking the gardens.

Next I called von Karsthoff's office and got Elizabeth on the phone. Only a second's hesitation in her voice indicated her surprise. After that it was business as usual. I arranged to be picked up that evening on the road outside Estoril.

Von Karsthoff himself came to the rendezvous point. "Good to see you, Ivan," he said as I ducked hastily into the back seat.

"Even better to see you," I replied as the car pulled away. "And to be back here after that mess in the States." I'd decided my best tack was to be friendly but aggressive.

"We'll talk in the house," von Karsthoff said, driving swiftly in the direction of his country place. I followed the familiar old routine, ducking down when we approached the property and not reappearing until the car was out of sight in the garage.

"Come," von Karsthoff led me upstairs to the drawing room, where Elizabeth was waiting. She greeted me warmly, and I knew at least on a personal level I was not in Coventry.

"Now, what happened?" von Karsthoff said as soon as Elizabeth had settled a drink in my hand and left the room.

It was the moment for one of Freckle's white elephants.

"That will take ages to tell," I evaded the question. "We've got over a year to catch up on. Before we go into that let me give you the new information I've collected."

Von Karsthoff nodded his agreement. I spieled off the stories Ian had coached me on in New York, first of all figures on materiel, particularly airplanes, delivered to England from the States. The information was not complete, of course, but it was partially true and would stand checking. I also related our deception plan for Operation Torch. Torch was the Anglo-American plan for the invasion of North Africa. In preparation, we were building up our military and naval forces in Gibraltar, a situation that couldn't be hidden. To delude the Germans about those reinforcements, I related to von Karsthoff that reliable informants reported Malta in a disastrous military position and its population close to starvation. The British, with American help, were coming to its rescue.

Coordinating with another deception plan on which Balloon and Gelatine were concentrating, I told von Karsthoff about rumors of a combined American and Canadian operation directed against France and Norway.

The white elephant worked. Von Karsthoff was mellowed by my returning with news of value, and I was able to answer his initial question under better auspices.

"About America," I told him, "it was a colossal error from beginning to end. Berlin should have known better. I wasn't equipped to work in the States. I was a specialist on Rolls-Royces, not Fords. In England I had connections from before the war. Every door was open to me. But in the U.S. —" I threw up my hands. "You send me there with no help whatsoever, no contacts, a few miserable dollars, although Berlin considered it a lot, and you expect me to produce results in no time."

"But that showed we had confidence in you." I had von Karsthoff where I wanted him, on the defensive.

"Confidence! It's not with confidence that you produce results. The whole mission was poorly thought out. I needed help, a lot of it. And about ten times the amount of money I was given. The last few months I hardly had enough for a subway."

"Berlin thinks you concentrated more on film stars than on your job."

"Of course I saw film stars. Those were the people I knew. That was part of my cover and my introduction around town. You never objected when I saw society people in London. Film stars are the society of America, and they can open doors, too. But it takes time if you have to start from scratch. Time and money. I'm not trying to absolve myself of all blame," I continued magnanimously. "I should never have accepted the job with the Yugoslav Ministry of Information. It was the wrong cover. It didn't leave me time for anything else. To end with, I bungled that job and the Abwehr's, too."

"So, what do you propose to do now?" von Karsthoff asked after I had expanded on my American sojourn.

"For the moment I'm going into hiding," I pretended. "I spent about eight thousand dollars in the States belonging to Bailoni, the Yugoslav banker. His family is in Lisbon now, and if I don't reimburse them immediately, my name will be mud. I won't be able to do anything."

"That can be taken care of." Von Karsthoff's conciliatory mood was more than I had expected. "What I want to know is whether you will go to England, to Dubrovnik, or do you want to stay here?"

"What would I do here?"

"I could use you here if you want, but I would prefer to have you in England. Müntzinger would like to have you in Yugoslavia."

"Well, I'll have to think about it," I hedged. The ease with which I was being reintegrated in the Abwehr made me slightly suspicious. I had come prepared for a thorough interrogation and at least a good dressing down. Apparently, the Abwehr placed greater value on my cooperation than I thought.

"Jebsen will be here in a day or two with instructions from the Tirpitzufer." Von Karsthoff revealed a swift reaction to my telegram. "We'd better wait for him before deciding anything."

In a car borrowed from a Portuguese friend, I picked Johnny up on the Estoril road, just outside of Lisbon, a few hours after his arrival. Except for a two-wheeled farm cart driven by a peasant with a weather-beaten face, there was no one around to observe our reunion. We clasped hands, and then I started the car moving.

"Cascais all right for you?" I asked. Cascais was then a small fishing village. The tourists and the smart set hadn't discovered it yet. It was an ideal spot for an undisturbed talk and a simple but good lunch.

"Fine," Johnny answered. "I've got a lot to tell you. News about your family and plans from the Tirpitzufer."

"Start with the family." I had had a few brief letters from them smuggled via Switzerland in which they didn't dare say much. There was always the possibility that such letters would fall into the wrong hands. Knowing that Johnny would tell the complete story faster in his own sparse manner, I refrained from asking the many questions that bubbled in my brain.

"Your parents and Ivo are in Belgrade. They had to flee from Dubrovnik, and they had a rough time for a while. At first, after the Yugoslav surrender, your people were safe enough in Dubrovnik. The local Ustachi were behaving themselves fairly much, and the Italians were being the very proper conquerors. They were hoping to win everyone's good will and eventually incorporate Dubrovnik into Italy. Then Anton Pavelic—he's the head of the new Croatian Independent State, in case you're not familiar with local politics these days—Pavelic brought in some Ustachi from another province and started a reign of terror. It was a blood bath of Serbs and Nationalists."

I could see my knuckles turning white on the wooden steering wheel, and I swore a thousand revenges.

"Your brother Ivo, being both a Serb and a Nationalist, was high on their list. He had a narrow escape. He managed to get false papers in time and escaped to Belgrade disguised as a monk.

"Your parents weren't bothered until early this spring, when there was a fresh wave of terrorism. The Ustachi decided to slaughter most of Dubrovnik's leading families. Probably they wanted to make an example of them for being pro-Yugoslav. Luckily, the afternoon before they were all to be arrested, someone got wind of the Ustachi plans and warned everyone. That night, other Dubrovnik people helped most of them to escape in small boats."

Tears, tears of gratitude, came to my eyes. I blinked them away as I drove.

"There was a bad storm that night. Its cover helped. They went to a small deserted island down the coast near Mlyiet. Your father, your mother, Ivo's wife, and his baby were in the escape party. They all lived on the island for five weeks without any food except what fish they could catch. Your mother is a great woman, I must say, Dusko. She saved the baby. Your sister-in-law lost her milk in the emotion of escaping, and your mother kept your nephew alive by chewing boiled fish and feeding it to him from her lips.

"When I heard about their escape in the boats, I started to look for them but couldn't get any information. Naturally, no one would trust me or anyone I could send. For a while we thought they had drowned. Finally I found a retired Austrian sea captain who speaks Yugoslav and sent him out with a search party. It took them several weeks, scouring every island, before they found them."

"Thanks, Johnny," I managed to whisper.

"That is the happy part of the story, Dusko. There is more. About your Uncle Jova and his family."

Uncle Jova had the reputation of being the kindest and most generous man in Dubrovnik. It was well earned, and he was loved by all.

"Your uncle refused to run away," Johnny sighed. "He was killed—hanged—together with his two sons in his own courtyard. Your aunt was put on a train for shipment to a concentration camp. Ivo learned about it through the underground. He called me, and I got your aunt off the train. She is in hospital now, recuperating, but I'm afraid it is not easy to recover from the wiping out of one's entire family."

The forty kilometers to Cascais were longer than ever, but I was glad of it. I wouldn't have known what to do if I hadn't been occupied with driving. Johnny continued talking, not bothering me with futile condolences.

"Conditions in Dubrovnik have improved now. The OKW instructed the head of the German army mission there that he will be held personally responsible for any terrorism. You can be sure he is keeping his eye on the Ustachi."

We drove in silence for a while. A compatible silence. Revenge was still in my mind. It would be in my brother's mind, too. And more than in his mind.

"And Ivo?" I asked. "What is he doing?"

"Ivo is practicing medicine. By day, he is the best friend of the Germans and a true believer in the new Europe. At night," Johnny smiled grimly, "at night he is blowing up barges and organizing every act of sabotage for a radius of fifty kilometers around Belgrade."

"How do you know?"

"He told me so. Not boasting, he had to. I heard my colleagues talking about certain suspicions they had, suspicions that could lead to Ivo. Ivo is the official doctor for the railroad, and some railroad workers were caught and arrested for sabotage. I had no choice but to warn Ivo."

"But he is continuing, you say?"

"I couldn't stop him. Nothing can stop Ivo. The only thing I could do was to advise him to be cautious and to give him my help, covertly."

"You, Johnny, you're helping in sabotage?"

"What else could I do?" he laughed. "The only way of stopping Ivo would be to have him killed. I like that brother of yours, so I'm trying to keep him alive."

"But if Ivo is burned, we'll all be burned with him," I said, realizing the ramifications of the game he was playing.

"Exactly. All the more reason for me to protect him. The discouraging thing is that I don't have much faith in the efficacy of these boy-scout actions. They won't help us to get rid of Hitler."

"To get rid of Hitler, no. But every little bit may help Germany to lose the war."

Johnny answered sadly, "Yes, but that is a second choice."

"There is no choice, Johnny. There are two Germanys, I'll grant you. One the Germany of music, scientists, writers, and gemütlichkeit; the other cruel, aggressive, and militarist. In wartime, there can be only one Germany, and it must be defeated."

"I know, Dusko," Johnny beat the dashboard with his hand. "I know it too well."

I looked for some way to turn the conversation. "Tell me more about Ivo. What faction of the resistance does he belong to?"

"It's hard to say." His reply was thoughtful. "There are only two really effective groups, General Mihailovitch and the Communist-led partisans. Knowing Ivo's philosophy, I'd say he's with Mihailovitch. More or less, anyway. Ivo is operating in Belgrade, and it is difficult to draw a distinct line in the cities. Both sides operate entirely underground, and from what I can establish, the Communists and the Royalists often work hand in hand. In the country it is entirely different. They both have paramilitary forces. They wear uniforms and have either long or short hair. It is easy to distinguish them and they often fight each other. In the cities, conditions frequently force them to cooperate. The rich bourgeois are known to the Germans, so it is difficult for them to operate. They must depend on the workers, who can go underground more easily. Anyway, as far as Ivo is concerned, I wouldn't be surprised if he is under British orders."

We arrived in Cascais and I stopped at a small inn, where we selected an isolated table on the terrace. Not that it was particularly necessary. Only a few people, obviously locals, sat around drinking vino verde. We ordered a cool bottle of that wine ourselves. I wasn't in the mood for lunch, but I agreed to share the traditional bacalao with Johnny. I think each was trying to encourage the other to cheer up and eat.

"Your situation has its humorous side," Johnny said, once we had settled our business with the waiter. "We had several conferences in Berlin, trying to fathom your very mediocre results in the United States. I gave my opinion that your poor work was probably caused by worry about your family's difficulties. Colonel Oster was shocked, but sincerely, when I told him the story. He dispatched Colonel Toeppen to Belgrade immediately to ask Ivo if he could be of any help. Being paymaster of the Abwehr, Toeppen offered financial assistance as well. As you can imagine, Ivo refused. But he charmed Toeppen so much, practically hypnotized him, that he got him to bear down on some overzealous officers. They were told to go easy or they would be transferred to the Russian front."

"That Ivo," I had to laugh. My brother's charm was legendary. And the wine, the sun, and the soft air of the coast were having their healing effect on me.

"Tomorrow"—Johnny returned to the business at hand— "I shall see von Karsthoff and Kamler. We're to decide how to employ you. What's your feeling? What do you want to do?"

I had made my decision in New York. "I think I would be most useful if I were reintegrated in the Abwehr and sent back to England."

"Consider it done."

"Just like that? Do you have the power to make final decisions now?"

"Sometimes. While you were getting soft over there in that decadent democracy," Johnny kidded, "I worked my way up. In the Abwehr. I'm far from a fair-haired lad with the S.D."

"And this Kamler you mentioned, who is he?"

The waiter came with our dish of cod smothered in a sauce of tomatoes, olives, and local herbs. Johnny waited until he was gone.

"Captain Otto Kurer is his real name. He used to be a kind of A.D.C. to Canaris. Now he's with Abwehr I in Lisbon. He evaluates the work of our agents. He gave you rather a bad mark in the United States." Johnny paused to sip some wine but looked steadily at me as he did so. "What was your trouble there?"

"Money," I said evasively.

"And what else?" Johnny wasn't being fooled.

"I'd rather not discuss it, Johnny." I didn't feel free to go into my difficulties with Hoover.

"Would you rather stay here in Lisbon?" he asked, perhaps sensing that I had had some sort of run-in with Allied authorities. "You could send new agents to England and run them from here."

"Where would I get them?"

"I'd furnish them."

I calculated that I could be more effective in London, where I could work closely with the XX Committee. "I'd rather go to England."

"Good," he answered. "In that case I'll select someone for this end or do the job myself. It would be too risky otherwise."

"I can stay if necessary," I offered, realizing that we would need a thoroughly reliable man in Lisbon. Kamler's power to evaluate us was an example of one of the dangers.

"No, go to London. You are the only person who can cover that end."

Johnny had the situation all arranged by the time of my next meeting with von Karsthoff. He sat in on the meeting as an adviser, but one could see that his advice carried much weight. The excuse he had imagined for my poor work in America was being accepted by as shrewd an operator as von Karsthoff.

"We are all sorry to hear how your family was mishandled," the Lisbon spymaster told me. "I hope you will believe that I knew nothing about it."

"Of course, Ludovico." I did believe him. Von Karsthoff and I were on genuine terms of friendship aside from our work. There, I couldn't expect any favors.

"Herr Jebsen tells me everything is under control now, so you can go back to work with a clear mind. He also tells me that you are willing to return to England. That is splendid. We shall have to get busy reorganizing."

"Oh no, not again."

Von Karsthoff laughed heartily. "No, nothing like in the United States. We just have to adapt ourselves to the new situation that exists."

"What has changed?"

"Nothing, basically. Nothing, that is, with the organization. It is the military situation I was referring to. We know, for instance, that the British are preparing some sort of move in conjunction with the Americans. Your agents in England, Balloon and Gelatine, have warned us about that, but there is much contradiction as to where the attack will come. Some agents indicate it will be Dieppe, others North Africa. Berlin has reasons to believe both would be too risky for them. There are other indications they may strike in Norway, especially since Churchill's trip to Moscow. The Russians want to make sure their convoys keep coming through, and having Norway would help secure the Murmansk shipping route. But that is only part of the picture.

"Our French friends"—his sarcasm was not veiled—"are clamoring that Dakar is going to be attacked. And now you come along with the possibility that the concentration of naval units in Gibraltar means a relief force for Malta."

"Perhaps all these counterindications mean that your agents are bad, including me," I said to protect myself. Better to be accused of incompetence than of betrayal.

"No," von Karsthoff corrected me, "it doesn't mean anything of the sort. It means that the British and Americans are employing diversions. Our agents, as is quite usual, are falling for external signs."

"And you want me to sort this mess out," I protested, "to determine where the real invasion will take place?"

"No, that would be asking too much. That is the OKW's job. Ours is to enable them to do so by supplying all the divergent information possible. Never mind if it is contradictory. Just get it here fast."

"I'll need a radio transmitter, in that case."

"I'll take care of a radio and an operator," Johnny put in hastily, presumably thinking of furnishing me someone trustworthy.

"What will your position be in England?" von Karsthoff inquired practically. "How do you stand with the Yugoslav government-in-exile now that you have resigned from the Ministry of Information?"

"I still have connections. I can arrange something," I boasted. "I'll have to see exactly what when I get there."

"If possible, find something that will allow you to come here often," von Karsthoff suggested. "We'll want you here." Not more than the British will, so no worry, was my private thought. I assured von Karsthoff that I would find some legitimate excuse, a business or government project to make repeated trips to Lisbon.

To wind up the tref, von Karsthoff presented me with tangible proof that I was back in the good graces of the Abwehr. Excusing himself, he left the drawing room where we were conferring and returned a few minutes later with a stack of bank notes. He held them out to me.

"Here. Ten thousand dollars. Eight thousand to repay the banker, the rest for your expenses here. You will get the money for your English expenses before going."

Johnny and I left together in the car he was driving. When we were some distance from the house, I climbed over into the front seat.

"Do you have someone in mind as a radio operator?" I asked Johnny.

"Someone!" His voice rilled with amusement. "I've just worked it out. A dozen, if you want. Plus other agents and a valid excuse for coming to Lisbon."

Stopping the car on the side of the road Johnny elatedly asked, "How would you like to run an escape route?"

For some time, he explained, he and Ivo had been trying to get some prominent Yugoslav prisoners out of the Nazis' hands. Johnny had been toying with the idea of an escape route but hadn't found a means of establishing it until tonight. Now it was the Nazis themselves who would help set it up.

The Yugoslav prisoners were serving as hostages for the good conduct of the resistance. They were held in prison on a rotating basis. If not executed during their term, they were released temporarily. Some had been through this mill several times and were near the breaking point. Awaiting death, being released, then picked up again, over and over again. It was a masterpiece of sadism, and Johnny and Ivo felt they should be rescued.

The escape route Johnny conceived would work two ways. The Abwehr would consent to it readily because Johnny would propose that it serve as a camouflage to send spies to England. They would be passed off as refugees. Not all of the latter were to be prisoners and certainly none of the former Nazi spies. They would be double agents and serve as much-sought-after reinforcements for my net.

Johnny started the car again and we rolled toward Estoril, chuckling like schoolboys over our multiple deception of the Abwehr.

Then, recalling von Karsthoff's analysis of Allied plans, I asked Johnny, "What makes the OKW so sure the Allies don't intend to attack at Dieppe or in North Africa?"

"Berlin estimates that the Allies don't have sufficient transport for those operations."

Later, when we invaded North Africa on November 20, I had a good laugh. The XX Committee had done its job well, keeping the Germans guessing.

19

British morale was high, higher than ever, I found on my return in November 1942. From the vantage point of over a year's absence, the difference was readily noticeable. Victory was considered certain, almost within grasp, if one kept on grasping. Until Montgomery's troops defeated the supposedly invincible Rommel in Egypt at El Alamein at the beginning of the month, the British had had constant defeats. Now it was one victory after another. Operation Torch with its successful landings in Algeria and Morocco marked the turning point in the war. People felt the Nazis had lost the initiative and would never regain it. The Royal Air Force had already made a comeback some months earlier, raiding Cologne with a thousand bombers and following that up with similar raids on other cities. On the eastern front, the Russians were taking the offensive at Stalingrad, where they had been under siege since September 1942. All this was reflected visibly in the humor and spirit of the Londoners, even if the city appeared more battered.

I was settling in for the long pull and rented a cottage in Rutland Gate—pretty much the center of London, not far from Hyde Park. Few houses on the square were still standing. Mine, Clock House, was one of about five out of a hundred still inhabitable. Since it was only a single story it was particularly vulnerable to even the smallest bomb or shrapnel, but I felt if it hadn't been touched during the great blitz of 1940–41, it had a charmed life.

Incidentally, some months after I moved in, Lillian Gregg, a beautiful English actress, rented the neighboring house, Box Cottage. Lillian was the fiancée of Prince Bertil of Sweden, grandson to King Gustave V. A commander, Bertil was sent to London as Naval Attaché as the result of an espionage incident.

The British suspected—unjustly it turned out—the former attaché, Captain Oxen Sterner, of leaking information to the Germans. He was removed, and to place the post above suspicion, Sweden delegated the irreproachable Prince to it. But the leakage continued.

A top German agent named Kraemer, running an espionage net called Josephine, was getting the Swedish Naval Attaché's daily report from London through a spy at the Ministry of Defense in Stockholm. To glorify his accomplishments, Kraemer led even the Abwehr to believe he had the reports directly from the attaché in London. Josephine continued to operate for a long time before the culprit was unearthed.

The War Office and the XX Committee were as eager to have me enlarge my spy net as were the Germans. D-Day, the invasion of the Continent, was in sight, and our flow of misinformation was increasing. Everyone, the Germans included, knew the invasion was coming. One might even deduce when it was coming. But not where. The object was to fool the German high command about that. My group and I were among those few double-cross agents chosen by the Committee to carry out this deception.

To quote the man who was holding the reins of the system, J. C. Masterman, "our mood in 1943 was one of gnawing anxiety." The XX Committee chief compared us to a man who starts a quarter-mile race; when he has run a couple of hundred yards those on the edge of the track shout to him that it is a half-mile race on which he has entered, and a little later it is borne in on him that the distance to be covered is a mile or perhaps three miles. Can he adapt himself, and will he last to the finish at all, let alone be in the lead when the last lap is run?

Continuing on the same theme in his book, *The Double-Cross System,* Masterman recalls:

No one can maintain a bluff indefinitely; sooner or later a blunder or sheer mischance will inevitably give it away. How should we feel if the whole of the double-cross system collapsed before it had been put to a test in a grand deception? The fear that this would happen was constantly in our minds, and was increased by the belief, which was probably at the worst only partially justified, that the collapse of one important case would destroy all the rest with it.

I set about setting up my end of the escape route by meeting with the Yugoslav Prime Minister, at that time Slobodan Yovanovic, and his aides. Without revealing its real purpose, I asked for their consent. As foreseen, they accepted the proposition eagerly. Too eagerly. They proposed so many candidates I would have had to run a commuter train to handle the traffic. I had to return to see Yovanovic secretly to tell him the truth. He agreed to go along with the plan anyway and named me Assistant Military Attaché in London, affording me diplomatic status and a diplomatic passport. Equally important, the Prime Minister saw to it that I was exonerated from any work attached to the title.

The Military Attaché, General Radovic, whose aide I was theoretically, took a dim view of my absence from the office. In keeping with the policy of secrecy on a "need to know" basis, Radovic was not told about my intelligence work. As with many others ignorant of my actual occupation, he, too, categorized me as a playboy with political connections. This reputation may not have won me friends in some quarters, but it certainly helped my cover.

The first agent to come through the escape route was Commander Tomas Sardelic, a Yugoslav naval aviation officer and test pilot. He was well known in British aviation circles, too, having completed an acrobatics course in England with, one might say, flying colors. A Croat—and from a prominent family in addition—Tomas was immune to being taken as a prisoner of war when Yugoslavia collapsed. But despite his soft manners, Tomas was iron-willed and a man of principle. He insisted on sharing the fate of his fellow officers and reported with them to be imprisoned.

After his release, Tomas returned to Zagreb, his home town, where his status brought him, unfortunately, to the attention of the head of the new Nazi state of Croatia, Anton Pavelic. Wanting to exploit the standing of the Sardelic family, Pavelic proposed to nominate Tomas to the post of Naval Attaché in Berlin.

Tomas was in a jam. In no way would he accept the post and swear allegiance to the Ustachi regime, yet to rebuff Pavelic would evoke grave consequences. Tomas put off Pavelic from day to day. It was too bad we weren't in contact with him at that point. We could have set him up as an invaluable M.I.6 agent in Berlin, allowing him to accept the Nazi offer in good conscience.

Tomas's only solution was to flee Croatia. He went to Belgrade, where he was out of Pavelic's reach. His immediate problem now was to earn a living, but his experience was limited to that of his military career. Here began a comedy with Tomas demonstrating his impractical but delightful character.

Tomas decided to become a businessman. It was the only road open to him. A job was either unthinkable or unfindable, and he did have a little money. Everything was in short supply in Belgrade, but somehow Tomas managed to unearth a stock of corks. He invested part of his capital in them, only to discover there was no market for corks because there were no bottles on the market. He combed Belgrade and finally discovered a cache of bottles, paying a good price for them. When he tried to sell the corks and bottles together, another problem popped up. No one had any use for them. There was nothing to put in the bottles. Not one to give up, Tomas ran around the city looking for a liquid product, wine or anything, to fill his bottles. On his rounds he ran into Ivo, who was an old friend. My brother didn't have anything to go into the bottles but he offered Tomas a good dinner instead, during which he listened sympathetically to his story.

Ivo didn't say anything to Tomas that night, but after checking his tale he called on him a few days later with a proposition. Ivo, now operating under the code name of "Dreadnaught," was looking for passengers for our underground railway.

"I have a way to get you to London," Ivo told Tomas. "Naturally, it is secret, but I promise you it is safe. Are you interested?"

It was a dream come true, a way to elude Pavelic for good and to get back in the war against the Nazis. Tomas accepted without hesitation even when Ivo warned him there were strings attached.

"You'll have to have confidence in me," Ivo explained. "I'm going to ask you to do something very strange and I can't tell you why."

"Anything. Anything to get to England."

"Very well. I'm going to introduce you to some Germans. They will put you through a training course to become a spy in England. No matter what you think of that—and I suppose you already may have a notion as to what's up—you'll have to take it all very seriously. You'll really have to apply yourself. When you get to London, you will see my brother Dusko first thing and follow his orders. That's all I can tell you."

Despite his innocence in business, Tomas was far from a fool. He knew Ivo, he knew me, and he knew explanations are not always forthcoming in wartime.

Realizing that one way or another he would be going into the service of a foreign power, Tomas made only one proviso: that he would never be asked to do anything against Yugoslavia—again, the invariable preoccupation of all the countrymen who passed through my hands.

Ivo turned Tomas over to Johnny. They got along splendidly, but then Johnny, in turn, had to pass him over to Müntzinger for training. Tomas got along much less well with the Nazi spymaster, particularly when Müntzinger proposed to send him to Berlin to learn the trade.

At that point Tomas had second thoughts. He foresaw certain hazards in going to England as a Nazi spy, even a spurious one. Supposing something happened to Ivo and to me. Tomas would be taken for a bona fide agent with no one to say the contrary. He decided to take out insurance.

Without disclosing the arrangements with Ivo, Tomas confided the escape plan to a friend who he had reason to believe was a member of the Serbian resistance movement. He asked the friend to get word to the government-in-exile in London that he was a genuine patriot cloaking himself as a Nazi spy only in order to reach England.

Tomas's friend, it developed, was a traitor, an *agent provocateur* for the Germans. Tomas, the last of the line of the Sardelics, was thrown into a Gestapo prison and summarily sentenced to death. Pavelic's fine hand had something to do with this as well. The grapevine brought the news to Ivo, who sought fruitlessly to contact Johnny. He was the only one who might possibly intervene. But Johnny was unavailable, being in some undisclosed spot in Germany.

For some reason Tomas was not sent before the firing squad immediately. Expecting each morning to be his last, he sweated in death row, his morale at rock bottom. After three weeks of desperation, Ivo finally managed to contact Johnny, who rushed to the prison where Tomas was living out his final hours. Under the guise of interrogating him, Johnny got to see Tomas alone. He found him haggard, bearded, not having been allowed to shave for almost a month, but above all distraught.

"Give me a pistol so I can kill myself," Tomas pleaded. "I'm afraid the Gestapo will get around to torturing me and I don't know if I can take it. I'm afraid I may talk and involve others."

"Nonsense," Johnny reassured him. "Hold on just a few days and I'll have you out of here."

Tomas could hardly believe him. Although he realized Johnny was somehow enmeshed with us, he wasn't aware of the extent. Nor could he guess at Johnny's influence in Germany. Proof of that came immediately. The same day he was removed from death row to more comfortable quarters, and three days later Johnny returned to escort him personally out of the prison.

The next step was to reinstate him in the good graces of the Nazis. Tomas would not be safe until his *faux pas* was explained away. To accomplish that, Johnny rushed him to Berlin.

Demonstrating his powers of persuasion, Johnny convinced the Abwehr to give Tomas a second chance, pretexting that he had had a change of heart and would act as a faithful German agent from now on. Johnny also invented a new role for Tomas that appealed to the Abwehr. Tomas was to confess on arriving in England that he was a German agent but pretend that he wanted to double-cross the Abwehr. Tomas was given not one but two formulas for secret ink. With one he was to write the information the British wanted him to send, with the other he was to pen the answers to the questions the Abwehr asked. Thus he became possibly the unique double double-cross agent of the war.

When he finally did arrive in England, Tomas tried to persuade us to allow him to join the Air Force. He had no taste for the devious role of an intelligence agent. But there was no turning back. Tomas, under the code name of "Meteor," fulfilled his job as a dual agent until the very end of the war, maintaining his integrity by refusing to accept payment from either the British or the Germans. The only coin that came his way was in the form of a medal from the British.

Another important agent whom Ivo selected for me came through the lines a few months later. Also a Yugoslav naval officer, a commander, he was the Count Nicholas Ruda, a childhood friend. Again, it was a tribute to Johnny that he persuaded the Abwehr to accept Ruda, whose family history was so tainted from the Nazi point of view as to make him a very dubious risk.

The history of the Ruda family is tantamount to the history of Dubrovnik, and it is unthinkable that a Ruda could break with tradition and turn traitor. It is possible that under certain conditions anyone may turn traitor, but under no condition could a Ruda break with tradition.

In the fifteenth century, one of Nicholas's ancestors was sent to Istanbul to pay the Turks the annual tribute for permission to trade in the Ottoman Empire. Sultan Surinam first accepted the gold he was bearing and then posed other terms. The Sultan demanded that Ruda sign a document recognizing Dubrovnik as a vassal state of the Ottoman Empire. Ruda refused. He was tossed in a cell and given a week to sign. At the end of the week his head was to be severed from his body.

Never for an instant contemplating submission, Ruda sought a way to warn his country. He found someone who was willing, probably for a fitting compensation, to smuggle a letter for him. Ruda wanted to write to the Rector of the Republic to advise the government not to send the tribute the following year unless Surinam recognized the city-state's complete independence. Since the Sultan was greedy for money, Ruda judged he would accept the terms.

Now to write this letter—which is preserved in the Dubrovnik archives—Ruda had a piece of parchment but no ink or other writing equipment. Usually under such circumstances prisoners resort to writing in their own blood. A simple scratch suffices. But although he was capable of choosing to offer his head to the ax, Ruda was incapable of drawing his own blood. Instead, with infinite finesse, he penned his advice and last farewell in a less painful product of his body: shit.

Nicholas, the direct descendant of this queasy hero, pulled a similar stunt. Although willing to risk his neck as an agent, he refused Müntzinger's request that he go to Berlin, saying that he abhorred the thought of being wounded in a British bombing raid. Our persuasive count prevailed upon his spymaster to send him to Paris for training. There he was put to studying to become a radio operator. He took that task seriously and learned his job well while at the same time thumbing his nose at the Nazis. Nicholas's delight was to parody the heel-clicking and Heil-Hitlering of the Nazi sycophants. Inexplicably, they never caught wise to the farce and instead treated him with favor as a 100 percent collaborator.

Finished with his schooling, Nicholas was embarked on the escape route. He crossed occupied and unoccupied France in the comfort of a first-class train, but at the Spanish border another farce began. Although the regime was sympathetic, the Germans couldn't let the Spanish police in on the supposed English escape route. There was always the possibility of an informer among them. Nicholas had to suffer the discomfort and, above all, the indignity of being squeezed into the trunk of an automobile and smuggled across the border at San Sebastian, the usual crossing spot.

Once in Spain, I took him in charge, still having to keep him hidden. Any foreign male caught without identification papers ran the risk of being interned in the Miranda, Spain's infamously uncomfortable prison, for the duration of the war, particularly if he was of military age. Our arrangement was to get the necessary documents from the British Consulate. To avoid risks, these would state that the man was either under twenty or over forty.

When I got Nicholas to Madrid after the rough ride from San Sebastian, I led him to one of the hideouts where we stashed away our escapees for the few days it took to prepare their papers. It was a room in a sixth-floor apartment in the slums of Madrid. The tenants, poor loyalist Spaniards, took these lodgers without declaring them to the police in return for a ludicrous payment.

Nicholas took one sniff of the malodorous courtyard, and that was it. He refused categorically to climb the six flights to view his lodging. "A Ruda voluntarily in such a place? Never. Jail first." I gave him a graphic description of the Miranda, the freezing, damp, rat-infested cells; no plumbing, swill, cruelty. Nicholas would not be moved.

A hotel was out of the question. I needed a place that operated outside the law. There was no help for it, Nicholas spent his days of waiting in one of Madrid's ubiquitous bordellos. "I never had a better life," Nicholas said contentedly when I went to fetch him a few days later. "The girls tucked me in bed at night, brought me breakfast in bed in the morning. It was like having a harem. I had several breakfasts every day with a different waitress each time."

Despite this royal treatment, Nicholas literally itched to get out of there. At the next stop on his voyage, Gibraltar, an obligatory medical examination disclosed that he had a minor by-product of Spain's houses of joy: crab lice. He was hairy, and the crabs had spread all over his body . . . and the story spread all over Gibraltar and beyond. At the dinner the governor of Gibraltar always gave for escaping officers, Nicholas was teased from *apéritif* to dessert. Even years later a guest at a party in London meeting him for the first time burst out laughing, explaining, "Oh yes, you are the Count who . . ." and he articulated his fingers crabwise.

But as with Tomas, once in London Nicholas buckled down to work. He became "Freak," my radio operator, and was awarded an O.B.E. after the war. My band now consisted of five major double-cross agents. In addition to Freak's radio, I had the use of the diplomatic bag to transport the sometimes voluminous information from such a bevy of spies.

The only difficulty my band of Yugoslavs occasionally had was with the government-in-exile. We had to avoid becoming involved in the intrigues inherent in that body. Also, since they ostensibly were working for their government, too much absenteeism provoked questions, and we feared eventual indiscretions.

In all, about a hundred and fifty people came through the escape route, not all of them as far as London. Some stayed in Paris.

Müntzinger foisted off three of his own candidates on us, and we were obliged to send them through. On their arrival in England we had them picked up and interned. Then, to avert Müntzinger's suspicion, Masterman cannily simulated the discovery and arrest of one of our own candidates.

20

One weekend in England I took a refresher course in political intrigue from a grand master: C. It was at the Menzies clan's country home, Tadley Court, near Basingstoke. We were a smallish group, the family and a few close friends. C sequestered me from the others and we sat in the inviolate seclusion of his study, temperately nursing our whisky-and-sodas while Menzies instructed me on his pet project.

"M.I.6 has much to catch up on," he said candidly. "We have an opportunity to do so now that your friend Jebsen will be headquartered in Lisbon and you'll have the possibility of seeing him often. The situation has changed considerably since last we spoke, and you must grasp it thoroughly, so listen closely."

He sipped the aged malt scotch we were drinking, savoring its flavor in his mouth for a moment before swallowing. Then he set his glass meticulously on the low table between us before continuing.

"There is much talk—you probably have heard it—of unconditional surrender. I personally dislike it. A phrase. It means nothing. It stands to reason that every surrender, even an unconditional one, must have conditions attached to it. But that is official Allied policy, and I can do nothing to change it. There is something else, however, that we may do.

"It would be . . . uh . . . beneficial if certain individuals in the right places in Germany were given to understand the proper meaning of that phrase: that no talks or bargaining with the Nazis will be accepted but that the Allies want to be guided after the cessation of hostilities by their conscience, by their democratic tradition, and by their honor, not by a hastily drafted scrap of paper that may be contested afterward. One should assure the proper-thinking Germans—and I think they will understand—that we do not mean to blot Germany from the map. That would be contrary to the ideal of freedom for which we are fighting.

"A friend of mine, a chap in whom you may have utmost confidence, will be posted to Lisbon. He is Mr. Cecil Gladhill. Gladhill can be of great help to all those who want to eliminate Hitler and start talking peace. Whatever information you come upon in that regard, report directly to him."

I drew from the conversation that Menzies was no longer as optimistic as he had been about arriving at a peace by circumventing Hitler. My impression was that he felt such a peace might have been feasible, particularly now that the tides of war were going against Germany, were it not for the "unconditional surrender" motif. Menzies' supposition was that the generals and marshals might have been persuaded to make a coup against Hitler to preserve Germany, but that faced with unconditional surrender, such an act was pointless to them. Still, the idea of ending the war a few years earlier was too attractive a goal for him to drop even if it had only the flimsiest chance to succeed.

When I saw Johnny next in Lisbon, I broached the *coup d'état* theme to him again. His response was a horselaugh.

"Why the hell should the Allies want to get rid of Hitler? He's winning the war for them. The German Army high command is absolutely frantic. They're dancing about in frustration. I can tell you, General Halder and many, many others are fit to be tied. Dusko, the German Army's victories at the beginning of the war came about because the campaigns were planned by the professional soldiers in the Generalstab. Then Hitler started putting his grubby hands in strategy and look what happened. First he delayed Operation Barbarossa against Russia for nearly two months by his attack on your country. It was a gratuitous campaign. There was no need to secure Yugoslavia, since there was no danger of a major British operation up through Greece. The English were too weak in April 1941. And they were alone. If it weren't for that delay, Russia might have been crushed before winter set in. But even aside from that, Dusko, Hitler made cardinal mistakes in the first stages of the Russian campaign. He overrode Halder and the general staff and insisted on pushing too far south instead of taking Moscow and Leningrad. And then he made that futile sacrifice in Stalingrad all for the sake of what he conceives to be glory. Von Paulus had an army of about three hundred thousand men there. If it had been withdrawn and sent to reinforce the southern front, it could have neutralized the Russian counterattack. No, Hitler is the Allies' best friend."

"Is he really that bad a military man," I asked, "or are the generals trying to shift the blame?"

"It doesn't require an expert in military strategy to answer that. A psychologist would be more qualified. The man is insane. Look at the Tunisian affair. Rommel was begging for more tanks and reinforcements for months. He hardly got any at all, and then they came too late. But after the Allied invasion of North Africa and the loss of El Alamein, Hitler rushed over a quarter of a million German and Italian troops to Tunisia to hold a bridgehead that was lost in advance. If he had listened to his generals, he would have done that several months before. Rommel would have taken Cairo and probably controlled all North Africa."

"If there is so much dissatisfaction, wouldn't this be the

moment to act?" I was obeying C's directive despite Johnny's opinion.

"I wouldn't want to hazard a guess on that. I'll try to get you a definitive answer from Oster—he's been promoted to Major General, by the way. Oster will know more than I do, and I can tell you he'll certainly be happy to learn that the way is still open for talks despite the unconditional surrender terms of the Casablanca meeting and the Atlantic Charter."

Johnny returned from seeing Oster with a discouraging report. "There is no hope. Any major-general who has the courage to oppose Hitler is cashiered immediately or retired. You need active generals in command of troops to overthrow a tyrant who is well entrenched."

"But even if they are retired, they must have some influence." I tried to sound out every possibility, no matter how remote. "They still have their colleagues, friends in active commands."

"Dusko, the reality of the situation in Germany is sadder than you know. There is a so-called resistance group, but it is centered around retired or cashiered generals. I say so-called because they only join it after they are kicked out, and then all they do is sit around and talk. They can't even agree on a program. Most of them want a Kaiser back, but they can't get together on which of the grandsons of William II should mount the throne or become Regent. They also disagree about the type of constitution they should propose. All that is bad enough, but in addition—and this is what would make them totally unacceptable—they want to hold on to what Hitler has won."

"What do you mean?" I asked, not knowing if I understood right.

"They want the pre-1914 frontiers, plus Austria, plus the Sudetenland."

"No." I blinked. "They don't seriously think . . ."

"They don't think, period. I don't want to discourage any possibility of hastening the end of the war, Dusko, but this is a waste of time. My personal opinion is that only external pressures will bring about a change in Germany."

Still, the decision wasn't mine to make. I dutifully recorded the names Johnny gave me and passed them along to Gladhill, who got them to C along with Johnny's comments. Despite the fact that both Gladhill and Menzies submitted to the evidence and agreed with Johnny, Menzies still felt his plan was worth a try.

During these days of 1943, our deception work involved mainly the planting of false alarms aimed at keeping a maximum of German troops in the west and so relieving pressure on the Russian front. A fairly typical one was Operation Starkey, in which we fed the Germans bits and pieces of information to lead them to believe a large-scale amphibious operation was being prepared in the Pas de Calais region. This attracted Luftwaffe reconnaissance and bombing planes to the RAF's backyard, where they could be attacked easily.

One of the most spectacular and successful deception plans was devised by my old friend, the brilliant Commander Montagu, who had put himself up for bait in Plan Machiavelli, the bogus naval-chart operation. This scheme was called "Mincemeat" and has already been described in detail in Montagu's fascinating book, *The Man Who Never Was*. I played only a very minor part in this first-class mystery drama, whose object was to distract attention from Sicily, where an invasion was being planned.

Montagu conceived the idea of planting fake documents and letters on the body of a dead English officer, which would be allowed to wash ashore in Spain as though from an airplane crash. The papers included a letter from Admiral Mountbatten to Admiral Cunningham, the Commander-in-Chief of the Mediterranean, discussing an attack on Greece.

My initial contribution was to report to the Germans that many Yugoslav officers had been called for parachute training in Scotland. We were sure the Germans would draw conclusions based on the similarity of the terrain in Scotland and in Greece. Then, Operation Mincemeat was executed, and my job was to determine if the Germans received the planted documents and what credibility they attached to them. Through the Abwehr on the Iberian Peninsula I got part of the story. Johnny learned the rest in Berlin.

The Spanish Police photographed the documents they found on the body before returning them to the British, who were deliberately setting up a clamor. As the British presumed would be the case, Spanish Intelligence passed copies of the photographs to their German allies. The Abwehr was completely taken in, judging the documents to be absolutely genuine. The riposte was immediate. Berlin sent reinforcements to Greece, particularly to the area indicated in Mountbatten's letter. Other reinforcements were sent to Sardinia, submarines were ordered to Crete, and the defense of Sicily was downgraded, although previously the Germans had recognized that it was a prime Allied objective. And even in the defense measures taken in Sicily, the Germans were misled. They placed mines on the northwest shore, whereas the eventual invasion came from the south.

The revelation of a German espionage exploit, which subsequently was much publicized in book and film, came about as a result of an inadvertent tip I had from von Karsthoff.

Going over my financial accounts with von Karsthoff one afternoon, I complained as I usually did that the funds he was giving me were insufficient for my growing network.

"Well," von Karsthoff remarked, "we pay for what we get. You could earn millions if you gave us something really spectacular."

"You're exaggerating a bit," I grumbled. "What the hell

more spectacular could you get than what my net and I are supplying you? Short of a detailed account of Churchill's digestive processes, we tell you practically everything of value in England. You're just inventing an excuse for the Abwehr's stinginess."

"Believe me, Dusko, I'm not." Von Karsthoff spoke with extreme sincerity. "Why, we've been paying a fortune to one of our agents, and he is a man of very humble origin and in a humble position, too. He's giving the Abwehr incredible information. And not only information, documents."

"What kind of information?" I still pretended to grumble, sneering slightly at the competition but feeling like a bird dog on the trail.

"The best. Military. Political. Even the minutes of the Teheran Conference."

"I don't believe it. No one in a humble position could get that. He'd have to be highly placed. Who is he?"

"I assure you he is," von Karsthoff replied to the challenge. "As a matter of fact he comes from down your way, not far from Dubrovnik."

"What, another Yugoslav?"

"No, he is not Yugoslav," Von Karsthoff told me, but then realized he had been indiscreet and switched the subject of conversation. I didn't insist. What he had said sufficed.

Working on the supposition that the man in all probability was from Albania, that being the nearest border to Dubrovnik, M.I.5 started combing the entourage of all persons having access to the minutes of the Teheran Conference. Very soon the circle closed around the Albanian valet of the British Ambassador in Ankara, Ilya Basna, dubbed Cicero by the Germans. Cicero was wily enough to escape at the last moment. And von Karsthoff hadn't been inaccurate, only slightly misled. Cicero had been well paid: one and a half million dollars worth of British pounds. But they were counterfeit for the most part, forged by Mr. Himmler. The Germans hadn't been that generous after all.

I found out later that most of Cicero's extremely valuable information did the Germans no good at all. Ribbentrop, the German Foreign Minister, was on his guard as a result of the success of Operation Mincemeat and feared Cicero was a plant as well. He discounted the Abwehr evaluation and never made use of his million-and-a-half-dollar purchase.

Chance, being in the right spot at the right moment, is as important for a secret agent as it is in other walks of life. Chance—and keeping one's eyes and ears open—such as happened when I was being picked up for a tref by a couple of Abwehr secretaries. The moment their car came to a stop I jumped quickly into the back seat, and the blond Valkyrie at the wheel got going again without losing a second.

"It's easier with him than with 'der Dicke Alois,' " her friend giggled.

The driver exploded into almost uncontrollable laughter, gasping out, "Ja, it takes him half an hour to maneuver his behind in."

Alois isn't an everyday name, particularly in Lisbon. I did know one, and he was a Fat Alois, as the girls indicated. My fat friend posed as an Austrian political refugee and worked in a lowly capacity for the United States Embassy. He should have been suspected before. A poorly paid minor employee, he was living at the Palacio Hotel on the Estoril, the hotel I stayed at.

Now that I thought about it, there was something else that was extremely suspect about Alois. Probably because he didn't have much success with girls, he usually would stick like a U-boat to a convoy when there was a group with an extra girl in it. Yet I recalled that on some occasions when he was invited to join a party or to go to the Casino, Alois made some silly excuse to go off alone. Something like going to the cinema or to bed early.

Before sounding the alarm, I followed Alois the next time he pretended going to the cinema. He led me to the movie house in the Casino compound. I bought a ticket and followed him in, taking a seat in the last row on the aisle. Alois also was on the aisle, about halfway down. After ten minutes he got up and walked out, passing me unseen in the dark. I was after him a few seconds later, in time to see him go through the lobby and out into the Casino park. It was night, so I had no difficulty staying with him. He walked along the sea road to Lisbon toward the railroad station, leading me practically to the spot I frequently used for a tref. There he was picked up by a car that I recognized as belonging to the Abwehr.

The next day, the Americans, acting on my tip via British Intelligence, grilled Fat Alois. He broke down easily. His story was that he had been blackmailed by the Germans. He was pathetic in his eagerness to accept the deal offered by the Americans. He would continue his work under OSS supervision. Alois also denounced a young Portuguese who was employed by the U.S. Embassy. He had come well recommended by a bishop, and when he was seized, the Americans found on him a newly made key to one of the Embassy safes. Perhaps another Cicero in the making.

On the other side of the ledger, we at times had close calls within our own organization. A Norwegian named Jeff was working under our control in Internment Camp WX on the Isle of Man. Jeff had been recruited as a German agent and put ashore by seaplane and small boat near the Moray Firth in Scotland, accompanied by a Norwegian of British origin. They surrendered themselves immediately and agreed to work as double agents. Not trusting Jeff's temperament, the XX

Committee decided to run him from the security of the camp, where he operated a radio transmitter. Also on the Isle of Man, interned in another camp, was a member of the German War Graves Commission, Erich Karl, who was taken prisoner in the Low Countries. Although we suspected Karl had Abwehr connections, he was repatriated eventually in accordance with the Geneva Convention. Shortly thereafter, M.I.5 discovered that the group of internees to which Karl had belonged was in secret communication with WX camp. There was a strong likelihood he had tumbled to Jeff's double-cross activities. That would burn not only Jeff but many others as well, including me. By correlating what Jeff sent with similar information passed by the rest of us, the Abwehr could draw damaging conclusions. For the others, who corresponded by secret ink or radio, it would mean their services were at an end. For me, it was much more serious.

I was in London at the time of the Karl incident, preparing nevertheless to return to Lisbon. It was a calculated risk. Two nights before my departure, Tar and Wilson turned up at Clock House wearing long faces.

"You may be walking into a trap in Lisbon," they told me. "Not Karl. It's the Worm this time. We have news of him. He's in Paris and has been seen at the Hotel Lutetia. He's been going there regularly."

The Hotel Lutetia was Abwehr headquarters in Paris. The Worm was our name for a Yugoslav agent who was being passed through the escape route. He had vanished en route, and unlike most of the others whom Ivo sent, the Worm was onto our secrets. He had worked in the underground with Ivo and knew he was being sent to London as a double agent.

"You're probably burned," Tar said glumly. "As a personal friend, I advise you not to go."

"As a personal friend," he said, not as an officer of British Intelligence and my superior. The inference, even if unintended, was unmistakable. I was needed in Lisbon and my duty was to go there. I didn't need anyone to tell me that; my own stiff-necked conscience sufficed.

I played it casually. "Well, they won't kill me first thing."

"You might wish they had." Ian was grim.

"We don't know for sure that I'm burned," I said, still trying to make the best of the bad situation.

"No, and there's no way we can find out."

"Then I'll have to go find out for myself." I showed my bravado with a laugh. "If I don't come back you can put on my grave: 'Here lies Dusko Popov who couldn't live in doubt.'"

Tar hugged me. "I knew you'd do it. To be utterly frank, Dusko, this trip of yours to Lisbon is extremely important, but we couldn't ask you to go."

I went but I disobeyed orders. I packed a Luger. Normally, M.I.5 agents were not supposed to carry arms, the theory being that they in themselves might give us away. I had my own personal theory, however. During that phase of my life I was not particularly frightened by the thought of dying. It was a possibility I viewed only with regret because I wanted to live to see the end of Hitler. A peculiar brand of curiosity, I'll grant you, but understandable. I was completely engrossed in the struggle and could no more think of abandoning it than, say, a Rembrandt could allow himself his final gasp while in front of an incompleted canvas. There was something I was determined to avoid, however, and that was torture. The heavy Luger was my insurance against that. I would shoot my way out of a tight situation or be killed in the attempt.

More resolute than ever before, I walked through the dark on the Estoril road toward the spot where I was to be met by an Abwehr car. I had the Luger in a shoulder holster, and while walking I drew it a few times to make sure it slid freely. When the car came along, I noticed with relief that a girl was at the wheel. At least, I was not being met by what is known in the trade as a garbage-disposal unit.

"Herr Ivan?" the girl I didn't know said as I reached for the door handle. "I am Friedl, a new secretary."

We went through the usual routine of entering the garage and going up the inside stairs. Friedl saw me to the drawing room and said, "I shall tell Herr von Karsthoff you are here." She went out, leaving me alone.

The room was large. I had been in it several times before but had never paid particular attention to its topography. We had entered by the hall door. There were two more doors. The one on the right-hand wall, I knew, led to the dining room, and the one on the left to the garden. It was a large double french door inset in the wall. In case I had to beat a hasty retreat, that would be my best exit. Reaching under my armpit, I snapped the safety off the Luger, then walked toward the french doors. I wanted to see where I would land if I dove through in a hurry.

"Turn around slowly, Popov, and don't make any sudden moves." Von Karsthoff's voice, very soft but firm came from in back of me. He had entered through the hall door without making a sound.

My hand sought the butt of the Luger. I was about to turn, shooting as I did, when I caught von Karsthoff's reflection in the windowpane. He was alone and unarmed. On his shoulder perched a small monkey. I dropped my hand and turned around.

"An agent from South-West Africa gave him to me a few days ago," von Karsthoff explained still speaking in an extra-soft tone. "He isn't tame yet, and if frightened he may bite."

Despite the warning, I couldn't help laughing.

"Do I look so ridiculous?" von Karsthoff asked.

"I'm afraid you do. Anyway, please take him out." I

wanted a chance to regain my composure. "I can't stand monkeys."

Von Karsthoff came back and said while pouring me a drink, "You look odd, on edge. Did something happen?"

I looked at von Karsthoff and saw the ghost he nearly had been. "I nearly killed a friend," I blurted out.

"You and your reckless driving." Fortunately, he misunderstood. "You'll kill yourself someday."

I learned later that both our alarms were false. Nothing materialized as a result of Erich Karl's repatriation, and the Worm was merely AWOL in Paris. He was having a good time and decided to stay awhile. As for his frequenting the Hotel Lutetia and Abwehr officers, the Worm thought it was good fun to have the enemy pay for his pleasure.

When I complained to Johnny about the lack of discipline on the escape route, he shouldered most of the blame. I think the Worm amused him in the same way as our escapades in Freiburg used to do. The Worm was an irrepressible and irresponsible rogue.

"When Jean (that was the Worm's first name) first arrived, I put him up in my apartment," Johnny recounted. "The flat was a bit overcrowded, and Jean didn't get along with an Egyptian prince who also was staying there. They were exact opposites. The prince was intellectual and always meditating.

"One morning I found Jean breakfasting on champagne and drinking toasts to himself. 'What are you celebrating?' I asked.

" 'My birthday.'

" 'Pity I didn't know,' I told him. 'I haven't a present for you. But it's not too late. Tell me what you want and it's yours.'

" 'Really?' Jean asked.

" 'My solemn pledge.'

"Jean gave me one of his crooked smiles and said, 'Then I want to throw this fool out the window.' He pointed to the Egyptian prince, who was dreaming away, probably not even hearing our conversation.

"Well, my flat is on the ground floor," Johnny continued, "and I didn't think he'd really do it anyway, so I said, 'Go ahead.' "

"He didn't!"

"He certainly did. The prince wound up with a dislocated shoulder, and I had him mooning around for another month."

"Very funny. How do I explain all these juvenile high jinks and delays to my Yugoslav friends?"

"Oh, sort it out with British Intelligence," Johnny said, nonchalantly.

"What?" I was taken aback. The words British Intelligence had never passed between us.

"Sort it out with British Intelligence," he repeated.

"I don't know British Intelligence." My tone must have been extremely convincing. Perhaps it was engendered by my annoyance with the Worm or by Johnny's breaking our unspoken code. It was one of those "I knew that he knew that I knew" situations where implicit silence seemed the easiest way.

Johnny gave me a sharp look. For the first time I saw fear in his eyes. I had overplayed my role. "God, oh God," he buried his head in his hands. "You don't mean you've really been working for the Nazis all these years? I must be going crazy. Dusko, what will Ivo think?"

Orders be damned, Johnny was truly in agony and I could understand why. Seemingly, I was betraying the ideals we shared and I was aiding Hitler in his mad war by the same token.

"Hold on, Johnny. It's not as black as it looks," I consoled him. "Everything's okay but just don't ask any questions. I'll explain tomorrow, I promise. Meet me for dinner, right?"

"You old bastard, Dusko." Johnny regained his aplomb. "You had me going for a minute. Dinner tomorrow," he punched my arm, "and a good explanation or you'll go out the window."

I put it on the line with Freckles Wren immediately. "You've got to clear it with London," I insisted. "I told Tar and the others back in 1940 when I first met them that Johnny knew I was working for the British. My God, he should have, he instigated the whole thing. So no more hesitation. Johnny has to be told outright or we risk losing him."

London conceded. Johnny was accorded full confidence and integrated into our ranks under the code name of "Artist." It was like a baptism—three and a half years late.

Around mid-April 1943, Johnny and I were asked by M.I.6 to investigate a purportedly devastating new weapon the Germans were developing. Reports about it came from various Allied agents in Europe and from interrogations of prisoners of war. M.I.6 established a connection between these rumors and the presence of some undefinable structures and earthworks spotted by aerial photography in Peenemünder, the German experimental station. Basing their estimate on the dimensions of these constructions, experts in London concluded that they might be dealing with a seventy-ton rocket capable of carrying a ten-ton warhead. More worrisome was the slight possibility that the weapon might be an atomic bomb.

Johnny's first report was reassuring. Otto Hahn, the top German scientist in nuclear fission, stated that research had not progressed enough to produce an atomic bomb. Hahn was critically placed, studying chain reactions with uranium taken from deposits at Jorhminstahl, in Czechoslovakia.

As far as a seventy-ton rocket went, Johnny combed the Greater Reich from one end to the other, yet he couldn't find the monster weapon. He did unearth two German firms, Argus and Fisseler Flugzeugbau of Kassel, which were receiving large orders and credits for the development of a new weapon, but both firms specialized in the construction of light airplanes and didn't have the facilities to produce something in the way of seventy tons. British Intelligence insisted we were on the wrong track, and Johnny went doggedly back to the task.

In September, after weeks and weeks of fruitless search for a seventy-tonner, Johnny came to me with definite information about a much smaller missile, the FZG-76. The British later called it the V-1, or the Doodlebug. His research showed that the two light aircraft manufacturers were constructing a small pilotless machine, a monoplane carrying a bomb of about one ton. It was in mass production at Fallerslaben. There were rumors about a rocket, Johnny found, but he hadn't been able to establish anything more than that.

When I passed the information on to M.I.6, they came back with literally hundreds of detailed questions. What was the range, weight, speed, source of power, fuel; was it radio-controlled, etc.? Johnny would go out and get the answers, and then the British would think of more technical details they needed. To end with, their probing became so technical that specialists were sent to Lisbon. Short of taking an accelerated course in engineering, I couldn't cope with passing their requests to Johnny intelligibly. Johnny was called in to confer with the specialists himself, but this caused some difficuties and friction with the XX Committee. They objected to his being used openly by M.I.6, fearing that his additional exposure endangered the entire organization. But there was nothing to do but continue the search—the V weapons were more important than the deception program. A successful attack with a new and unknown weapon could mean a change in the course of the entire war and obligatory cancellation of D-day. To avoid that, there was no choice but to risk compromising the Committee.

Around this time, many Germans, particularly those in the Abwehr, started to realize that the Nazi ship was sinking and sought to defect openly. Normally, defection would seem desirable, but in this instance it was, again, something that could threaten the XX Committee. The Germans would presume that a deserting Abwehr officer was likely to name their spies abroad. Their exposure was the last thing we wanted. By the end of 1943, all those in Great Britain were ours, willingly or unwillingly. So we were not only discouraging defection, but openly refusing it. It was an attitude that appeared stupid and unbending to many uninformed British officials as well as to the would-be deserters. Actually, the direct ruling against defections came as the result of a case that did us no harm. It was a fortunate warning.

Erick Vermehren and his extremely beautiful wife, the former Countess Plattenberg, were Abwehr spies in Constantinople when they decided to defect to the British. The case generated a lot of publicity because the Vermehrens were notable social figures among the foreign set in Turkey, and because von Ribbentrop exaggerated its importance, using it to feed the fires of his feud with Canaris.

Luckily, none of our controlled agents had anything to do with Constantinople, which is why the Vermehrens caused us no harm on that score. But they did cause some slight annoyance. They gave British Intelligence the Abwehr's telegraphic code, which we already had. The Abwehr naturally suspected as much and changed the code immediately. We got it again within a matter of days, but it was still a nuisance.

And then there was a pseudo defection, which was a thorny proposition on both sides of the fence. Johnny came to me one day with the problem. Two friends of his were in Lisbon on Abwehr orders to become friendly with the British and the Americans and eventually use their positions to go abroad and spy. They were both sons of prominent men whom the Allies would naturally seek to court. One was Otto Wolff von Amerongen, whose father was the most important steel manufacturer in Germany. The other was Rudi Enders, son of the former Austrian Prime Minister.

"Great," was my reaction to their proposed defection. "Perfect material for the XX Committee."

Johnny shook his head. "No, it's a hell of a dilemma. They're both anti-Nazi, they never considered spying against the Allies, but they won't work against Germany either. Their names mean something in Germany, and they feel it would be a stain on the family escutcheon if they become traitors."

"Bullshit." I had little patience with such types. "How about you? You're not worried about your name. Anyway, I should think it would be a help after the war to be known as a genuine anti-Nazi, to be someone who actually did something against Hitler."

"That's not the way a lot of my countrymen see it. Those boys are going to inherit their fathers' positions—at least, Otto will—and he's going to have to work with many people who have their own particular notions about patriotism. It's not my attitude, but then I'm a sort of rugged individualist and I don't give a damn. Anyway, in the final analysis, they may be more useful in Germany after the war if they're not considered traitors."

"Well, then, why are you coming to me, Johnny?" I asked impatiently. "If they don't want to come over, there's nothing I can do for them."

"That's part of the dilemma. They may find themselves going over willy-nilly. Once they start circulating in Lisbon, chances are the Allies are going to woo them. In fact, in the

few days they've been here, the Americans already seem eager
to offer them asylum."

"So? They can say no, can't they?"

"No, they can't. Not if the Abwehr finds out—and they're
likely to. That sort of story could become choice gossip for
the cocktail party set. There's only one solution. You've got
to short-circuit any offers."

I agreed to do so, but it was a delicate matter to explain
and caused me much hassling with M.I.5. Otto Wolff and
Rudi Enders would have made a prize catch, except they
weren't going to be caught. Not to help them, I pointed out,
would cause gratuitous trouble.

Johnny's own situation had many perils. He had been
spinning a devious and complicated web in Germany. To
gain a hold on influential Nazis, particularly those in the
S.D., Johnny was using the oldest bait in the world: money.
He was making investments abroad and depositing money,
mainly in Switzerland, for these bigwigs. The transactions
were illegal and therefore bound his clients to Johnny. Out of
self-interest, they would warn Johnny of any plots or intrigues against him and use their influence to sidetrack them.

"I also get a lot of information that way for your friends
in M.I.6," Johnny told me when we discussed the advisability
of his financial skulduggery.

"You're privy to too many people's secrets, Johnny," I
objected. "You know where too many skeletons are buried.
That can boomerang on you."

Johnny shrugged. In a way I think the operation appealed
to the businessman-adventurer in him. "It can go either way.
On the one hand I'm protected, on the other I'm vulnerable.
But the balance is tipped by the information I get. So . . ."

"No arguing with that. But anyway, there's one good thing.
M.I.5 insists that you stay here in Lisbon. If anything goes
wrong, they can't get at you so easily," I said, innocently.

Something in Johnny's face, I don't know what, a sharp look, the ghost of a cynical smile, made me ask, "What is it Johnny? There's a hitch somewhere, I can tell by your poker face."

"It's nothing."

"Johnny, for Christ's sake, no heroics. We're working together. I've got to know the score."

"Well," he hesitated, "the fact is I'm safer in Germany. Here my antennae don't catch every warning and the situation could get out of hand."

There was no way to alter things. I tried, taking up the problem with M.I.5 only to be forced to agree that Johnny was essential to them in Lisbon. Also to M.I.6. British Intelligence used to boast that we read the German cables before they did. That was the literal truth, and it was Johnny's doing. Through a friendship with one of the girls in the decoding section, Johnny read and copied these messages daily. The girl couldn't have helped suspecting his motive. Discreetly, she never questioned him, and although we knew her to be anti-Nazi, it was uncomfortable to have her hold both our lives in her hands.

In a way, the element of danger had an unreal quality. Until or unless it hit, it only existed in our minds. No one was shooting at us, and we weren't living under front-line conditions. Far from it. I had my apartments at the Palacio and Clock House. Johnny maintained a luxurious villa on the Estoril, catered to by four servants. Johnny's Silver Ghost Rolls-Royce was like a chariot of Eros, ferrying the most beautiful women on the Estoril—with special emphasis on the useful secretaries of the German Embassy—to candlelight dinners at the villa.

Our indulgences were perhaps symptomatic of the unseen danger. We were smoking more—particularly Johnny, who was never without a cigarette dangling from his lips or between his fingers—drinking more, and sleeping less. I became dependent on sleeping pills when I felt I could no longer go without a night's rest, and I was taking Benzedrine regularly to keep me in peak performance during waking hours.

The very fragility of our existence was pointed up to me by the action of a most casual acquaintance. While in New York I met a woman named Celia Jackson, the wife of a British film producer, who was weathering the blitz on the lee side of the Atlantic.

On my return from the States, I ran into Mrs. Jackson in Lisbon awaiting transport to London. While she was still awaiting a place on the plane, I went to London and back again. When finally she got to London, Mrs. Jackson took the trouble to go around to M.I.5 and tell them that she found my conduct and constant traveling suspicious. She was convinced I was a Nazi spy. M.I.5 told her that they knew about me, intimating that they would pounce when the time was ripe. They requested Mrs. Jackson not to say a word to anyone.

21

During the second half of 1943, I spent much time finding out what the Germans thought of their agents in England. The XX Committee was trying to decide which of its double agents to employ in the most important of its deception programs, that of D-Day, code named "Overlord." Naturally, the Committee wanted to use those whom the Germans trusted most.

Lieutenant Kamler, the Abwehr I man who was Johnny's friend, was a prime source. Part of Kamler's job was to evaluate and pass on to Berlin the information sent by agents to Lisbon. Kamler was shrewd and good at his job. I cultivated him.

Frequently, Kamler was not on good terms with von Karsthoff, Kramer, and Schroeder, the new S.D. man in Lisbon. Kamler did not curry favor with the Nazis, and he at times put a monkey wrench into the operations of the spymasters simply because he was too good at his job.

To boost their own prestige—and purses—or simply to hold onto their comfortable posts abroad, practically all spymasters tended to exaggerate the value of their own men. Kamler saw through their estimates. Incidentally and unwittingly, he helped us in our evaluations. He enabled us to know which of our controlled agents were benefiting by the personal protection of the persons running them.

While nosing about on this activity, Johnny discovered the existence of a special Abwehr ring in Lisbon called Ostro. The discovery temporarily upset our notions of having a monopoly on German spies in England.

"Ostro is run by someone named Paul Fidrmuc von Karmap," Johnny told me worriedly, "but I haven't much of a line on him. I don't know his background and I don't know if that's his real name, although I rather doubt it. He's running three agents, Ostro 1, Ostro 2, and Ostro 3. One and two are in the United Kingdom. Ostro 3 is in the United States."

"How long has Ostro been operating?" I was trying to figure out how much damage the group might have done.

"Don't know. The Abwehr has been keeping Fidrmuc under cover. Even von Karsthoff and Kamler don't have any control over him. They have orders only to collect his information and send it by special courier to Berlin. Usually Kamler's secretary, Fräulein Kran, the one with the cute upturned nose and the delicious ass, takes it." Even in an emergency Johnny didn't neglect primary information.

M.I.5 got on the job immediately, sending Kim Philby to Lisbon to work on the case. By our combined efforts we soon knew more than the Abwehr about Fidrmuc.

Ostro was a magnificent hoax. Fidrmuc was operating alone. Ostro 1, 2, and 3 were ghosts. They were what is known in the trade as notional. Furthermore, Fidrmuc never did any actual spying. He based his reports on rumors, on what he could cull from periodicals, and, foremost, on his fertile imagination. And for this he milked the Abwehr royally and ingeniously, accepting only part payment in cash, the rest being in art objects, which he sold at a high profit.

Although Fidrmuc was a hoax, he still represented a danger to us, and for a while Intelligence considered eliminating him. The problem had many facets. At first glance, it would seem Ostro could do us no harm. On the contrary, he could mislead the Germans. Yet supposing he made some good guesses, particularly about Overlord, and the Germans believed him rather than our double agents? On the other hand, to destroy Ostro might provoke undue curiosity and inquiries, which could endanger our own organization. Finally, we decided to undermine him. To destroy his prestige in Berlin, I sent true information based on proven evidence, which was contrary to reports sent by Ostro.

Kamler, with his keen analyses, almost caused the fall of two of the Committee's double agents and, at any rate, seriously hindered their work. Luckily, Kamler told Johnny about his suspicions concerning the two. Even more fortunately, Berlin and the outpost in Belgium to which he reported both ignored his evaluation.

With his keen perception, Kamler also sniffed out a particularly embroiled situation involving a trio of double agents. It concerned a double-cross net run by an elderly Austrian ex-cavalry officer named Dr. Kösler, who was now in the Abwehr.

Dr. Kösler was a man of mystery. To this day, there are many unexplained things about him. In a way he typifies intelligence dealings, which are frequently maddeningly illogical and opaque. They leave loose ends trailing and are full of contradictions.

For one thing, Kösler was a Jew. How he came to be an Abwehr officer is not known. And he was more than an ordinary Abwehr officer. Kösler had the ear of many high-ranking German generals, supposedly anti-Nazis—what I would more accurately label non-Nazis. This Jewish Abwehr officer also was an inventor and a manufacturer. Or perhaps that was merely his Abwehr cover. But that is only my conjecture.

Kösler started his career as a spy with the Abwehr Amt in Brussels, at the time the most important outpost in Europe.

When in 1941 events made the Lisbon Amt the center of espionage, Major Kratzer, chief of the Brussels Amt, sent Kösler to Lisbon to infiltrate British Intelligence. It was not a transfer, however; he still remained under Kratzer's wing. The Brussels outpost was trying to justify its continued existence.

Kösler came to Lisbon with a Mr. Fanto, formerly a European manager for the Colgate-Palmolive Peet Company. There he formed a business corporation and sent Fanto to represent his interests in England. He also gave him an intelligence mission: Fanto was to ask British Intelligence for information that Kösler could feed to the German generals to persuade them to break with Hitler and sue for peace.

The XX Committee found the prospects enticing and took Kösler and Fanto on as double agents, dubbing them Hamlet and Puppet. Later Kösler added another agent to his net, Mullet, a British insurance man from Brussels. The Committee organized a British company for Kösler as a cover for Mullet's and Puppet's frequent voyages between London and Lisbon. The net became particularly active in furnishing the Abwehr with deception reports on production and industry.

Probably prompted by the rivalry between the Lisbon and Brussels Amts, Kamler scrutinized the activities of Kösler's net closely. He concluded that their frequent voyages and reports were suspicious and that they might be British agents. He passed that opinion along to Berlin and to Johnny. Berlin never acted on Kamler's suspicions. Perhaps they discounted them, perhaps they had their reasons. I, of course, advised British Intelligence that the Kösler net was under a cloud.

Actually, I suspect Kösler was a genuine double agent, furnishing valid information to both sides impartially and milking both as well. M.I.5 cut down on Kösler's activities, perhaps because it had the same feeling I did. Probably it had ulterior motives for not cracking down on the net.

For petty bureaucratic reasons, Kamler's relations with von Karsthoff deteriorated to the point where the latter had him recalled to Berlin toward the end of 1943. This lost us an observation post in Lisbon, the importance of which was underscored by Kamler's farewell advice and warning to Johnny:

"Don't go back to Berlin," Johnny quoted him as saying. "I can't give you the source of my information, but I can tell you for certain that you are on the S.D. blacklist."

The source didn't matter this time. There was no doubting its authenticity.

22

From the end of 1943 to June 1944 was like one never-ending session at the roulette wheel for Intelligence. The analogy is the most accurate I can think of. It was a gamble in all senses. We had spent the earlier days of the war perfecting our system, building it up. Now we were wagering everything, going for broke. The armed forces were gambling, too. They were wagering on us to play the right numbers so that their long-awaited disembarkation in Europe might sweep the board with minimum expenditure.

On a personal basis it was like a continuous five-month roulette game, too. The tension generated by the constant play mounted, mounted, mounted to almost unbearable heights. It was a period of utter concentration, and I was convinced that if the invasion had to be postponed, I would collapse under the strain of another few months. In addition to the strain of the job, the double-cross game had now reached the point where I was expendable. "We always expect," Masterman commented, "that at some moment, all the agents will be recklessly and gladly blown sky high in carrying out the grand deception." For most of the XX Committee organization sitting in England, being blown meant an end to their usefulness. For me, spending most of my time among the Germans, being blown could be much more uncomfortable.

The Germans knew the grand lines of the projected invasion. That stood to reason. They were impossible to conceal. Johnny and I had confirmed this in conversation with numerous Abwehr officers. It was certain that they wouldn't be taken in by a deception indicating that the attack would come from Greece, from the much-talked-about soft underbelly of Europe, or from Norway or Denmark. They knew the attack had to be made somewhere between Ostend in Belgium and the Cherbourg peninsula. Von Karsthoff showed this to me in a clear "Generalstab"-type lecture. Drawing circles on the map, he demonstrated the areas where the British could provide the fighter cover essential to the invasion. Von Karsthoff also pointed out to me other elements indispensable for a landing: the tides and moonlight. It stood to reason the invasion was not likely to take place in full moonlight, but a certain minimal amount of light was necessary for the complicated movements of large convoys without giveaway reflectors. It was equally impossible to disguise the enormous preparations and troop concentrations on the British Isles, which made it evident that the attack had to come on the northern shores of France. Von Karsthoff's lecture, of course, was intended as a guideline for the spying I was to do on my return to England. All these factors narrowed the margin of deception possibilities. Yet, from the Admiralty point of view, Operation Neptune, the naval portion of Overlord, was too hazardous to undertake without a successful deception.

The main lines of the deception plan were blocked out as follows: Above all, it was necessary to convince the Germans that the attack would start in the northeastern extremity of the expected area—in other words, in the vicinity of the Pas de Calais, and that the first landing would be followed by a second one, a much more powerful one, in the same area. We inferred that there might be a landing around the Bordeaux area but that it would be merely a diversion to draw the Germans away from the Pas de Calais. We tried to make the Germans believe that the main attack in the north would come toward the end of June and that the Normandy beachhead (on June 6) was another diversion.

Never did we say anything directly about the Pas de Calais. Naturally, we couldn't say things right out. We had to give the Germans indications that would make them draw these conclusions themselves. Thus we indicated that the main body of our troops was concentrated in Scotland and on the east and south coasts of England opposite the Pas de Calais. In reality, the main concentration was in the Midlands. We also created notional armies, similar to notional agents. We simulated one army group named FUSAG (First United States Army Group), another dubbed the British Force Army Group, and a third, the United States 14th Army Group.

Like in a game of hare and hounds, we planted small signs to lead the Germans on the trail of the nonexistent forces. We gave them information about divisional signs, troop movements, materiel, storage, repair shops, and the like. To augment the credibility of these false trails, we larded them with bits of real information, usually not too damaging, which could be verified by other means.

Shortly before Overlord went into operation, we received fairly conclusive proof that the enemy was being taken in by our deception. A German map, dated May 15, was captured in Italy. It showed what the Germans conceived to be the British order of battle in the forthcoming invasion. They had fallen for the geographic falsehoods and notional army groups we had sown. Their normal conclusion had to be that the main attack was scheduled for the Pas de Calais area.

On the basis of the German spy appreciation reports, some of which I had had from Kamler, my Tricycle group and another net named Garbo were selected to carry the brunt of the deception plan for Overlord.

"You and Garbo vie for the number-one spot on the German spy list for over a year," Tar told me on giving us the assignment.

Garbo was a Spaniard who, on his own initiative, had insinuated himself into the German service and run his own sort of deception plan. He started his career as an independent working in Lisbon. He ran about a dozen imaginary agents supposedly located throughout the United Kingdom, and even a few in the Dominions. He reportedly was rebuffed when he tried to link up with British Intelligence until, at last, his exploits forced his acceptance.

Garbo worked on the Iberian peninsula for a few years and came to England only as the aftermath of a confusing run-in with Johnny, which almost cost him his life.

While having lunch one day at the Jockey Club in Madrid with a Spaniard he found sympathetic, and with whom he was dealing as an Abwehr officer, Johnny committed an indiscretion. He let drop a few anti-Nazi remarks. Foolhardy as well, the Spaniard confided that he was duping the Nazis by selling them worthless information. Casually, Johnny replied, "It doesn't matter, so do I."

After he left the man, Johnny realized that he had been an idiot. He called Freckles Wren immediately, and Freckles got on the scrambler and informed London. Johnny had no logical explanation for the incident. Perhaps it was combat fatigue.

I was in England at the moment, and on returning to Clock House after lunch, I found Tar and Ian, both very upset, waiting for me. The three of us held a rapid conference and concluded that if it weren't already too late, Johnny might be saved only by drastic action. We put the matter up to C, who immediately said, "Carte blanche."

When someone was to be eliminated—as did happen at times—Intelligence never used one of its own agents to do the job. The killing was always done by specialists, the garbage-disposal squad, called in from the outside. We phoned Freckles to tell him to get on with the job.

While in the midst of making the arrangements, Freckles somehow stumbled on the fact that the Spaniard who Johnny knew under an alias was in reality our own man, Garbo. But for that we would have eliminated one of our best agents.

Still, it was too dangerous to allow Garbo to remain on the Continent knowing Johnny's affiliation. He was smuggled into England and continued to operate his net of nonexistent agents from there, but now under the close supervision of a case officer.

After long hesitation, a Polish officer with the sobriquet of Brutus was assigned to aid Garbo and my net in the Overlord deception. Brutus had run a resistance net in France until he was arrested by the Germans. He managed to convince them that he was converted and was allowed to "escape" to England, where he promptly came over to us.

From time to time other agents in the Committee's stable gave us an assist as well, and other deception machinery played a very heavy role. I'm sure some were equally as important as we were. For the benefit of Nazi eavesdroppers, a vast wireless service working on a round-the-clock schedule simulated the traffic of the nonexistent army groups, sending messages from divisions to headquarters. To fool the Luftwaffe's observation planes, camouflage units constructed dummy concentrations of assault craft, airfields, and army camps. And to consolidate our reports of preparations in certain coastal areas, stories were leaked to neutral embassies and from them to the Abwehr.

Amidst this fevered and optimistic ambiance in England, I made ready for another of my trips to Lisbon in December 1943. Like everyone else, I was straining at the leash, feeling I was helping deliver the final blow. In that peculiar and contradictory spirit of British fair play, C saw fit to tell me,

"If everything goes well, you'll share the glory. But if you have any hesitation, no one will blame you for backing out of the Lisbon trip."

If I had any qualms—what person with a normal sense of self-preservation wouldn't have?—they were counterbalanced by other factors. The white feather that would have been accorded me—British fair play or not—was not one of them, however.

I replied that I definitely would not contemplate throwing in the towel. More realistically than before, C warned me, "I didn't think you would, but no overconfidence, Dusko. One false step and you'll bugger everything, yourself in the lead."

23

Christmas eve in the enemy camp. I spent it with von Karsthoff, Elizabeth, and a few of his friends. We foregathered in
his new weekend house near Sintra, a modern imitation of an
ancient Portuguese *quinta*. We drank champagne, sang Christmas carols, and exchanged small presents, but the Christmas
cheer was artificial. Our conversation centered mainly on the
eventual invasion.

After dinner we sat around the huge fireplace. The logs refused to burn properly, so von Karsthoff threw a full package
of candles on them and they blazed beautifully.

"That is what Hitler ought to do," remarked one of the
guests, a naval attaché at the embassy. We all looked at him
curiously and he hastened to explain his remark.

"We are facing the most heterogeneous coalition one can
imagine, composed of extreme Bolsheviks and hardened capi-
talists. We should sacrifice some of our gains to burn up the
most hated enemy."

"And just who are these candles to be?" I asked.

"Everything south and west of Germany," the pundit replied. "They are either unreliable allies or restive conquests.
It would be no real loss to toss them back in the pot in exchange for peace on the western front. No American politician could say no to such a deal. The Americans are realists
and would not die to save Russia."

He went on to play the old Nazi record. Germany was the savior of Europe and its civilization. Germany was shielding the world against Russian Communism. I almost threw up my captured caviar, *foie gras,* and champagne, restraining myself from asking about this savior's slave laborers, concentration camps, and mass executions. The grooves of the record were so warped, it constantly amazed me that anyone could believe them.

Back as I was in enemy territory, Masterman's remark about recklessly blowing all his agents sky high was haunting me. Ivo was a very active part of the system, and he was deep in enemy territory with no recourse, not even Johnny to fall back on any more. My fears were something I couldn't even confide to Johnny. They were too personal. I wanted to get Ivo out, but how justify nepotism? There were others in the same boat, so why should only Ivo be spared?

My obsession won out. Without telling him expressly why, I asked Johnny if he couldn't bring Ivo out with the next group on the escape route.

"Nothing easier." Johnny didn't ask why. "How about the rest of your family?"

It was a tempting offer, but that would be asking too much. The XX Committee would be within its rights to court-martial me on the spot.

"No, that would really be abusing my position. I just want Ivo here for a few days. Together we'll figure out a way to safeguard the rest of the family."

On my next trip to the Continent, Johnny told me he had a surprise for me. Ivo had already reached Madrid. We decided it was preferable to have our reunion in Portugal, so Johnny arranged a quick change of identity for him, and in no time at all, Ivo materialized in Lisbon with a false German passport.

After over three years of separation from my brother, I

burned with impatience to greet him, but an airport encounter in Lisbon was not indicated for such an illicit traveler. Wanting to be free of all observation and intruders, at least for this first meeting, I arranged a tref with Ivo as carefully as with the Abwehr. The rendezvous point was on the Lisbon-Estoril road, and I stayed at home in the Palacio until I had confirmation of the arrival of the plane.

At a halfway point, I parked my recently acquired S.S. Jaguar on the shoulder of the road and waited. I had bought a car to have more freedom of movement. The Standard Swallow was far from anonymous, but then anyone interested in me would know what make of car I was driving, and the sports car had the advantage of being able to shake almost any pursuer. Our timing was well coordinated. After only a few minutes, Johnny's Rolls arrived from the direction of Lisbon. I unjackknifed myself from the S.S. and crossed the road. Ivo was out of the Rolls before it stopped moving, and we enfolded each other in a tremendous bear hug. The three years and the underground hadn't changed Ivo physically. He was unmarked, still dapper, handsome.

We exchanged family news first as I drove him back to the Palacio, where we literally shut ourselves into my apartment, ordering our meals sent up and talking for two days on end.

Ivo began his work in the resistance by organizing sabotage. Some of his patients being railroad workers, he arranged for the derailment of trains. In reprisal, the Nazis started taking and shooting hostages. Ivo sought another field. In Yugoslavia, as in most of Europe, river transport is important. Ivo and his friends developed a delayed action bomb to explode barges after they were safely out of Serbian waters, frequently in enemy territory.

Some of his sabotage was more subtle and vastly more ingenious. One scheme in particular was so comical, yet so effective, that as Ivo recounted it, we broke into gales of much-needed laughter. "You know how the Germans boast about their neatness and cleanliness," Ivo related. "Well, we got it to work against them. The more they licked and polished boots, the worse it was."

A relative of ours was the director of the Egü shoe-polish manufacturing company. Like most production in conquered countries, Egü's output was requisitioned by the Germans for army use. A friend of ours, a professor of chemistry, developed an additive for Egü to mix with its shoe polish that caused leather to crack at below-freezing temperatures. The thought of those "Good Soldier Schweiks" on the Russian front was hilarious. The more they brushed away to make their boots waterproof, the more they leaked.

In countless small ways, Ivo harried the Germans, and I shared with him the pleasure of the immediate tangible results. Sabotage gave more personal satisfaction than espionage. Even when Ivo's brother-in-law was arrested for stealing a few pounds of wax, Ivo turned the incident to profit. The wax was for his father, who was Rector of the Belgrade Cathedral and who needed it to make candles.

"It's not the quantity or the purpose that counts but the principle," Colonel Toeppen said when Ivo tried to get him to intercede. After being introduced to him by Johnny, Ivo had developed a friendship with the Abwehr officer, which frequently proved useful in his resistance work. But in this instance, Toeppen insisted he was powerless. "I'm sorry," he said, "there is no mitigating factor. Your brother-in-law will be shot."

"Shot because he is a Serb, not for stealing. A German officer can steal tons and get away with it," Ivo said angrily.

"Do you have proof of your accusation?" Toeppen asked.

"I can get it."

"Give it to me and I'll free your brother-in-law immediately." Toeppen pounded his desk. "Any German officer who steals will be court-martialed."

Nothing was easier for Ivo than to return with the proof. Many occupation officers were deeply involved in the black market. That meant involvement with local civilians, and Ivo had only to select his cases with care to avoid harming our people. Toeppen kept his word. He released Ivo's relative and arrested many officers.

"Not that Toeppen's own hands are clean," Ivo commented. "He's not stealing that I know of, but he is participating in Johnny's currency deal."

"I didn't know you were in on that. Johnny never told me."

I must have displayed my anxiety because Ivo answered, "Oh, I'm sure he was trying to avoid worrying you."

"I suppose. He hasn't told me much at all about the operation."

"It's a complicated racket," Ivo said, explaining as much of it as he knew. For some economic reason, the value of the occupation mark differed in relation to gold or hard currencies from country to country. Johnny figured out a way to use this discrepancy to corrupt high Abwehr and S.D. officers so as to bind them to him. Of course, it was illegal, but he arranged to shift money from one country to another, making a profit on each transfer. For those officers who had money, he merely facilitated the business. For those who didn't, he set them up in the black-market operation by lending them funds from his own considerable private fortune. Johnny had no personal interest in the transactions and left the mechanics to the others. Sometimes a single operation doubled or tripled the original investment. Johnny also arranged to transfer these profits—and other monies—to Switzerland and other neutral countries.

Johnny worked his spider web around Colonel Toeppen

early in the deal. As Abwehr paymaster, Toeppen was a key conspirator, being in a position to use his Abwehr consuls to shift the funds. They crossed the frontiers with impunity.

Toeppen entrusted Ivo with the leg work in Belgrade. Since his first encounter with the Abwehr paymaster, Ivo had gradually insinuated himself into his confidence. Toeppen gave him the job of gathering occupation marks. It was an easy one, since Belgrade banks were quite willing to accept Yugoslav dinars in exchange for the German scrip they were holding.

From Ivo's point of view it was a perfect setup. It obligated Toeppen to him, and Ivo also reaped a commission on each transaction, which he used to support the sabotage operations of his resistance group. It became the group's favorite joke that the Nazis were financing their own destruction.

When we finished our remembrances, and after Ivo had a long session with Cecil Gladhill to acquaint him at first hand with the situation in Yugoslavia, I broached the subject that had made me bring Ivo to Lisbon. I had avoided it as long as possible. Ivo is a man with a well-defined concept of morality and duty. He is capable of drastic decision, surgeonlike, regarding not only others but himself as well. I was uncertain of his reaction and was hoping that time would play on my side.

I took Ivo to my favorite spot for private conversation, the Boca do Inferno, and there on the cliffs above the waves, which were particularly wild that afternoon, I told him how our entire organization might be blown.

"The invasion is coming soon. I don't know when, but soon. Even the Germans know that."

"The sooner the better," Ivo answered.

"Yes, but when it happens, your life may not be worth an occupation mark. And I won't have time or permission to warn you beforehand even if I know when it is going to happen. So," I paused, "let's plan something now, a way to make sure you're safe."

Those familiar green eyes of Ivo's flashed. "You want me to stay in Lisbon." It was almost an accusation.

I answered without prevarication. "I do but I'm not sure that could be managed. The British may object. The slightest thing could cause the Germans to have second thoughts about our whole net. But I've thought of another way. You're here on a false passport. Where does the trace of Ivo Popov disappear?"

"In Paris. From there on it is pure Jebseniade." That was a word I hadn't heard in a long time. "From Madrid on, there's definitely not a trace of me. Only Jebsen knows I'm here. On the German side, I mean. Of course, there's Gladhill."

"The British aren't likely to object as long as you don't compromise them. I think you could return to Madrid and, with our contacts, get lost there for the duration."

Ivo took a long puff of the cigarette he was smoking and let the smoke out slowly, considering the suggestion. "I could. It wouldn't affect the family. They're too dispersed. Father is in Dubrovnik, Mother in Belgrade, and my wife and son are safe enough with relatives in Serbia. None of them are mixed up in my affairs."

We let the matter rest there. The idea had to germinate. It was already a giant step to have had a conditional response from my idealistic brother. For the first time since his arrival, I went to bed with a fairly light heart and slept relatively well. I did hear Ivo get up several times, saw the flicker of a match, and knew that he was smoking. That meant he was still pondering the matter and I could hope for a favorable decision.

Over morning coffee Ivo announced, "It's no go, Dusko. I've got to go back. There are too many others involved. I can't desert the resistance."

"But you won't be able to protect them," I objected. "You'll be the first one arrested and put up against a wall."

"Then that will be their warning."

I tried to object, but Ivo stopped me. "Let's not talk about it any more, Dusko. My mind is made up and talking will just cause us pain."

Ivo left the next day. I went back to the routine of life in Lisbon, which despite its seriousness, the constant contact with the enemy, the unnerving pretense, seemed too frivolous. Where is the line of demarcation between pretending to be a playboy and actually being one?

One afternoon, I drove for refuge to the Bailonis' home, a converted monastery in Carnaxide. I used it often for meetings with Gladhill or when I wanted a place to get away from it all. It was a sort of second home for me, only a few miles out of town yet with enormous beautiful gardens, a swimming pool, and horses. When I was away from Lisbon I would leave my car there. Bailoni's two daughters, beautiful, joyous creatures, delighted in using the S.S. Jaguar rather than their sedate family vehicles.

Hardly had I pulled into the courtyard than Lillian, the younger daughter, rushed out and proposed, "Let's go to the shore for a swim. It is so hot."

"Thanks, no." I wanted solitude. "Some other time."

"Oh, you're no fun any more," Lillian scolded, and spotting another visitor, a young American officer, she cried, "Bill, how about a swim?"

"Great."

"I'll take your car." Lillian slid under the wheel. "At least that's fun."

"Any time."

She was an expert driver. I could hear her smooth gear changes as she sped down the twisty lanes of the estate.

Four hours later Lillian and Bill returned in a taxi.

"Your car, Dusko, it exploded," Lillian gasped as she ran toward me. "It wasn't my fault, really. We were in swimming and it just exploded all by itself."

"I think someone helped it," Bill amended knowledgeably.

I thought so, too, and an examination of the twisted remains left no doubt.

"Who would want to get rid of me?" I propounded the question to Cecil Gladhill. "It couldn't be the Germans. I'm graded number one with them, and anyway, they'd put me on the grill first if they suspected I was double-crossing them. And the same with you." I grinned at him.

"No, we'd draw and quarter you in the Tower of London. We're traditionalists." He smiled back. "And I agree, it couldn't be the Germans. But . . ."

"But you have another idea."

"Well, yes," Gladhill said reluctantly. "Some weeks ago an American service showed some curiosity about you. They asked if you were working for us. Naturally, we said no. But I doubt that they would do anything like that."

I didn't press Gladhill for more details about the unnamed American service. It wouldn't have done any good. He was the type who said as much as he wanted to without questioning and never any more. I went around looking over my shoulder more than usual for several days, but there was no repeat attempt. Someone must have put in a discreet cease-and-desist order. Whatever the case, when I replaced the Standard Swallow with a hairy Talbot, I kept it not so selfishly for myself, resolving never to lend it, except to an enemy.

Not too long after, another unidentified service got interested in me, but their intervention was of an entirely different nature. While exaggerated, fictional accounts of the sexual adventures of espionage agents have some basis in fact. What could be more normal than to employ this basic drive as a trap?

I was at the Estoril Casino playing baccarat for unlimited stakes and winning about three or four thousand dollars. A group of friends passed by and said hello. With them was a statuesque, dark-blond Belgian girl. They introduced us. Her name was Louise, and the handshake she gave me was so inviting that it was obvious it would be more amusing to be with her than to follow my winning streak at the table. I proposed a drink at the Casino's Wonder Bar. She accepted. I swept my chips off the table and jammed them into the pocket of my jacket.

From the bar to my bedroom was a matter of natural progression. Nothing to arouse suspicion, not during that period in the Estoril. After a delightful end to the evening—Louise's handshake was not misleading—I awoke at about three or four in the morning to find myself alone in bed. Perhaps it was the daylight that woke me, it being midsummer. Or perhaps it was a rustling in the salon, the door to which was open. I listened attentively for a moment and heard the noise of my desk drawers being opened. I never kept any papers of importance in my apartment, so I let Louise go on searching. If she was going to turn in a report on me, better to have it a complete negative.

Several minutes more and I heard Louise tiptoeing back to the bedroom. I pretended to be asleep but watched her through slitted eyes. Nude, she approached the bed and softly slid in beside me. I propped myself up on one elbow, somewhat amused.

"Restless, darling?"

Louise turned on her side and slithered over against me. "Didn't mean to wake you. Looking for a cigarette."

I reached over her and picked up the package on the night table.

"Try again. The truth this time."

"It's embarrassing," she murmured, still pressing against me. "I'm broke. I was looking for money, but Dusko, please, I'm not a thief. This is the first time . . ."

I pushed her away from me. "You can do better than that! My jacket is over there and the pockets are full of chips. You saw me put them there. All you had to do was to take some and cash them at the Casino. I don't even know how much I have. So now, let's try again. Whom are you working for?"

"I don't know what you mean. . . ."

I slapped her. For the form, not too hard. She began to cry but still wouldn't explain. I gave up. As for her, she turned the other cheek.

24

In mid-February 1944, our smoothly functioning organization was hit by the shock waves of a disaster to our opposite number in Germany. Admiral Canaris was removed as the chief of the Abwehr, the opening stroke of a general reorganization of that German espionage organization for inefficiency and political unreliability. At least to some degree the charges were true. We had infiltrated the Abwehr to the point of knowing all its important officers, how to influence them psychologically, and how to foresee their reactions. The shake-up was somewhat of a blow to us.

Johnny came up with the inside story of how Canaris was sacked. Hitler summoned Canaris to Berchtesgaden and asked him for a detailed account of the situation in Russia. Canaris gave him the truth, a pessimistic report that threw Hitler into a rage. The Führer had reached the stage of tolerating only what he wanted to hear. Hitler, Johnny heard, threw himself at Canaris, overturning the table separating them and grabbing the tiny admiral by the lapels.

"Are you trying to tell me I lost the war?" he yelled.

Maintaining his calm as much as possible, Canaris answered, "I'm not trying to tell you anything, mein Führer, about losing or winning the war. I'm only transmitting the reports of my agents."

"Your agents," Hitler swore violently. "Are your Russian agents as trustworthy as the Vermehrens?"

On being sacked, Canaris was placed more or less under house arrest in a castle near Frankfurt. Some of his close collaborators were dismissed, others arrested. Canaris himself emerged from disgrace temporarily in June when he was appointed head of Economic Warfare, but after the July 20 attempt on Hitler's life, Canaris was arrested again.

The Abwehr continued as a unit under the new name of Military Amt with Schellenberg commanding. Some of the department heads retained their positions, and the O.K.W. maintained a degree of influence, but all and sundry were now responsible to Kaltenbrunner, chief of the S.D.

Von Karsthoff was one of those affected by the shake-up, although not seriously. He was transferred to a post in Austria. Later, however, I learned he was arrested by the Russians and executed. He was no longer in Lisbon when I returned from London in April and I had to face a new set of spymasters.

Before going to a tref with them the evening of my arrival, I hastened to see Johnny to find out who they were.

"You will report to our S.D. friends, Schroeder and Nassenstein and," he added worriedly, "a new man is being sent out from Berlin specially to interrogate you. He will be either Major Kuebart, a General Staff officer, or his assistant, Weiss. That's the word as of a few hours ago from my Mata Hari in the cipher department.

"The report you're making tonight has top classification: important and urgent. They'll pick your brains down to the last curlicue, and they won't be gentlemen like von Karsthoff."

"Just in case, then, perhaps we'd better meet afterward. We may have to patch up my story. Here." I gave Johnny the key to my hotel room. "You'll find a bottle of Black Label in my shoe bag. Haven't had time to unpack yet."

The tref with Schroeder and Nassenstein was for 19:30 in a rented villa in Estoril. It was a barren place, the furniture typical of summer rental bungalows, nothing like the luxurious houses of von Karsthoff. The two S.D. men were Spartans, conducting the interrogation with only a short break for dry sandwiches and beer. Without any frills or social amenities, I recited all the information that had been prepared for me in London. I drew them the insignia of the divisions poised in England for the invasion, both the real ones and the nominal, and gave them the names of their English or American commanding officers, again both real and invented. The information was designed to cause the German General Staff to form the picture of the battle order we desired. Schroeder and Nassenstein took turns at cross-examining me until three in the morning, but were by no means as probing and wily as von Karsthoff.

As he was seeing me out, Schroeder sprang what he thought was a surprise. "A superior officer from Berlin will be here tomorrow to meet you. He'll have some additional questions. Same time tomorrow night, yes?"

"Preferably, no," I answered, shocking him. I wanted more time to prepare. I said that I would rather see the Berlin envoy the day after tomorrow, explaining that I had to make my report to the Yugoslav Ambassador the following day and he usually insisted that I stay for dinner. This was true enough, and Schroeder accepted the delay, saying seriously, "Yes, your cover. We must not neglect your cover."

When I got back to my apartment, Johnny was wide awake, reading, I noticed, *Point Counterpoint*. The bottle of Black Label was still two-thirds full, which astonished me.

"All ideas sound naïve when thoroughly cross-examined," he said by way of greeting.

"Are you referring to my tref or Huxley?"

"Both. How did it go?"

"They were a couple of faithful party hacks, not at all as smart as von Karsthoff. Or as dangerous. You got the wind up unnecessarily."

"I may have the wind up but you keep a tack in your sails, you old Dubrovnik pirate. Wait till the lord high executioner from Berlin gets hold of you. I'm not sure you appreciate the extent to which the O.K.W. is banking on what you've gleaned in London. They trust you but they'll want to be double sure that you haven't been misled. I can't put it strongly enough, Dusko: be on your toes."

I held up the bottle of scotch. "This speaks for you, Johnny. You stayed cold sober." I poured us both a decent ration. "Here, nothing will go wrong."

"Bloody sure of yourself, aren't you?" Johnny's doubts and pessimistic attitude were unlike him, so I answered, "Yes, I'm sure of myself. I've been in the game for four years and I'm a smarter fox than they are. I'm alive, aren't I?"

"Oh, you're bright and bushy-tailed, Dusko, a real fox. You can outwit them as long as your head stays clear, but what happens if they give you the truth serum?"

"Truth serum? What's that?"

"The newest wrinkle out of the laboratory. Sodium thiopental. A new drug that destroys a man's will. While under its influence, the patient is supposed to be incapable of lying. And it might interest you to know that the Abwehrstelle in Lisbon got a delivery of some of it recently."

"You think they'll slip some in my food or a drink?"

"No, it is administered intravenously. I don't believe they'll truss up their favorite agent and give it to him by force, either, but they may suggest you demonstrate your sincerity by submitting to it voluntarily."

The problem called for another scotch. I sat looking morosely into space for a while, as did Johnny.

"Johnny, you sure about this drug? Not everyone reacts in the same way to drugs, you know." One of my minor prides is that I am the master of myself.

"Well, I'll admit your resistance is damn good to alcohol, but that's been in your veins for a hundred generations."

"Can you get some of this sodium pentol . . . whatever you call it?"

"Could be."

In Johnny's language, "could be" means yes.

"We'll try an experiment, then. I'll find a doctor to administer it to me."

Dawn was well up over the Estoril hills as Johnny left to doubletalk the Abwehr out of its truth serum. I had hardly slept for two days and I had another busy forty-eight hours in front of me and wanted to catch a few hours sleep, but first I had to leave the hotel to call Gladhill from a public phone. When I told him it was urgent and I was dead tired, Gladhill came to Estoril to see me immediately.

"I need a doctor who doesn't ask questions." I described the new drug to him. Gladhill was alarmed, too.

"A Dr. Pinto will call on you at eighteen hundred hours in your rooms. And Dusko," he shook my hand, "good show. You are serious when the chips are down." I felt as though he were writing my obituary.

I stumbled back to the Palacio and got a few hours' sleep. Johnny woke me shortly before Dr. Pinto was to arrive. He tossed several capsules at me and explained how he got them.

"The great god, money. Luckily, most of my confreres appreciate hard cash. It replaces idealism in the Nazi world."

Dr. Pinto was a young Portuguese who had studied in London and knew what it was all about in more ways than one. He obviously knew what Gladhill's job was and enjoyed being a cloak-and-dagger medico. He also knew about sodium thiopental.

"Twenty-five grams." He checked the level of the solution on the graduated scale of the hypodermic syringe. "That should be the dose to give partial paralysis of the nervous system." Carefully, as though I were made of crystal, he shot the drug into the vein of my left arm. Then he withdrew himself as discreetly as he did the needle. "I'll be in the hotel bar if you need me. Don't hesitate to call. You should start feeling the effects in a few minutes."

Very shortly I started feeling dizzy, then sleepy. With it all, everything seemed gay and funny. I loved everyone.

"Okay, Johnny"—my tongue felt too big for my mouth— "You're on. Make like a Gestapo man."

Johnny started with innocuous questions. Stuff about my background, childhood, then led up to Freiburg and why I had left there under a cloud.

"Did you dislike the Germans?"

"No."

"The Nazis?"

"No."

"Hitler?"

"No."

I was slumped in a large Morris chair. Johnny was standing over me, looking fairly hazy.

"Why did you disrupt the meetings at the Auslander Club?"

"A lark," I answered fuzzily.

"You knew what you were doing. You made political speeches."

"Course I knew, wouldn't have been funny otherwise. Anyway, wasn't a serious time." I could recall justifying my university record exactly as I had in conversations with Müntzinger in Belgrade when I was recruited. I knew I was still in command.

Johnny switched to England, to my activities there, to the people I knew. I parried, denied, lied. My brain functioned although my tongue had some difficulty.

"It's wearing off, Johnny," I said at the end of an hour. "I'm not even sleepy any more. But Christ, do I have a hangover. Worst one in my life."

"I'll treat you to a better one," Johnny was jubilant.

"Either this truth serum is for frightening children or you have a will of iron."

It cost me an effort to speak. "Perhaps the dose wasn't strong enough. Get Dr. Pinto."

Johnny fetched the faithful doctor from his post. "It's the prescribed dose," he said as he examined me. "Do you drink a lot?"

Johnny answered for me. "Like a bloody big whale."

"Okay." I was resigned. I was at last paying for my abuses. "Let's have a larger dose."

Dr. Pinto shook his head. "Not now. Better have a reasonable interval. I'll come back tomorrow morning."

"Too late," I gritted my teeth. "This hangover. If it leaves me with another like this, I'll need a day to recuperate."

The doctor felt my pulse, listened to my heart, and finally pronounced, "All right, but not before one or two in the morning. No alcohol now, and if you are hungry, eat very lightly."

"All I want to do is sleep." I pushed them both out the door.

Pinto and Johnny let me have till two o'clock, then jacked fifty milligrams into my vein, double the prescribed dose. This time it hit me almost immediately. I was aware of being conscious for a while but had no idea how long. It could have been thirty seconds or two hours. Johnny was questioning me. I don't know about what, I don't know if I answered. Then I had the impression of doing a somersault in the midst of which I do remember falling asleep.

I came out of a sleep so deep it was more a state of unconsciousness. Johnny was shaking my shoulder.

"Dusko, Dusko," I heard him from the end of a long cavern, "you must get up."

I blathered a bit, slowly coming back to an awareness of what had happened, where I was, and what I had to do.

"What time is it?" were my first intelligible words. I knew I had an appointment.

"Five in the afternoon."

There was a knock on the door. It was the hotel waiter pushing a tea trolley loaded with the breakfast Johnny had ordered before awaking me: an extra-thick steak, a huge pot of black coffee, and a chilled bottle of rosé in case I needed some mild hair of the dog. He rolled it to the bed.

"You've just got time to get this down you and have a cold shower." Johnny shook out the napkin and handed me the plate with the still smoking steak.

"Fattening me up for the slaughterhouse?" I joked, worriedly. "How did I do last night?"

"I'm recommending you for a Hollywood Oscar: the best unconscious actor in the world. I questioned you at several intervals. When you first got the shot and later when you were in a deep sleep. Nothing can shake you, you didn't reveal a thing."

Speaking of sighs of relief, I never realized to what extent they really do come from the depths, not only of one's lungs but of the whole spirit.

Johnny's eyes radiated his relief and pleasure as well. "If this war doesn't end soon, you'll be the most complete case of schizophrenia on record. You'll be a candidate for electric-shock treatments."

"As long as the Gestapo doesn't try it on my balls first."

"Well, we won't carry our experiments that far, but I can assure you, you can volunteer for the truth serum."

Freshly shaved and bathed, restored by about twelve hours of sleep, I left for my tref with the gentleman from Berlin. He went by the name of Major Muller. I never learned his real name. I don't know if he was Kuebart or Weiss or someone else, but he was a specialist in interrogation, no doubt about that.

Muller was aided by his appearance. No Gestapo brute, he looked kindly and interested. Very patient, he would dissect each phrase I uttered with never the undertone of a threat. He appeared to seek only to understand, to help one express oneself. It was a technique calculated to put the interrogatee at his ease, softening him for the ostensibly innocuous but potentially dangerous questions that would follow. Occasionally Schroeder, who was seconding him, would take over to try to throw me off by varying the pace.

After six hours of questioning, at about two in the morning, both Muller and Schroeder started showing signs of fatigue, yawning occasionally, stretching, rubbing their eyes. My day had started ten hours later than theirs after the equivalent of two or three nights' sleep, but I gloated, feeling as though I could go on almost indefinitely or at least until I drove them both into the ground. I also blessed Masterman and Wilson for having prepared me by putting me through almost equally wearing sessions and Tar, that imperturbable British gentleman, for teaching me to look nonchalant in the face of death.

Nine hours of interrogation and Muller and Schroeder couldn't hold up any longer. You Nazi supermen, I've done you in, I rejoiced.

Muller started packing up, meticulously placing his notes in his briefcase. "One more thing," he said, looking up, "we would like your consent . . ." he paused to straighten a recalcitrant sheet of paper.

Here it comes, I thought, the truth serum.

". . . your consent to contact Guttmann and to ask him to gather some additional details. We shall need them in a hurry, so it can't wait until you return to England yourself."

Guttmann was the German code name for Freak, my radio operator. I gave my consent willingly.

A few days later, Schroeder handed me a substantial bonus to give to Freak. It was reassuring, indicating my good standing as well. Pictures—those on bank notes, that is—spoke more than a thousand words in the language of the Nazi Secret Service. The conclusive indication of their confidence came shortly thereafter. Reversing von Karsthoff's project to keep me in Lisbon, the S.D. requested me to return to England as soon as possible to orchestrate my spy ring there. We were in the last days of April. The invasion was expected at any moment, and there were rumors of a travel ban to and from England to go into effect shortly.

The night before leaving, I had the last in a series of futile discussions with Johnny about his tenuous situation. Since speaking to Ivo I was more concerned than ever about him. But I was looking for guarantees where none could exist. There was no way to do Johnny's job and play it safe.

"In theory," Johnny tried to console me, "the people I'm doing business with will protect me. They have to in order to protect their own interests and their own safety."

"But they could try to silence you . . . forever."

"It's a horse race." Johnny pretended fatalism.

"But if you've backed the wrong horse?"

"I'm not backing, I'm the horse."

There wasn't anything to be done, and talk was useless. This was one race that couldn't be scratched. We spent that last evening together at the Casino, avoiding what couldn't be said. The glitter, the games, the brittle chatter around us seemed like a Roman circus, and the prospect of winning or losing money left us both coldly indifferent. When the last players straggled out of the Casino, terminating the spectacle for the night, I restively proposed to Johnny, "I'll walk you back; to hell with the car."

His villa was about two miles away. The spring night was

too balmy, too peaceful, it didn't seem right for this world. We strolled in a community of silence. We parted on the steps of the house with a handshake. I turned and walked away.

"Dusko," Johnny called.

I faced him from about ten feet away.

"Nothing. I just wanted to have a good look at you. It's going to be a while. I feel we are going in different directions." He was speaking to me in German. I could see him start to say, "Auf Wiedersehen," but only the first syllable came out. "Goodbye," he said in English, leaving the interpretation to fate. It makes a difference, a farewell. Somehow, if you are not going to see a friend again, you want to tell him "adieu," but it is a hard word to say, particularly when it may indicate pessimism. Yet "Auf Wiedersehen," "au revoir," stick in the throat.

I said, "Goodbye," too, thankful for that ambiguous English expression.

25

The early days of May 1944 were a dress rehearsal for the biggest performance ever to be staged. The actual play was written. We were now polishing the lines, making last-minute changes and additions, verifying that there were no holes in the construction.

The recent questions asked by the Germans had to be analyzed to see what had prompted them. The answers had to be created, studied to ensure that they meshed with our deception program and the limits of credibility. New information had to be sent by radio to reinforce the erroneous image of the order of battle that we had already built up. Every man on the staff was working at fever pitch, checking, double-checking, coordinating, making 100 percent sure that there were no holes in the complicated weave. But there always seemed to be something we had overlooked. I pointed out to Tar that the Germans would probably get around to asking me for my guess at the invasion date.

"Well, I don't think we should suggest anything to you. Make your own guess; you've been observing things around here long enough."

I calculated a bit and then came up with "the fourth or fifth of June."

Tar turned white.

"I'd advise you to forget your guess, Dusko. Say you don't feel competent to give an opinion."

Returning late one night in mid-May to Clock House, I noticed light winking through a carelessly drawn blackout curtain. Friends frequently dropped in and made themselves at home. All my intimates knew that I left the front-door key on the right-hand window ledge and that the bar was well stocked even if the refrigerator was frequently empty.

Tar and Wilson stood up awkwardly as I entered the salon. I could see bad news smeared all over their faces.

"Dusko, Artist has been arrested," Tar said immediately. My heart gave one huge thud and then seemed to stand still. I stood looking at them dumbly.

"We had a signal from M.I.6 in Lisbon two hours ago. Jebsen was kidnaped by the Gestapo. Our agent in the German Embassy just got the story. It happened last week. They invited him to tea at the embassy and put knock-out drops in it. Then he was given an injection, placed in a large trunk, and driven that way to Madrid in a motorcar with diplomatic plates. From there he was taken to Biarritz and then flown to Berlin. He's in the Gestapo prison in Prinz Albrechstrasse."

"Prinz Albrechstrasse," I repeated in a whisper. We all knew what went on in those cellar dungeons.

"He won't talk, not Johnny." I answered the question I knew was uppermost in their minds.

"We hope not," Wilson said. "For the moment, M.I.6 in Lisbon tells us we're not implicated. The Gestapo took him in because of his financial dealings. But he's under what they so nicely call 'reinforced interrogation.' You know what that means. If Jebsen cracks, if he reveals he is working for us, every agent he's passed to you will be blown."

"Worse than that," Tar added, "the Germans will read every message we've sent these last few months in reverse. Our entire deception plan will go by the board."

"Johnny won't crack," I repeated furiously, furious not at their understandable doubts but because I could visualize him under torture. "He'll stand up to anything, physical or moral. I know Johnny."

Wilson sighed lengthily. "Dusko, we can't take any chances. The Committee has decided to suspend your net's activity."

"But that's locking the barn after the horse is stolen," I protested, then regretted the simile as I recalled Johnny's description of himself as the horse in the race. "Who will carry on the work?"

"Garbo."

"Garbo is in the same position I am." I argued. "If the Gestapo knows Johnny is with us, they'll make the same association for Garbo as for me. There's no logic in dropping just one of us."

"Perhaps," Tar agreed, "but the Committee decided we've got to minimize the risk, and that's the way they're doing it."

To deactivate my net, Meteor and Freak were sent on naval missions abroad. Their assignments supplied an explanation for the discontinuance of their spy missions.

Inadvertently I supplied my own reason for breaking off. Cudgeling my brains for a way to help Johnny, I decided to try blackmail. I notified the Germans in a letter in secret ink to Lisbon that I had heard Jebsen was arrested, and unless he were liberated, I would not continue to work for them. It was a ruse that might work, I figured, if Johnny were being held only for financial manipulations.

June 6, 1944. D-Day. The panic caused by Johnny's arrest dissipated. Obviously, he hadn't divulged our deception program. The success of our landing indicated that the Germans had fallen for it. Rather than reinforce the Normandy beachhead, they sent the 116th Panzer Division from the northwest of Paris to the Somme, retained the 85th Infantry Division near the Somme, canceling previous orders to move it, and ordered the 1st S.S. Panzer Division from Turnhout to Ghent. To complete this bolstering of the Pas de Calais area, some four other divisions that were expected to be transferred to the Cherbourg front were retained there.

Hitler's Chief of Staff, General Alfred Jodl, stated later, according to newspaper reports, that the situation was even worse for the Germans. Jodl said that not seven but fifteen divisions were held in the Pas de Calais to counter our threatened landing there and to protect V-weapon launching sites. And he was quoted as saying that this strategic error was fatal.

All these divisions were held in place for two weeks while the Allies drove in through Cherbourg. Obviously, the Generalstab stuck with their impression that we were planning a second front in the north. Intelligence kept the fires burning by passing bits and pieces of information to reinforce that presumption. When the Generalstab finally realized they had been deceived, it didn't blame me or their other agents for the error. It apparently felt we had been taken in just as it was.

While the battle was still raging on the Normandy beachhead, Ian Wilson came around to ask me to a "little dinner" with some of the Military Intelligence boys at the Hyde Park Hotel. On entering the dining room, I encountered a surprise, a gala banquet with most of the top intelligence officers from headquarters attending. I was led to the seat of honor and was so confused and embarrassed that Ian had to whisper to me to sit down when a toast was made to me. It would be false modesty to say I wasn't gratified, although I did squirm in my seat at the exaggerations of some of the feats attributed to me. I felt like Horatio at the bridge when General Petrie described me as the man who by himself had held up seven to fifteen German divisions during the invasion. Then to top it all came the announcement that I was getting an O.B.E. It would have been a splendid evening if I could have kept my thoughts on the festivities and not on Johnny.

A week or so later—although it seemed like ages—Tar rushed into Clock House, excitement flustering his customary aplomb.

"News of Jebsen, Dusko. Your ruse seems to be working. We've had a report that the Abwehr is trying to obtain his release. The Gestapo is blocking it, but there's hope."

"How is he? Did they say?"

"Only that he is still in prison and obviously hasn't talked."

"That's not much to go on."

Tar tried to raise my spirits. "It's one hell of a lot, Dusko. It probably means that Jebsen wasn't tortured, or at least, not badly. And it also means that the Abwehr has no reason to doubt you."

"The way you put it, it sounds good. But the Abwehr is one thing. The Gestapo is another."

My forebodings proved more realistic than pessimistic. M.I.6 came through with some more news from its secret agents in occupied Europe. My brother Ivo was arrested a few weeks after Johnny. The charges were similar: participation in illegal financial transactions.

Ivo was arrested one afternoon at his office. A squad car of Gestapo men erupted into his waiting room, ordered the several patients there to leave, and hardly gave Ivo the time to change his white jacket before hustling him out. During the drive to the Glavnyaca prison, nothing was said to him and, naturally enough, he was under the impression that the Germans had discovered his role as Dreadnought. It wasn't until the interrogation progressed for some time that he realized the Germans knew nothing about his underground activities. They asked nothing about the resistance, about sabotage, about me. All the Gestapo wanted to know was when, where, and how many occupation marks he had purchased and under whose orders he was acting.

Ivo answered their questions frankly, since they concerned only his relationship with Germans, and he hoped that when it came to more serious matters his open cooperation and apparent collaboration would make them believe his innocence. He protested that he had been working in good faith for the Germans, and he gave as reference Colonel Toeppen. Ivo knew that unauthorized dealing in currency was punishable by death, but for the moment he could only feel relief not to be questioned about his other activities. Also, he nourished the hope that Toeppen would eventually extricate him.

Placed in a cell, he lived with this hope for a few days. The cell had the usual arrangement, a fold-down cot, a stool, and a bucket, but at least it had the advantage of not being underground. High on one wall was a small window. Ivo spent a good deal of his time standing tiptoe on the stool, looking out into the courtyard, where prisoners were allowed a few minutes' exercise each day, walking in a circle. One morning, Ivo recognized Colonel Toeppen among the shuffling prisoners, shattering his hope of aid in that direction. His only possibility of rescue now, he thought, was Johnny, not knowing that our friend had been arrested, too.

Periodically, Ivo was allowed to receive parcels. One of them from a patient, actually a member of the Dreadnought net, contained a box of a hundred cigarettes. Ivo examined the box thoroughly. On the paper separating one layer of cigarettes from another was a simple drawing, apparently of a locale. At first the drawing meant nothing to Ivo, but after studying it for hours he recognized it as a sketch of the first-floor corridor of the Gestapo Headquarters' building where he had been taken for questioning. Two doors in the corridor were heavily marked. One was that of the interrogation room, the other led to a flight of steps in front of which was drawn a forest, a symbol of freedom in our language. Now the regular interrogations to which he was subjected became his hope.

Eagerly, Ivo awaited the next time he was taken to be interrogated. It was a dry run to study the routine of the place. In their stockinged feet to hinder escape and also without a tie or a belt, some fifteen prisoners were crowded into a flat-bed truck. The drive from the prison to the Gestapo building took about a quarter of an hour. Once in the first-floor corridor, Ivo confirmed the emplacement of the two doors indicated in the sketch. There was no doubt, one was the door of the interrogation room, the other a sort of service door through which people passed fairly often.

The prisoners were lined up in the corridor facing the wall. Each was given a slip of paper, which he had to hold against the wall with his nose, a disciplinary measure that ensured security by preventing the men from turning their heads to observe what was going on. At the end of the line, next to the service door, sat their only guard, armed with a Schmeisser machine pistol. When the signal light over the interrogation room flashed on, the guard would walk to the head of the line, enter the room, and return the interrogated prisoner to his place. Then he would take the next man and lead him into the room. Ivo concluded that on his next trip he would have to arrange to be the last man on the line so as to be near the service door. Also, this would not leave a suspicious hole in the line when he made his break. With any luck, the guard would not notice his absence immediately.

A few more days and it was Ivo's turn to be questioned again. Mainly, these repetitious sessions were calculated to wear a man down psychologically, to see if he wouldn't make a slip and reveal more than he had previously.

On the drive from the prison to the interrogation building,

Ivo counted noses. There were eleven other prisoners. He decided to make his break at the first opportunity before the guard became accustomed to his presence on the line.

By pretending to have injured his stockinged foot, Ivo managed to be the last man out of the truck. He fell limping into place at the end of the line. They were marched into the building and stood up against the wall. About fifteen or twenty minutes elapsed, the prisoners holding their bits of paper against the wall with their noses, until Ivo, out of the corner of his eye, saw the guard get up from his chair and move down the line. The light must have gone on. Ivo strained to follow the guard's progress without letting the small piece of paper drop. That would cost him heavy punishment. The guard walked without turning around. Ivo risked holding the paper with his hand so that he could see and time the guard as he took the first prisoner into the room and came out again. Ivo hurriedly put his nose to the wall again as the guard returned to the end of the line. Another quarter of an hour wait, and the guard set off again.

Ivo counted the seconds. This time the guard would have to return the first man and bring in another. As soon as the guard entered in the room to fetch the first prisoner, Ivo made his move. Five steps and he was through the door. On the way down the stairs he encountered a secretary and casually gave her a "Guten Morgen." Exactly as drawn on the sketch, he found the exit to the street. A guard was stationed before it. Another "Guten Morgen" got Ivo through the door. Probably the guard was there to prevent people from entering and didn't pay attention to anyone going out.

"It was like a dream," Ivo related to me much later, "a miraculous dream. There I was without shoes, without a tie, without a belt. My pants kept slipping and I had to hold them up with one hand, yet no one seemed to notice. I passed right by all of them. The most difficult part was not to start running once in the street.

"I walked a few blocks to where, fortunately, I had a friend living. He wasn't home, but his wife gave me a pair of shoes, a tie, a belt, and a few dinar. The shoes were a couple of sizes too small, but I only had to walk as far as the corner, where there was a streetcar stop."

Ivo's flight to safety took three weeks of dodging and hiding. He eventually reached the headquarters of a resistance group in the thick forests of inner Serbia. From there he was able to send a radio message to London to tell me he was safe. Ian Wilson rushed over to Clock House to bring me the news.

"I hope he has sense enough to stay in the woods now," I remarked to Ian. "He's too well known to go gadding about."

"Why don't we bring him over here?" Ian proposed. Seeing the incredulous expression on my face, he explained, "We have some secret airstrips in the region. I think we can put on a plane in a case like this. That's the least we can do for Dreadnought. It may take a bit of time, but it is possible."

As a result of both Ivo's and Johnny's adventures, my nerves were stretched to the breaking point. I hadn't realized my state of exhaustion until Ian brought the news about Ivo, then I felt I had to let go for a while. "I think I'll ask for a short leave," I told Ian. "Do you know a place far away from everything where I can hole up and just read and walk and forget about the war?"

"I know just the place, quietest in the world, in the north of Scotland about fifteen miles from Tain. There's a small inn. Maybe you'll see five or six other boarders, but aside from that, only sheep for miles around."

In less than a week, my leave and reservations were confirmed and I was off to Scotland. It was just as well I was making the move, since Clock House was uninhabitable for the moment. A doodlebug had hit nearby a few days before, shattering all the windows.

A train ride to Edinburgh, several changes of buses to reach Tain, and at last a battered taxi and I arrived at the Fisherman Inn. It was shortly before dinner. One of the guests, an elderly retired colonel, saw fit to take me in hand.

"There's nothing to do here but trout fishing. Are you equipped?"

"I don't fish." I tried to discourage him, wanting to be alone.

"Nonsense, you'll love it. I have some extra equipment. I'll have you knocked up early and I'll show you the best spot on the stream."

He was so enthusiastic and warm that I had to agree.

Around three in the morning, insistent banging on the door awakened me and I cursed the colonel and my softness. I shouted, "Yes, yes," and the innkeeper entered followed by a policeman.

"Sorry to disturb you, sir," the policeman said formally, and in my torpor I thought, This is a hell of a fishing expedition. "A telephone call came to our station; you are to report to the War Office in London immediately. I can take you to the airport on my motorbike, sir. If we hurry you can catch the military plane leaving in about three hours' time."

I hung onto the back of the motorcycle in the freezing Scottish night, clutching my valise between us and wondering what calamity had caused the cancelation of my leave.

The Citroën and my racing-driver friend Jock were at the military airport near Epsom to meet me.

"What is the emergency this time, Jock?" I asked as he started the car.

"No idea, sir. I have instructions to take you directly to Waterloo Station, where Mr. Wilson will be waiting for you. I don't think you are going anywhere though, since I am to wait for you. I imagine we are expecting visitors."

The visitor was Ivo. He had landed at another military airport and was just reaching London.

"How the hell did you arrange it so quickly?" I asked Ian excitedly.

"Nothing to do with me. C ordered it himself and pulled the necessary strings."

In a few more minutes I was reunited with my brother, hale-looking from living out in the woods, still dressed in rough clothing, and still using the assumed name of Pedrag Ivanovitch, under which he had lived in hiding and flown to England.

Ian left us at Waterloo, and we started out with Jock in the Citroën for the Savoy Hotel. Even using pull, it was going to take several weeks to get the windows of Clock House repaired. As I was explaining the bombing to Ivo, we heard the buzz of a doodlebug overhead. Old Londoners, Jock and I knew what to expect. There was no danger as long as one heard the motor. It was when the motor cut out that the buzz bomb would glide down and explode in the immediate vicinity.

The noise stopped. Jock slammed on the brakes, and we both threw ourselves out of the car onto the pavement, forgetting that we were with a backwoods innocent. Ivo remained sitting in the back seat. The bomb hit a five-story building a couple of hundred yards away, collapsing it completely. By extraordinary chance we weren't touched at all, not even by flying debris. Ivo grinned as we brushed ourselves off. "I should have brought you to the woods. It's safer there."

Once in the Savoy and Ivo's own story recounted, I acquainted him with what happened to Johnny. It was the first he knew of it.

"You worked with him, Ivo," I said hopefully, "perhaps you can help. Johnny told me any number of times that he had involved many important people in the scheme and he was depending on them for protection. If only I knew who some of them were, perhaps I could do something. Did he ever give you any names?"

"I may have one lead," Ivo reflected. "When Johnny passed me through Paris on my way to meet you in Lisbon, he took me to dine at the home of the fiancée of one of his partners in the financial operation. She was a French girl, but he was German, apparently fairly high up in the Reichsbank or the Ministry of Economics, I'm not sure which. His name was Frederick Hahn."

"Was he stationed in Paris?"

"No, he was always on the move. He was in charge of controlling the national banks of the occupied countries."

"And how about his fiancée?"

"She seemed to stay in Paris. Her apartment was on the Rue de la Pompe. I don't remember the number, but the house was opposite a small restaurant. Her name is Jacqueline Blanc."

"What kind of a man is Hahn?"

"He wasn't a Nazi, from what I could judge. Around forty, good-looking."

Paris had been liberated about a week at that point. I was scheduled to go there shortly for Intelligence, so I speeded matters up. The girl was too good a lead to let get away. Hahn, I was sure, must have fled with the retreating German Army.

A simple inquiry at the Police Commissariat of Paris's fashionable 16th arrondissement, in which the Rue de la Pompe is situated, got me Jacqueline Blanc's street number. The house was one of those small mansions that had been broken up into apartments, still very chic and expensive. Mademoiselle Blanc lived on the second floor. I walked upstairs and listened in front of the door. I could hear someone moving about and the murmur of voices. I knocked. No answer. I knocked several times more, loudly. Absolute silence in the apartment.

Trudging heavily down the stairs so as to be heard, I left

the house and crossed the street. Suddenly I turned and saw a movement of the curtain of the second-floor flat.

I returned to the second floor. This time when I knocked at the door I called, "Mademoiselle Blanc, I am a friend and want to talk to you for a few minutes. I know you are there. Please let me in."

Still no answer. I became more insistent.

"I shall stay here until you are forced to come out. If you want to be discreet, you'd better let me in."

I heard a key turn. The door opened two inches, retained by a chain.

"What do you want?"

"It's a private matter. I doubt that you'd want to discuss it in the hall."

The door closed as she undid the latch, then opened fully. Jacqueline Blanc was in her mid-twenties and fully as beautiful as one invariably imagines beforehand under such circumstances. She was wearing a dressing gown which didn't spoil anything, her long brown hair was flowing freely, looking as though it had just been brushed, but her eyes, also brown, didn't harmonize with the alluring aspect. They showed profound terror.

"I am a friend of Johann Jebsen's, a very good friend." I used Johnny's name to try to win her confidence. "My name is Dusko Popov."

Her eyes narrowed, scrutinizing my face. "I have the feeling we've met before."

"No, you met my brother. There's a family resemblance." Jacqueline went stiff again and I realized the blunder. "Oh, of course, you weren't introduced to him under his real name, but you entertained him here for dinner. He was invited by your fiancé Mr. Hahn along with Mr. Jebsen."

She nodded as though recalling. "What can I do for you?"

We were standing in the foyer. "May we sit down?" I asked.

"Sorry." She led me into an overfurnished drawing room and waved toward a sofa, seating herself in a small armchair next to it.

"What I have to say is confidential. I hope we won't be disturbed." I was thinking of the voices I had heard, not wanting to hold our discussion within range of strangers.

"I am alone," she lied. All the better, I thought, perhaps it is Hahn in the next room. If it were anyone else, she probably would not want to be overheard discussing Johnny.

"Cigarette?" I proffered my case.

"Thank you, I don't smoke." I glanced at the ashtray. There were cigarette butts in it. Jacqueline blushed. There was also the very distinctive smell of Balkan tobacco smoke floating in the air, but I didn't want to force her hand prematurely. I tried to give her a chance.

"The Gestapo has arrested Mr. Jebsen and I'm trying to help him. I know he was collaborating with Mr. Hahn, and every bit of information you may give me could be of assistance."

"I haven't seen Mr. Hahn for over a month," she said hastily. "He is in Germany. Besides, I know nothing about his business affairs."

"Mademoiselle Blanc," I said with exaggerated patience, "let me be very frank with you. I am determined to save Jebsen by any means necessary. If you refuse to help, I shall have to take disagreeable steps. You are quite vulnerable, Mademoiselle Blanc. Please don't force me to take action."

"What sort of action, Mr. Popov?" she said provocatively.

"Yesterday, I was walking on the Champs Elysées and saw a revolting sight. Some girls were being marched through the street naked with their heads shaven and swastikas painted all over them. They had been associating with Germans."

With a gesture and a whiteness of face that reminded me of a Japanese Kabuki actor, she gasped, "You wouldn't . . ."

"To save a friend's life, Mademoiselle Blanc, I'd go much further than that."

The bedroom door burst open and a tall, handsome man, also in a dressing gown, bore down on me menacingly, a revolver in his hand. "You . . ."

"Good afternoon, Mr. Hahn," I interrupted him cheerfully. He fitted Ivo's description closely. "I thought we'd draw you out of hiding. Please put the gun away; there's no reason to shoot me. I don't mean any harm to Mademoiselle Blanc or to you."

He kept the gun pointed at my chest. "I'm a friend of Johann Jebsen's, Dusko Popov, as you probably heard through the door."

"Doesn't mean anything to me. I don't know you." He was nervous, a German in hiding in liberated Paris. Probably he was more than nervous; desperate, ready to risk anything, his grim expression indicated.

"I can help you, Mr. Hahn," I said to relax that tense finger on the trigger. "I appreciate your position. I don't think you are a Nazi or a war criminal. Not very likely you'd stay on here in Paris if you were, unless you were left behind to spy or for sabotage, and then you wouldn't be staying with your financée. Too easy to identify you."

He lowered the revolver. "What exactly do you want? How could you possibly help Jebsen?"

"I want the names of the important people involved in your financial transactions. Johnny told me he was counting on them to protect him. If I know who they are I may be able to blackmail them."

"From here?" he sneered unbelievingly.

"Lines can be crossed, Mr. Hahn. There are neutral countries. And I have some connections in the Abwehr. I can help Johnny if I have the right information."

"You think so?" He was being cautious, but he relaxed

enough to take a seat and put the revolver in his pocket. "One of the reasons I didn't retreat with the troops was that if I did I would be sharing Jebsen's fate now. You're too late to help him. Since the twentieth of July most of the people Johnny was involved with are in prison themselves. Those who aren't are afraid for their own skins. They won't become involved."

"What was your part in the operation?" I had him talking and wanted him to go on.

"Oh," he began reluctantly, "it wasn't complicated. When an officer was transferred, say for instance from Greece to France, he could walk into a German-controlled bank and change his Greek occupation money for French currency. But he could only do so for a thousand or two thousand marks, certainly not any appreciable sum like fifty or a hundred thousand marks. He'd have to explain how he came by it. I arranged large transactions for them through the Reichsbank under the cover of Abwehr requirements."

"Then you must know the names of those who profited by your arrangements."

He started to shake his head. I persisted. "Look, Mr. Hahn, I'm not trying to incriminate you. All I want are a few names."

He took out one of his Balkan cigarettes and looked at me calculatingly while lighting it. "You mentioned that you might help me. How?"

We were at the bargaining stage. I knew I would get what I wanted. "You can't expect to stay in hiding forever. Sooner or later someone will learn you are here, and then not only you but Mademoiselle Blanc as well will be in trouble. I'm not going to promise you the moon. As far as I know you haven't done anything for which you may be held guilty by the Allies, but others will have to judge that. What I can do for you is to sort of regularize your situation. I can place you in a position of security until the hysteria of the hunt for Germans has passed."

"That's not very much."

"It's a damn sight more than you have now." I made my position firm. "You can take it or start shooting."

Hahn didn't have any intention of shooting. He got up and walked to the window as though reflecting. He was one of those stiff-necked types who had to save face. He had no reason for refusing to give me the information. Jebsen was his friend, or at least a good business acquaintance; he was supposed not to be a Nazi and he was no longer in danger of them, not being in German territory. What's more, I had arrived like a protecting angel.

"I'll return tonight at eight," I said, getting up. If he wanted to play games, it didn't hurt me to soothe his ego. "Make up your mind by then or start running."

By eight o'clock, Hahn had made peace with his ego and talked freely. Or perhaps he was hungry and wanted to be rid of me fast. With some types, the stomach takes preference. There was an exquisite aroma of coq au vin coming from the kitchen, and a small table in the salon was set for two.

Hahn knew more than I expected. He confirmed that Johnny was being held in the Gestapo's cellar prison in Prinz Albrechstrasse. "The man directly in charge of his interrogation," Hahn related, "is an S.S. officer named Sondar Eggar, but Stawitzki, the chief commissar, often questions him and so do his assistants, Baumert and Günther. They are a couple of butchers, Baumert and Günther, real sadists."

This wasn't the information I had asked for, but I let Hahn tell the story in his own way. The more information the better. I noted the names in my memory against the day I might meet them.

"I've been thinking about your problem," Hahn said with

all the suavity of a bank director. He looked like one, too, now that he was out of his dressing gown and clothed in a dark-blue suit of excellent cut. "I could give you many names that would be of no use whatsoever. What you need are the names of men in power now. I can think of three. The one who might be the most amenable to pressure and at the same time in a position to do something is Dr. Schmidtt, Schellenberg's aide-de-camp."

Schmidtt sounded like an ideal candidate, being the current chief of Military Amt. Johnny's tentacles went high indeed.

"Then there is S. D. Standartenführer Dr. Knocker. He had dealings with Jebsen while he was stationed in Paris. I don't know where you'd find him now.

"To end with"—Hahn massaged his jaw thoughtfully—"there is Walter Salzer. Obersturmbahnführer Walter Salzer. He is Kaltenbrunner's Mädchenfüralles." The man who did Kaltenbrunner's dirty work—that could be interesting, I thought, as Hahn continued with his description. "I don't know Salzer very well, but I do know that before the war he worked for one of the Jebsen companies. Salzer was Jebsen's go-between with the S.D. on all financial transactions. Jebsen never dirtied his hands with them himself."

I paid off Hahn with a phone number: that of the new British Intelligence office near the Trocadero. My friend, Peter Hope, was heading it.

"If you run into trouble, phone this number, you or Mademoiselle Blanc, and leave a message saying where you are and, if possible, the nature of your trouble. Someone will see to you. I suggest that you stay put here for the next few days, although this apartment is not too safe for you. You're known here. If the British agree, I'll arrange another place for you. Meanwhile, you might spend your time writing a complete report on all your wartime activities. I know the

British will want one. You'll probably be questioned but, as I said before, if you haven't done anything that could bring you up on charges as a war criminal, you have nothing to worry about."

"I'll write the report," Hahn declared ponderously. Was he being cooperative or selfish?

Jacqueline looked relieved and begged, "Please don't let us down."

I promised to do what I could and meant it, but she didn't strike any real cord of sympathy in me. Paris had just been liberated, we were still fighting the Germans, and I was bitter. Or was I paying him back for his pigheadedness at the beginning.

"You don't need money, do you?" I looked at Jacqueline in her haute couture dress and her luxurious apartment.

"No. Thank you," Hahn hastened to say. At least he had enough sensitivity to be put out by my facetiousness.

Reviewing the evening, I walked all the way back to my hotel, the Scribe, down the street from the Opera. Hahn hadn't been on the side of the Nazis, but that didn't make me like him any better. As far as I could see, he was an opportunist. He certainly had been in on the mark exchange for personal gain, and he hadn't had the decency to come to Johnny's assistance without bargaining. Knowing that Johnny was in prison—where but for the grace of God went he—Hahn would keep silent unless he could turn his knowledge to his own advantage.

I composed a letter to Dr. Schmidtt. Hahn was right, Schmidtt was the most likely prospect. Basically, the letter repeated what I had said before: that I was not interested in becoming involved in the internal problems of Berlin—all I wanted was Johnny's safe delivery to Lisbon or Switzerland, in return for which my net would resume operation immediately. It wasn't until the postscript that I planted my threat, saying that I knew a number of others were involved in Johnny's financial transactions and would hate to see action taken that would cause other heads to fall. I was sure Dr. Schmidtt would get the allusion. I signed the letter "Ivan" and sent it via special courier to avoid censorship.

Shortly after Dr. Schmidtt received my letter, Johnny was transferred from Prinz Albrechstrasse to Oranienburg, a concentration camp for transients near Berlin. Reputedly, it was better than most, and certainly not as brutal as the Gestapo cellar prison.

Following the transfer, Schmidtt summoned Captain Kamler and ordered him to go to Oranienburg, visit Johnny, and negotiate with the Gestapo for his release. Kamler was one of those from Lisbon who survived the Abwehr office cleaning and was now with the Military Abteilung. Schmidtt instructed him to insist that my services were essential and that the only way to get me back to work was to release Jebsen.

Kamler found Johnny physically debilitated but strong in spirit. Dressed in prison clothes, he was starting to take on the look of the typical concentration-camp victim. His flesh and muscle had melted away, and his head looked enormous sitting on top of his wasted neck and shoulders. His hair had fallen out in patches. But his eyes flashed as of old when Kamler told him I was effecting his release.

"Tell Dusko I knew he wouldn't forget me," was his message for me.

I got a similar description of Johnny's unbreakable spirit from Hjalmar Schacht after the war. Schacht was imprisoned in the cell next to Johnny's in Prinz Albrechstrasse. He caught a glimpse of Johnny once as he was being brought back from an interrogation. His shirt was drenched with blood. As the guards were about to lock him into his cell, Johnny turned to them, haughty as ever, saying, "I trust I shall be provided with a clean shirt."

Despite Schmidtt's initiative, months passed—September, October, and most of November—without any word. There was no further way for me to speed up or force the action. At best I'm not a patient man, and this frustration plus the perfunctory jobs I was doing for Intelligence—mainly clean-up work: "de-Nazification"—had me pawing the ground. Then, at the end of November, the postman delivered a curious letter to Clock House. It was from Switzerland, handwritten and signed "Ulla." The name didn't mean a thing to me, nor did most of the contents, personal chitchat. At the end, Ulla mentioned that Johnny would be coming to visit her in Zurich a week or two before Christmas. He would be staying at the Hotel Baur au Lac and would love to meet me. If I couldn't manage to come, Ulla added, Johnny would certainly write to me himself.

I timed my arrival in Zurich for exactly two weeks before Christmas. Catching a military plane in England, my first stop was Paris, where I bought an automobile, one of those sturdy front-wheel drive Citröens that were so handy in the snow. Switzerland, to a lesser degree, was like Portugal: neutral but infested with the secret agents of all powers. I wanted mobility in case I had to get Johnny out quickly.

Via Geneva, staying in the valleys, I drove straight through to Zurich with the weather holding good. Johnny hadn't yet arrived at the Hotel Baur au Lac, but it was only the tenth of December. I didn't put up at the Baur au Lac but got myself a room at the Zum Storchen, not far away. During the first few days I visited the Baur au Lac twice a day to ask for Mr. Jebsen. The clerks and the porters got to know his name and me. I wanted them to. Quite likely some of them were in the pay of the Abwehr—and others of British Intelligence—and I wanted the Abwehr to know I wasn't giving up on Johnny. As the days passed, I started haunting the Baur au Lac more and more, taking my meals there and even attending the boring *thé dansant* without dancing and without taking tea. Finally, I moved into the hotel and practically never put my nose outside it.

With Christmas only a few days away, Johnny still hadn't put in an appearance. I was tempted to drive to Berne to see the Abwehr man I knew was stationed at the German Embassy, figuring I might get some information from him. It was a dubious long shot, and I hesitated, having to take into consideration that I might mess up some unknown project of the XX Committee. Gelatine and Balloon were still operating, still fooling the Germans. I didn't go to Berne.

On Christmas Eve, long past the deadline, I gave up my vigil in Zurich and headed back for London, nursing a last-ditch scheme. It required the Committee's consent, since it risked blowing Garbo and his network of notional agents. I wanted to go to Lisbon and blackmail Schroeder openly, trading Jebsen's release for the Arabel network, as Garbo's outfit was known to the Germans. Otherwise, I would threaten to reveal to the British all I knew about Arabel. The Gestapo, I felt, would consider Arabel more valuable than Johnny's hide. With the Tricycle net on strike, it was their only major contact in Britain outside of a few independent agents.

The plan looked infallible. I pushed the Citröen through the gray winter landscape, caught a military plane in Paris, and headed straight for the office as soon as we arrived in England. Tar and Wilson were in. Not even giving them a chance to speak, I started to tell them my plan. Tar cut me short.

"It is too late, Dusko. Sorry, old man, Johnny is dead."

I stood with my mouth gaping open, the unspoken words of the plan in which I had so much faith still trying to brim out, colliding with Tar's.

"How?" I managed to croak.

"Shot . . . while trying to escape."

"While trying to escape," that overworked official version of murder. "He was about to be released. Schellenberg's office had given the order. An Abwehr officer was detailed to pick him up at Oranienburg. When he got there, he was informed that Johnny was shot while trying to escape." There are times when you can't say anything. I walked out of the office. Jock was outside with the Citröen. I opened the door and plopped in. "Home." He drove me without a word. I brooded in Clock House for the better part of a week. Before, during the entire war, my feelings were objective and fairly unemotional. Now they were purely subjective, nothing theoretical about them. It is one thing to know that people are being murdered, another to know the person murdered. Hate, cold bitter destructive hate, rose in me like fury. I wanted vengeance. Whoever was responsible for Johnny's death wasn't going to enjoy the warmth of the sun, a woman's body, the beauty of living. Not when he had robbed Johnny of that. The war was my private vendetta now. I was hunting Johnny's killers.

My job facilitated the hunt. I was mopping up for Intelligence. I accomplished most of what I had to do mechanically, not caring about it except where it touched my personal interests, as when it concerned the tracing of war criminals. Somewhere in the heap was at least one I would settle with by myself. At times in uniform as a lieutenant colonel, at times in mufti, I followed the troops, searching.

I had a pretty good idea where to start. The Gestapo was behind Johnny's arrest and his murder. Kaltenbrunner, the head of the Gestapo, signed the warrant for his death, gave the order to have him shot "while trying to escape." But Kaltenbrunner hadn't inspired it. Kaltenbrunner wasn't connected with Johnny; he had no reason to fear him. Kaltenbrunner rubber-stamped an order. There was one direct link between Johnny and Kaltenbrunner: Walter Salzer. Walter Salzer, Kaltenbrunner's handyman and a former Jebsen employee. Salzer, who dealt with the S.D. people for Johnny.

Johnny had been dealing with two groups, the Abwehr and the S.D. The Abwehr was protecting him, trying to get him freed, so it had to be the S.D.—or the Gestapo, with which it was linked—that feared him, wanted him silenced for good. The S.D. and/or Salzer. From all that Hahn had told me, there was little doubt that Salzer was my man.

I went back to see Hahn. He didn't know where Salzer lived or where he might be in these last days of the war, but he was able to furnish me with a graphic picture of him. Salzer was in his early forties, about five foot ten, had thin brown hair, a receding forehead, and small blue eyes, wore glasses, and was fairly corpulent. He had a saber scar on his left cheek, which deformed his smile, and his left hand was so badly burned that he almost always wore gloves. If ever I came upon Salzer, there would be no mistaking him.

When the war ended in May, I set out to scour the whole of Germany. At the wheel of a jeep I crisscrossed the country, visited all the zones—British, American, French, and Russian—inspecting every camp, every prison where S.S. or S.D. officers were being held. Deliberately, I would stay around for roll call, scrutinizing every man for a saber scar that deformed his smile, for the badly burned left hand.

In searching through the records in each camp, I pulled out the cards of every officer who had had something to do with France. Then I would have the man brought to me for questioning. I must have interrogated a few hundred of them. Some admitted having known Salzer, but not one knew, or admitted knowing, where he was. Others said they thought he was dead. Some deliberately gave me false leads, undoubtedly out of a sense of solidarity.

I also checked with the German civilian authorities, visiting the police registration office in every city and town through which I passed. Nowhere was there a record of Walter Salzer. If anyone knew of Walter Salzer, he wasn't talking, and I tried every means possible. In postwar Germany, where a few cigarettes would buy a woman or a family heirloom, I must have distributed half a wagonload without results.

Kaltenbrunner was the one man who might have had the information I wanted, and he was unapproachable. He was being held in the Wiësbaden jail as one of the principal war criminals, and all contact with him was forbidden. I was advised to pose my questions through official channels, but that wasn't the route I wanted to travel. Johnny's killer was mine.

On my rounds, I arrived in Freiburg, haunted by the memories of our university days. Freiburg was in the French zone, and war criminals were the province of the Deuxieme Bureau, as their Intelligence section is known. I checked in with the commanding officer, a major, who furnished me with a list of about two hundred suspects rounded up in the area.

Seated at a desk temporarily assigned to me, I started going through the cards, extracting those of officers who had been in France. About halfway through, I came upon a card that had the name Friedrich von Kaghaneck on it. No room for error, only one man in the world bore that name. It was a shock to find him on a list of suspected war criminals— almost unbelievable.

Extracting Freddy's card and those of three others, I returned to see the major and asked to be taken to see the four prisoners. Although at that point I was only interested in seeing Freddy, I couldn't single him out. It would appear strange that a British colonel should have a close personal relationship with a suspected Nazi war criminal. I was a complete stranger to the French major, he having accepted me simply on the presentation of my identification papers.

"I'll call the jail and have them brought here," the major offered.

"No need to bother," I said. "I prefer to see them alone in their cells." The truth was I didn't want Freddy to be confronted with me unexpectedly in front of witnesses.

"Very well," the major agreed, "but this von Kaghaneck chap may be dangerous. He's scheduled to be condemned to death, and you never know . . ."

"What's the charge against him?" I pretended only professional interest.

"He was head of the S.D. in Monte Carlo and is responsible for sending many of our people to concentration camps or to their death."

Head of the S.D. in Monte Carlo! I had imagined Freddy safe in his berth in the Vatican all throughout the war. Johnny and I had never discussed him after our meeting in Rome, and I don't know if he was aware of Freddy's assignment to Monaco.

The Freiburg prison hadn't changed for better or worse during the war. It was still the ugly place that I remembered from my days of incarceration there. Except that the jailors had changed. A French captain and two sergeants conducted me to the cells. I left Freddy for last, interrogating each of the others alone in his cell. One of them admitted knowing Salzer, but that's all he knew. Or all I could get out of him.

"We'd better not leave you alone with this one," the Captain said as we stopped outside Freddy's cell. "He's dangerous."

"My responsibility," I said. "Just make him stand face to the wall and leave us."

The two sergeants unlocked the heavy steel door and entered the cell, coming out again after a few seconds.

"He's all yours."

I walked in and closed the door after me. The cell was

similar to the one I had been in. A high window, an iron cot, a stool, and an unadorned toilet. Freddy was standing with his face to the wall.

"Freddy," I said softly, "don't show any excitement. It's Dusko Popov. You can turn around now but careful how you act."

"Dusko!" he said in an explosive whisper. "But what are you doing in that?" Freddy pointed at my uniform. It seemed to astonish him as much as my presence. It was the only time I ever saw the Graf von Kaghaneck's composure ruffled.

"Don't look for explanations now, Freddy. I'm here to help you if I can. Tell me about yourself."

I offered him a cigarette, then turned out my pockets to leave him all the packs and the bars of chocolate I usually carried with me. Freddy puffed deeply, and we both sat down, he on the cot, I on the stool.

"It's true I was the chief of the S.D. in Monte Carlo. Not of my own choosing," Freddy explained. "But luckily it was me. I did what I could. I saved some people, but it was impossible to save them all. That would have only resulted in my removal and someone worse in my place."

"Can you prove what you're saying, Freddy?"

"These idiots haven't allowed me to," Freddy said angrily. "They won't let me communicate with anyone. I managed to get a number of people, most of them Jews, away to North Africa and arranged hiding places for others. If I could write letters, I know I could find them. Many of them were prominent."

I arranged for Freddy to send about twenty letters. The people he had helped replied, giving their thanks for his having saved their lives. Some of the letters contained money in repayment of funds Freddy had given those who were broke. Freddy was exonerated on all counts and freed.

26

Clutching at straws, having exhausted normal channels, I decided to try to trace Salzer through his past. I drove to Hamburg, where he had worked for one of the Jebsen family's main companies. The firm's offices were in the Avelhofstrasse in the center of the city, and I found nothing left of the building but a mass of rubble. Allied bombings had destroyed half of that important port city and practically the whole of the Avelhofstrasse.

I sat in my jeep and stared at the pile of brick and mortar. Walter Salzer had once worked there. His name, his address, his *curriculum vitae* had been in a filing cabinet somewhere in that wreck of a building.

As I tried to figure out what to do next, a child mysteriously materialized from the ruins of a building across the street. I got out to investigate and discovered an entrance to the cellar, half hidden by a pile of charred stone.

"You live here?" I asked the child.

"Yes, my father is the janitor . . . was the janitor."

I gave the boy a chocolate bar.

"Call him up here for me."

The chocolate worked its miracle. The boy ducked into the cellar and returned immediately with a man who looked too old to be his father. Literally, he had been through the wars. A pack of Players in my hand, I asked if he knew anyone who could tell me about the former tenants of the building opposite.

"Herr Mayerdorf, my former colleague." His eyes never left the cigarettes. "He is living with his daughter-in-law in the suburbs—in Marienthal, Am Neumarkt 27."

Herr Mayerdorf, I found, occupied a decent apartment, and the sight of a packet of Players didn't stir his memory. He couldn't remember Walter Salzer, although he had worked for the firm for over ten years. A carton of Chesterfields and a promise of more gave him total recall.

"Ah yes, Herr Salzer. He hasn't been with the firm since 1939, I remember now. No, I don't know where he lives, but maybe the Herr Direktor, Dr. Ziegler, would know. Herr Salzer was friendly with Dr. Ziegler. He used to visit him at home."

"Where is that?"

He shook his head. "Dr. Ziegler has moved to Cologne. I don't know the address."

Every German was supposed to be registered with the police of his community. I made the eight-hour drive to Cologne but had to wait till the following morning to see the undernourished clerk in charge of the registration cards. Dr. Ziegler, he found, had moved back to Hamburg.

Following the same procedure, I got Ziegler's new address in Hamburg. The mighty had fallen. Ziegler occupied one room in what formerly had been a private house. He wasn't in, but his haus-hälterin was glad to gossip for a few bars of chocolate.

"I'm not really looking for Dr. Ziegler," I lied to the landlady. "I'm looking for my sister-in-law. She is married to a man who used to work in the same firm as Dr. Ziegler, Herr Salzer."

No, she didn't know Herr Salzer, but when I described the burned hand and the saber scar, she recalled him.

"Yes, a man of that description came to see Dr. Ziegler shortly after he moved in here. He even spent the night with the Herr Doktor. He couldn't leave because it was after curfew."

That was all she knew about him, but it gave me something to go on. Salzer was alive. The bombs had spared him, and he hadn't been swallowed up in a Russian prison camp.

This time I wasn't going to rely on a carton of cigarettes. I rushed to the British Military Intelligence office. The C.O. was Captain Clive Aldridge, a cousin of Ian Wilson's, which saved a lot of precious time. With a minimum of explanation, I asked for two reliable soldiers, motorized, and the use of an office for twenty-four hours.

I instructed the two men to go to Ziegler's house and pick him up as soon as he returned. They were to take him to Military Intelligence and not allow him to speak to anyone.

"You'll find me in the Officers' Club," I instructed.

Several times during that afternoon I had to restrain myself from going to Ziegler's place, the two soldiers not returning until the evening. They found me having dinner in the club. "We have him locked up in the Military Arrest Room," they reported. "He was out all day."

"Fine, thank you." I felt like a spider contemplating his dinner. "Let him spend the night there. It'll soften him up. Please report to me in my office at nine tomorrow morning."

The office Captain Aldridge placed at my disposal was exactly the window dressing I wanted. It was huge and well-furnished, I imagine one of the few of its kind in bombed-out Hamburg. A real director's office, heavy with leather and dark polished wood. If I could prejudge Ziegler's type correctly, it would impress my authority upon him. I was going to need every advantage I could find to get him to open up. A smartly uniformed A.T.S. sat before a typewriter in the outer office. I explained my requirements to her.

"I shall be interrogating a man here this morning, and I want him to have the impression that I'm a regular staff officer. Please ring through to me from time to time and never mind the nonsense I say to you. Also, it would be a good idea if you came in occasionally to give me a file or a paper to sign. And dress up the desk in there, give me a few dossiers, some papers, anything you can find."

The A.T.S. enjoyed the game. She prepared the office in no time, piling the desk high with files. Selecting the thickest one, I placed it before me and wrote SALZER on it in block letters. The two soldiers appeared a few minutes later for their instructions.

"Bring the prisoner up, but first try to find out of he speaks English."

"No doubt about that, sir. He squawked like a real toff last night when we brought him in. Speaks better than I do," the corporal answered.

"Good man. Put on a show for him. Prod him a bit."

They returned marching the former Herr Direktor into the office at a clip that ruffled his dignity.

"Mr. Ziegler, sir." Their hands quivered in salute.

I pretended to be reading the file. It may be an old trick, but it does disconcert.

"I protest strongly . . ." Ziegler began in German.

"Shut up," I cut him off, also in German. "Sit down and wait till you are spoken to."

He sat in the hard-backed wooden chair I indicated in front of the desk. He was in his late fifties, small, slim, and dark. He hadn't been allowed to shave, and the stubble on his face made him look—and undoubtedly feel—shabby. He also looked frightened, for all his arrogance, but there was no doubt that he was intelligent. He wouldn't have been a director of a Jebsen company otherwise.

Still pretending to read, I held the file so that he could see its title. Then, opening it in front of me and picking up a pen, I asked in German, "You know Walter Salzer?"

"Yes. He used to work for our firm," he answered readily.

"When did you see him last?"

"End of 1944, here in Hamburg."

I tapped the file. "He visited you at your home about a month ago, Herr Ziegler." I got up and walked around the desk to stand looking down at him. "No more lies. Where is Walter Salzer now? What is his address?"

"I don't know."

"Ziegler, perhaps you don't understand. I want Salzer. I know you know where he is, and you'll never walk out of here unless you tell me. If you don't cooperate, I'll find him another way, but it will take longer. You're intelligent enough to understand I won't be kindly disposed toward you." I strolled back to my seat and looked at him. "Now, where is Salzer?"

Ziegler looked worried but he probably didn't quite believe I would do anything to him. "I told you I don't know where he is," he blustered. "Your threats can't change that. I have nothing I can tell you. Besides that, what you are doing to me is illegal. Who is your superior? I shall complain to him."

"Get up, Ziegler," I ordered roughly. "Go over to the wall and stand with your face to it. Go on," I snapped as he was about to protest again, "or shall I have the guard help you?"

He tried to comply with dignity, but no man can be very dignified being placed in a corner like a naughty schoolboy.

"You have a half hour to change your mind."

I busied myself pretending to read, answering a telephone call from the A.T.S., and signing some dummy letters she brought in. I passed her a hastily scribbled note saying I would be placing a dummy call to London. She was merely to stay on the line and not be amazed at anything I might say.

At the end of the allotted time I said, "Half hour, Ziegler. Anything to tell me?"

He didn't turn his head, and his unnaturally high voice bounced back from the wall. "I don't know anything."

I don't know what made him so stubborn. Was it loyalty, was he defying the conqueror, or did he fear being implicated himself?

I picked up the telephone. "Miss Harley, get me London, priority call. I want to speak to General Menzies."

She rang back in a few minutes. "General Menzies on the line, sir."

I said, "Thank you, Miss Harley," then, with listening pauses, "Good morning, sir. . . . Yes, sir, I'm working on it. I have a civilian in my office now, sir, who knows where Salzer is, but he won't talk. . . . No, I caught him lying, there's no doubt about it, he knows where Salzer is. . . . No, I don't think I can break him down, sir, not even that way. Either he's a dyed-in-the-wool Nazi or he has something to hide himself. Anyway, I don't believe we need him. I have another lead. Should have an answer in a few days. . . . Very well, sir, but I should like your consent about the man I have here. There's no charge we can make against him, so I can't hold him, not without the risk of a stink being made. But I can't let him go either. He'd warn Salzer. Matter of fact, he might even find a way of warning him if we hold him. You know these prison tom-toms. I would like to have a free hand. . . . Yes, sir, splendid. I certainly shall take all the necessary precautions."

I rang off, then jiggled the bar to get Miss Harley again. This time I asked for a nonexistent Captain Smith.

"Bill?" I went into my soliloquy again. "I have a case for the garbage disposal unit. . . . Yes, I have an okay from the boss. . . . As soon as possible . . . but it has to look like an accident. And look, take him right out of here. He isn't booked, and I don't want him seen any more than is necessary. I'll hold him in my office till you can arrange things. . . . Right, we'll have a drink on it. See you at dinner."

I went back to my supposed work. Ziegler didn't say a thing. A half hour passed, an hour. He stood there without moving. I was sure he was calling my bluff. Perhaps my acting wasn't very convincing or my scenario was weak or he knew or guessed that we didn't use such methods. I glared at his back. One way or another he was going to tell me what I wanted to know, but I didn't like the thought of the methods that would have to be employed.

At eleven fifteen he cleared his throat. "May I talk to you, please?"

"Only if you've decided to tell me what I want to know."

"What will happen to me if I help?"

"You know that better than I do. If you're not guilty of anything from the Allied point of view, you'll be released."

"Then I want to speak."

"Come over here and sit down."

Ziegler turned around and walked uncertainly toward the desk. My skit had touched its audience. He was gray and sweating.

"Ziegler," I said, "I'm not interested in you. Tell me where Salzer is, and you can walk out of here a free man as soon as I check your story."

His lips quivered. "Salzer is hiding in a house called 'Schloss' on the outskirts of Minden. He goes under the name of Ingenieur Hugo Ulrich."

"Do you know what happened to Johann Jebsen?"

"He was killed in a concentration camp. Salzer told me. He said Kaltenbrunner ordered it. Herr Jebsen knew too much about some currency deals."

"Who thought he knew too much? Salzer or Kaltenbrunner?"

"That I wouldn't know."

"Is Salzer living with someone at 'Schloss'?"

"No, he lives alone. He rented a room there."

I called the corporal and had Ziegler escorted back to his cell, then I arranged with Aldrich to turn him free the following night if there was no news from me.

27

Killing a German in Germany in August 1945 presented no difficulties. Many accounts were being settled, and in the state of turmoil that existed no one was going to carry an investigation very far. Particularly when it concerned a war criminal. I acted cautiously primarily to avoid a scandal that might reflect on Intelligence. I wasn't in the least concerned about my own reputation, no more than I would be if I were exterminating a nest of rats.

That evening I set up my alibi. I drove to Bad Oenhausen, where the main headquarters of British Intelligence were located. Bad Oenhausen was about four hours from Hamburg and one hour the other side of Minden. At headquarters I dined with several officers and then went to bed early, saying I wanted to leave for Paris early in the morning so as to arrive there by nightfall.

I occupied an enormous mansion in Paris requisitioned for me by the army, as was the practice. During the war it had been seized for the residence of a high German officer, and its owner hadn't yet returned. The house was far too large for my own personal use and had become a way station for a crowd of Dubrovnik refugees. I knew my guests would testify willingly that I had arrived in Paris at any hour or day I specified.

At five in the morning, I was on the road for Minden. Oc-

casionally I crossed or caught up with another military ve-
hicle, but a jeep and a man in uniform were the most
anonymous things in the world. On the outskirts of Minden
the highway passed through a large wood and at one point I
found a dirt track which suited my purpose. It ended in the
thick of the forest and was probably a fire lane. It didn't lead
to a house or have any other justification. The weeds in the
middle of the track looked as though they had been undisturbed for ages.

Minden was a port city of less than fifty thousand at the
junction of two canals. There wasn't too much of it left
standing. To get my bearings, I circled through the center of
the old town. Its eleventh-century cathedral had fallen down
and the thirteenth-century city hall was a broken shell. Minden felt as empty and devastated as I did. I experienced no
elation even though my quarry was in sight.

Not wanting to ask my way, I quartered the suburbs for
about an hour until I came upon the 'Schloss.' It was a large
house, not difficult to spot. I knocked at the gatekeeper's
lodge and asked for Herr Ingenieur Ulrich.

"First floor, fourth door on the left," the hausmeisterin
called out, "but he's not in. He's out shopping. I saw him go
by with his basket. Can you come back later?"

"I prefer to wait," I said, choosing a chair in the hall that
gave me a good view of the entrance, the lodge, and the wide
staircase.

"It may be a long time," the woman said. "Shopping nowadays . . ." She shrugged her shoulders expressively.

It was a long wait, but I was prepared to stay forever to
meet Herr Salzer. I noticed that it was a lovely August morning, and it seemed the greatest of ironies. I was thinking of
Johnny, and it didn't seem just that his murderer should be
alive and enjoying it. How could the sun shine on him? I
wanted a Walkyrian storm and freezing cold.

Many people passed, mainly elderly or children. They looked at me covertly, astonished to see a British lieutenant colonel seated in the hall, and scurried on. I smoked one cigarette after another, covering the floor with butts. Around noon I opened the small overnight case I was carrying. One couldn't leave anything in an open jeep. In it were a couple of sandwiches that had been prepared for me the night before at the Officers' Club. Travelers in Germany carried their own food. My stomach was rumbling, but the sandwiches didn't go down easily. Each swallow was a deliberate action.

At nearly two o'clock, my man entered the hall. I didn't need anyone to point him out. His left hand was gloved despite the summer heat, and the saber scar stood out on his face. He was carrying a basket of potatoes and looked at me with feigned indifference as he started up the stairs. I knew he had to be at least curious. Everyone else had been. British officers didn't normally sit on your doorstep.

"Salzer," I called from my chair.

His body stiffened but he continued to climb the stairs at the same pace, not turning around.

"Salzer," I called again, following him up the stairs.

He turned this time. I couldn't have been addressing anyone else.

"You are making a mistake, sir. My name is Ulrich, Ingenieur Hugo Ulrich."

I undid my pistol holster. "Come down, Salzer. I want to speak to you."

He gave me a long look as though trying to remember if he had seen me before and walked slowly down the stairs. His shambling, flabby figure revolted me. This was what had been exchanged for Johnny's life.

"Leave your sack there in the corner and take off your glove," I ordered. He did so without a word of protest, exposing a badly scarred hand.

"We'll talk more comfortably in my jeep." I motioned him to precede me.

At the jeep, I handed him the key. "Get in and drive." He slipped under the wheel like a beaten man. I think his little room and potato diet had defeated him. Gone were the days of glory of the Third Reich. I drew my pistol and held it across my lap, pointing at him.

"Drive. I'll tell you where to go."

He drove slowly, his face a gray blank as he followed my directions through the city and onto the highway. As we turned off onto the lane he glanced at me, fear showing in his puffy eyes. I motioned with my pistol, and he held his tongue. When the track petered out he had no choice but to stop. I reached over and switched off the ignition.

"Get out."

He moved with difficulty, hoisting himself out of the driver's seat as though his legs were paralyzed. Keeping my gun on him I walked around the jeep. Get it over with, I said to myself. Shoot him right now and leave. I couldn't stand the sight of this cowering subhuman object. I only wanted to be away from it. This wasn't a man any longer, it was a sack of excrement. The fury that had sustained my search for months turned into disgust. Vengeance is a dish which should be eaten cold, according to a French proverb. I was thoroughly cooled off, but how can one put a bullet in a sack of shit?

"Do you know why you're here?" I half-whispered to the object.

He shook his head.

"Why are you hiding? Why did you change your name?"

"I never did anything, nothing wrong." He trembled as he spoke. "But they . . . I was in the S.D. They're arresting everyone who was in the S.D."

"Johann Jebsen. . . . Why did you have him kidnaped in Lisbon?"

He was so dulled by fear he looked at me like a cow. "I didn't order it. Kaltenbrunner did," he replied.

"At your suggestion," I said accusingly.

"No, I acted on orders."

"Whose orders?"

"My superiors."

"Superiors! Always superiors. Always the same excuse. Their names? Who were they?"

"S-Superiors," he stuttered.

"And his killing at Oranienburg? Who ordered that?"

"Th-They did. My superiors."

My anger started building up again. I seized him by the front of his shirt, shoving my pistol hard into his stomach. "And they don't have names either?"

He was properly terrified now. "No, yes. I mean, I can explain. Jebsen was doing illegal things. Black market. Currency transactions. But it wasn't against you. Not against the Allies. We didn't do anything against you."

I was twisting the shirt harder, my fist sinking into his flesh. "Please, I can explain, I tell you," he gasped.

"I'll explain," I said and could feel my face contorting in rage. "You had Jebsen murdered to protect your own stinking skin. I'm going to kill you for that. Now. Right now. Later I'll get everyone else, anyone else who was responsible with you."

Salzer's knees sagged. I had difficulty holding him up. I shoved him backward against a tree, pinning him to it. He gave forth a foul odor, causing me to let him go and step back. He had fouled his pants. He stood there, his legs slightly apart, shaking. I lifted the gun but couldn't pull the trigger. I threw it into the jeep shouting, "You son of a bitch, I'll kill you with my own hands."

I smashed his face with my bare fist. The blow was very hard. It broke the skin on my knuckles. I was in such a towering rage I can't say if I was disgusted with myself for not shooting him or more disgusted by the contact with his vile body. My head seemed to have swollen ten times and my eyes had a film in front of them. I saw him in a haze. I punched him again and he fell on his knees.

"Fight, you bastard," I yelled.

He stayed on his knees. I found myself launching a tremendous kick at him. My heavy army boot landed in his ribs. There was a thud and a cracking sound at the same time. I was aware of them but they didn't seem real. Nothing did. I just had to destroy this monstrosity in front of me. I grabbed him by the throat, but looking down at him that way, looking at this sack of meaningless, stinking flesh, my fingers wouldn't close. I held him, paralyzed, wanting to let go but unable to do so. We remained in that position, both of us unmoving, for I don't know how long. Finally I threw him from me. I knew I wouldn't—couldn't—kill him.

I turned and, half running, stumbled to another tree, feeling as though a volcano were erupting in me. I heaved and started vomiting. The sandwiches I had had for lunch came first, then, as my heaving continued and my mind cleared, what came out, it seemed, was all I had lived through in the past five years, all the intrigue, the political manipulations.

I vomited my sins and my shame and my pain. At the end I felt empty. Empty and somehow free. Free of all that. It was behind me. I got in the jeep and drove off. I think Salzer was still lying on the ground. I didn't turn to see.